The Unexpected
George Washington

Also by Harlow Giles Unger

The French War against America: How a Trusted Ally Betrayed Washington and the Founding Fathers

Lafayette

John Hancock: Merchant King and American Patriot

Noah Webster: The Life and Times of an American Patriot

The Unexpected
George Washington

His Private Life

Harlow Giles Unger

WILEY

John Wiley & Sons, Inc.

Published by John Wiley & Sons, Inc., Hoboken, New Jersey
Published simultaneously in Canada

Library of Congress Cataloging-in-Publication Data:

Unger, Harlow G., date.
  The Unexpected Washington: His Private Life / Harlow Giles Unger.
    p.   cm.
  Includes bibliographical references and index.
  ISBN-13 978-0-471-74496-2 (cloth)
  ISBN-10 0-471-74496-4 (cloth)
  1. Washington, George, 1732–1799. 2. Presidents—United States—
Biography. 3. Generals—United States—Biography. 4. Washington, George,
1732–1799—Family. I. Title.
  E312.U29 2006
  973.4′1092—dc22

Printed in the United States of America
10 9 8 7 6 5 4 3 2 1

To my good friends Hana Umlauf Lane
and Edward W. Knappman

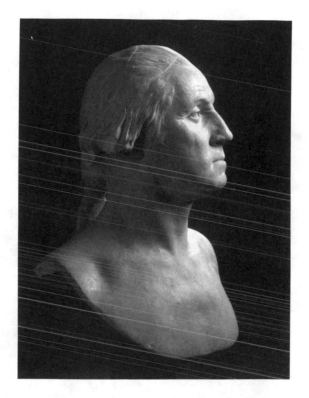

I am now enjoying domestic ease . . . under the shadow of my own Vine and Fig-tree, free from the busy scenes of public life . . . I am retiring within myself; and shall tread the paths of private life with heartfelt satisfaction. Envious of none, I am determined to be pleased with all.

— *George Washington, February 1, 1784*

Overleaf:

Bust of George Washington by the French sculptor Jean Antoine Houdon from a life mask he took in 1785.

Contents

Maps and Illustrations

Acknowledgments

Philander D. Chase, senior editor and longtime editor in chief of *The Papers of George Washington*, was kind enough to encourage and guide me from the outset of my research for this book and went beyond the bounds of generosity by reviewing the finished manuscript. I shall always be grateful.

My deep thanks, too, to James C. Rees, executive director, and Richard B. Dressner, who was associate director, of George Washington's Mount Vernon Estate & Gardens for their graciousness in placing the vast research materials of Mount Vernon at my disposal. I owe especial thanks to Mary V. Thompson, research specialist at Mount Vernon, for vetting my manuscript so carefully and suggesting many improvements. Dawn Bonner, the manager of Mount Vernon Library's Photo Services, deserves special recognition for her effort and skill in culling the magnificent illustrations in this book from the thousands of photos in the library's huge collection. And Kathleen Kleinsmith, book buyer at the Mount Vernon Book Shop, was most kind in helping me find valuable reference works.

The magnificent estate and gardens at George Washington's Mount Vernon that inspired this book are a monument not only to the Father of Our Country but also to a group of great patriots who have restored and preserved Mount Vernon for more than a century—namely, the regent and vice regents of the Mount Vernon

Ladies Association. They are heroines, and I—and all Americans—owe them deep thanks.

A number of people devoted long, difficult hours to improve this book and prepare it for publication—none more than John Simko, senior production editor at John Wiley & Sons; William D. Drennan, copy editor; and Alexa Selph, who prepared the index. My deepest thanks also to two friends whose names never appear on the covers or title pages of my books, but who are as responsible as I (more so at times) for their publication: my editor, Hana Umlauf Lane, at John Wiley & Sons, and my literary agent, Edward W. Knappman, at New England Publishing Associates. To honor all they have done and tried to do on my behalf, I have dedicated this book to them.

Author's Note

All extracts and other quoted material in this work appear with spellings and syntax of the original manuscripts—for a good reason. In an era before standard dictionaries, men and women—educated or not—spelled phonetically, and, by reading letters of the Washingtons and their friends aloud, slowly pronouncing each letter, it is, at times, possible to hear their voices, their accents. At the time, English accents varied dramatically, from village to village, and the accents of Virginians were still evolving from a cacophony of English, Scottish, Irish, African, and West Indian sounds that would eventually blend into the soft, melodic tones still heard in some parts of the state.

A note about money: the currencies cited are, of course, eighteenth-century units, whose values fluctuated widely and wildly, depending on the abundance or scarcity of commodities and whether the currencies themselves were "real" or "imaginary." Real money meant real coins minted from copper, silver, and gold, while imaginary money was "money of account," which consisted of only figures jotted onto countinghouse ledger sheets to track complex barter arrangements. Rarely did a merchant in far-off Britain translate the real money he received dockside for Virginia tobacco into the same amount of imaginary money on the ledger sheet of the tobacco grower's account. Making matters more confusing was the existence of various

colonial currencies, including the Virginia pound, whose value fluctuated between 1.35 and 2.45 British pounds sterling in 1759, the
year of George Washington's marriage, and rose to 1.20 by 1775, before collapsing during the Revolutionary War. Attempts to convert
eighteenth-century currency values into today's dollars are difficult
at best. In chancing to inject (in parentheses) approximate modern
equivalents in this book, I've relied largely on Professor John J.
McCusker's two works *Money & Exchange in Europe & America,*
1600–1775: A Handbook (Chapel Hill: University of North Carolina
Press, 1978) and *How Much Is That in Real Money? A Historical Commodity Price Index for Use as a Deflator of Money Values in the Economy
of the United States* (Worcester, Mass: American Antiquarian Society,
2001).

Introduction

A GREAT STONE FACE stares silently from a South Dakota mountainside, unable to express the genius, warmth, and humor of the man it depicts. For more than two centuries, artists and historians have portrayed George Washington as cold, stern, and distant, with a face—and teeth—as stonelike as the Mount Rushmore sculpture. But the real George Washington—the private, personal George Washington—was human to the core: laughing, loving, and living life to the fullest, from earliest childhood to his last hours at his beloved home in Mount Vernon, Virginia.

A dashing giant of a man, Washington rode across the Virginia landscape in war and peace, chasing Redcoats and red foxes with equal passion. He loved women, children, flowers, plants, dogs, horses, and fine wines; he slept on forest floors as soundly as in mansion beds. A loving, loyal husband, father, and friend, Washington evoked the love and loyalty of almost all who knew him—family, friends, soldiers, slaves. His courage in battle and daring on horseback rallied ordinary men to heroic deeds. His social graces left ladies swooning as he spun them 'round the ballroom. And his silly, funny tales sent children convulsing with giggles as he bounced them on his knee. Left fatherless at eleven, he instinctively reached out to children in the same strait, befriending, harboring, often raising as his own the nieces, nephews, and children of other relatives or friends, including his wife's two children by her first husband and two of her grandchildren. Generous, hospitable, concerned for others, he left all who knew or met him in awe. He inspired trust. He inspired love. He was hardly the "mysterious abstraction" that one historian called him and certainly not distant, stony, or wooden.

And he was so much more—scientist, inventor, architect, scholar. More than Franklin, more than Jefferson, his boundless intellect and ingenuity pioneered advances in agriculture, agronomy, animal husbandry, architecture, and mechanics. A century before Luther Burbank, Washington grafted fruit trees, grape vines, and other plants and trees to produce tastier, hardier varieties of fruits and vegetables. He pioneered crop rotation and methods of breeding livestock. He invented new tools and processes that made farming easier and more productive. A brilliant entrepreneur, he expanded a relatively small tobacco plantation into a diversified agroindustrial enterprise that stretched over thousands of acres and included, among other ventures, a fishery, meat processing facility, textile and weaving manufactory, distillery, gristmill, smithy, brickmaking kiln, cargo-carrying schooner, and, of course, endless fields of grain, tobacco, fruits, and vegetables. His agricultural sector boasted three types of crops: cash crops (oats, corn, wheat, tobacco, etc.), table food (every variety of fruit, vegetable, and herb), and utility crops (hemp, flax, and the like). His livestock operations produced wool and mutton from sheep, dairy products and beef from cattle, tens of thousands of pounds a year of pork from hogs. He was a pioneer in animal breeding, perfecting breeds of racehorses, hunters, riding horses (Jefferson called him the greatest horseman of his day), hunting dogs, and work animals, including oxen, Conestoga horses, and mules.

Like Franklin, Washington was a brilliant autodidact—a scholar with little formal education, but so hungry for knowledge that he consumed hundreds of volumes of great works, ranging from Caesar's *Gallic Wars* and Cicero's *Orations* to Gibbon's *Rise and Fall of the Roman Empire* and endless technical books and manuals, ranging from military strategy to the construction and maintenance of a stercorary, or compost heap. He loved literature and theater, relishing works such as Sterne's *Tristram Shandy* and attending plays with

Martha three, four, or five consecutive evenings at a time in Philadelphia, Annapolis, and New York.

And like Jefferson—indeed, before Jefferson—Washington was a brilliant designer and architect. Before Jefferson's beautiful but unoriginal Monticello, Washington designed and expanded the stunning mansion at Mount Vernon into the unique masterpiece that is one of the nation's architectural crown jewels. He constantly sketched—designing buildings, tools, clothes, furniture—even his own tomb and false teeth!

Historians divide Washington's life into five periods: *The Colonial Years* (1732–1775), during which he became a surveyor, wilderness explorer, soldier, husband, stepfather, planter, and colonial official; *The Revolutionary War Years* (1775–1783) as commander in chief of the Continental Army; *The Confederation Years* (1783–1789), which he spent as farmer, husband, grandfather, guardian, and behind-the-scenes political activist; *The Presidential Years* (1789–1797), spent largely in New York and Philadelphia; and *The Retirement Years* (1797–1799), in Mount Vernon as a full-time farmer, adoring husband, doting grandfather, and surrogate father.

During each of these periods, Washington's public and private lives frequently blended indistinguishably. In his early twenties, for example, he devoted his entire life, public and private, to fulfilling two driving personal ambitions: acquisition of land and the military skills to help protect the Virginia territory that embraced that land. In an era without police forces, Virginia property owners depended on their own weapons to fend off predators and on the colonial militia to repel raids by organized forces of Indians, French, or settlers and militiamen from other colonies such as Pennsylvania and Maryland, whose territorial claims overlapped those of Virginia.

After Washington married, clear distinctions appeared between his public life and private life, with the latter involving mundane activities that many biographers ignore as being of little consequence to American history. As a private citizen, after all, he was but a farmer—like 95 percent of Americans then—plowing, seeding, fertilizing, and harvesting his fields, then riding home to dinner with his wife and children. Not much history in that. Indeed, Washington himself seldom distinguished between his private and public life.

The grounds and Mansion at Mount Vernon were open to all—and almost always teeming with friends, relatives, and strangers, along with children of all ages. Only the bedroom and canopied bed that Washington shared with Martha were sacrosanct—and, indeed, quite isolated at the top of a narrow, private stairway.

It was the private George Washington, however, whose innermost thoughts, emotions, and incomparable mind fashioned the public man, and the private George Washington was nothing less than a genius. Always on the hunt for knowledge, he studied all the available literature and consulted every expert he could find before pursuing a plan of action—on the fields at Mount Vernon, on the fields of battle, and in the fields of politics and international diplomacy. A master of social as well as scientific skills, he seldom forced new ideas or plans of action on others. Instead, he suggested them in subtle ways that let others seize on them as their own. That is how he built his huge Mount Vernon enterprise; it is how he won the Revolutionary War; and, most remarkably, it is how he created the Constitution and forged the government of the first free nation in the history of man.

The greatest Washington biographer—Douglas Southall Freeman—realized long ago that the key to understanding Washington's genius lay in understanding the whole person, private as well as public. The result of Freeman's efforts was a massive seven-volume work, whose first volume appeared in 1938 and whose last emerged posthumously twenty years later. A staple in libraries, Freeman's *George Washington* was, unfortunately, too voluminous for the average reader. Subsequent biographers succumbed to marketplace realities by limiting their works to single volumes on cataclysmic public events in Washington's life that left little space for more than one-dimensional, thumbnail sketches—mere glimpses—of the private man: his occasional outbursts of temper, for example, and his *apparent* military and political miscalculations. And, of course, his bad teeth.

In this volume, however, Washington's public life will serve as the backdrop, while the private Washington—the multidimensional and marvelously human—steps forward center stage to reveal himself. And what a revelation. Far from stumbling and bumbling his way to glory, the private George Washington emerges as a brilliant planner—at home, on the battlefield, at the Constitutional Convention, and in the president's chair. He also shows himself to be a grand, wonderful man, with a boundless sense of humor. He often laughed at himself, as in this letter to his brother:

> Dear Jack: As I have heard . . . a circumstantial acct of my death and dying Speech, I take this early oppertunity of contradicting [both] . . . I had 4 bullets through my Coat, and 2 Horses shot under me yet escaped unhurt. . . . Please give my compliments to all my friends. I am Dear Jack, your most affectionate brother.[1]

. . . or teased friends:

> A wife! I can hardly refrain from smiling to find you are caught at last . . . that you had swallowed the bait. . . . So your day has at last come. I am glad of it, with all my heart and soul. . . . I assure you, that I love every body that is dear to you.[2]

In contrast to his playful moments are the tender, loving thoughts for his beloved "Patcy"—which was Martha's nickname. As he was about to march off to war, he wrote:

> My dearest, As I am within a few Minutes of leaving this City, I could not think of departing from it without dropping you a line; especially as I do not know whether it may be in my power to write again. . . . I return an unalterable affection for you which neither time or distance can change. . . . Yours. entirely,[3]

Only in such personal letters, and in his diaries and little notes to himself, does the *private* George Washington reveal himself. His voluminous correspondence with family members and friends and their letters to each other reveal still more. Washington adored his wife, wrote to her weekly when he was away at war, and she reciprocated his love—and letters. Theirs was a deep, lifelong romance filled with tenderness, tragedy, anger, frustrations, but marked largely by boundless happiness and mutual understanding. Martha shared George's love of dancing, theater, concerts, expensive clothes, fine furnishings, and lavish dinners—and she put up with his passions for drink, cards, horse racing, hunting—and bawdy jokes.

Both reveled in the society of relatives, friends, and small children, and Martha filled the Mansion at Mount Vernon with all three. There was seldom an empty bed for the night at Mount Vernon or at their two presidential mansions, in New York and Philadelphia. Like Martha, George was irrepressible with little ones. Together they "adopted" and helped raise or shelter about a dozen orphaned youngsters. Mount Vernon swarmed with squealing children, singing songs, playing games. He'd bounce them on his knees, regale them with tall tales, and, inevitably, envelop them in his strong arms in warm embrace and kisses. He even put several of the children through college. He grew as angry as any father (sometimes unfairly) at adolescent misbehavior, but was equally quick to envelop the youngsters in his family with "the warmest assurances of my love, friendship, and disposition to serve you." He was, in other words, eminently human—and far from perfect.

Among his frailties were his relentless personal ambitions. He was not ruthlessly or unethically ambitious, but cleverly and determinedly so. From his earliest years he set his eyes on acquiring property, wealth, and power, and he remained constant and untiring in obtaining all three. And he was incorrigible in attempting to implant his personal ambitions in his stepson, stepgrandson, and nephews; only one—Bushrod Washington—ever fulfilled his uncle's expectations, by winning appointment as a United States Supreme Court justice.

Washington was fallible in other ways, often erring, but always evolving emotionally, intellectually, and philosophically—as in his relationship with his hundreds of slaves (whom he freed in his will) and, again, in his transformation from an unbendingly strict, young disciplinarian, who ordered soldiers lashed to the bone, to a mature, caring commander who could not contain his tears saying farewell to a comrade in arms.

Above all, Washington—the great and gallant immortal most Americans know only from a distance—was a warm and tender mortal seldom encountered in the pages of most histories and biographies. Behind the stone face (and mythical wooden teeth) were the laughter, love, and tears of a vulnerable man, one whom millions of Americans have, with good reason, embraced for more than two centuries—none, perhaps, more than Mason Locke Weems. It was Weems who, shortly after Washington's death, created the beloved myth that some parents and teachers still recount to children to instill the love of God, country, and moral rectitude that characterized George Washington.

> One day, in the garden . . . he unluckily tried the edge of his hatchet on the body of a beautiful English cherry-tree, which he barked so terribly, that I don't believe the tree ever got the better of it. The next morning the old gentleman, finding out what had befallen his tree, which, by the by, was a great favorite . . . asked for the mischievous author. . . . Presently George and his hatchet made their appearance. "George," said his father, "do you know who killed that beautiful little cherry tree yonder in the garden?"
>
> "I can't tell a lie, Pa; you know I can't tell a lie. I did cut it with my hatchet."
>
> "Run to my arms, you dearest boy," cried his father in transports . . . "such an act of heroism in my son is worth more than a thousand trees, though blossomed with silver, and their fruits of purest gold."[4]

I

A Quest for Power
and Glory

THE WASHINGTON CLAN EMERGED from the mists of the Pennine Mountains in northern England as thirteenth-century sheep herders who settled along the rich, rolling meadows of Wessyngton, about 120 miles north of London near Chesterfield, in Derbyshire. Lingering Norman custom added the geographic family name of de Wessyngton (from Wessyngton) to distinguish residents—related or not—from those of nearby hamlets. By 1500, Lawrence de Wessington had become a successful wool merchant and moved to the market town of Northhampton, where he acquired considerable property, became mayor in 1532, and assimilated the local accent that corrupted his name to Washington. Three generations later, another Lawrence Washington advanced the family's social status by enrolling in Oxford, getting a master's degree, and entering the church in Essex. Before he could climb the next rung of the Church of England hierarchy, however, Oliver Cromwell's Puritan Revolution sent the Anglican clerical ladder crashing to the ground. Left in spiritual, emotional, and financial despair, Lawrence Washington died a drunk at fifty-four.

In 1657 his two sons, John and Lawrence Washington, sailed to Virginia to escape the harsh puritan regime at home and, in doing so, profit from the British craze for American sweet tobacco. Virginia's

John Rolfe had developed a curing method that cut spoilage on long Atlantic crossings and made tobacco so profitable that Virginians planted it in the streets to use for money.

John Washington's subsequent marriage into the Maryland gentry entailed a dowry of six hundred acres on Virginia's fertile Northern Neck, a two-hundred-mile-long peninsula stretching between the Potomac and Rappahanock rivers into Chesapeake Bay. Like other planters, he quickly learned that tobacco exhausted soil nutrients in about four years and forced farmers to acquire new, more fertile land or face bankruptcy. In partnership with a brother-in-law, Washington exploited a British law that awarded fifty acres of royal land, or "headrights," for each immigrant—each "head"—they brought to America. Owners of property used the tactic to acquire thousands of acres by importing indentured servants or any other souls they could buy, coax, con, or kidnap onto Virginia-bound ships. After collecting headrights, the wiliest landowners sold or traded surplus servants to buy more land and develop huge plantations. As unskilled slaves worked the land, indentured servants—some of them skilled craftsmen—built and maintained ornate mansions for the owners and an array of outbuildings for servants, slaves, livestock, and other purposes.

The result, after several generations, was a near-medieval society of self-sufficient fiefdoms. Lord Fairfax owned more than 1 million acres; his agent, Robert "King" Carter, more than 200,000; the Lee family, more than 150,000. Several dozen lesser families owned "middling" plantations of 5,000 to 10,000 acres, and, by 1668, George Washington's great-grandfather John Washington had joined this group, having accumulated more than 5,000 acres scattered along the Northern Neck.

As heirs divided their fathers' properties, successive generations inherited less. George Washington's father, Augustine—in the third generation of Washingtons in America—inherited only 1,100 acres in upper Westmoreland County, along the south bank of the Potomac, where it widens before emptying into Chesapeake Bay. His wife's dowry raised his holdings to 1,750 acres, but, like other tobacco growers, acquisition of additional, more fertile land became Gus Washington's lifelong obsession. Using self-taught skills as a surveyor

and a gift for shrewd trading, he accumulated scattered tracts totaling 8,000 acres in different parts of eastern Virginia.

Augustine Washington's first wife died in 1729, leaving the twenty-
nine-year-old Virginian with two sons—Lawrence, twelve, and Augustine ("Austin"), eleven—and a nine-year-old daughter. Widowered
farmers could spare no time from their fields to care for young children, and, within a year of his wife's death, Gus Washington married
Mary Ball, a twenty-one-year-old orphan.

Self-centered and demanding, Mary Washington lacked the cul-
tural and social skills of her husband's first wife, and Gus sent his
sons away to boarding school in England. On February 22, 1732,
Mary Washington gave birth to the first of six children in seven years.
She named her firstborn for her former guardian, lawyer George
Eskridge. George Washington was born on a property later known as
Wakefield, on Pope's Creek, less than a mile from where it empties
into the Potomac, in Westmoreland County (see map on page 12).

From the first, George's father was absent most of the time,
either working his fields or away for days on end searching for more
land. Alone at home, Mary Washington turned more unpleasant
with each pregnancy. George learned to tolerate his mother's ill temper silently, obediently, stoically. He would never express love for his
mother; even fifty years later, he would grumble that his mother "still
continues to give me pain."[1]

Washington's first home was typical of second-tier Virginia farms—
a twenty-four-foot-square, one-story structure topped by a half-story
attic. A narrow central hallway that served as a dining room bisected
the ground floor. Two small rooms lay on either side, one of them a
kitchen, the others bedrooms. Whitewashed, with only a framed
mirror for wall decor, the hallway eating area offered little joy, and
Mary Washington's immutable scowl discouraged the type of merri-
ment that light many memories of childhood.

By 1735, when George turned three, two more babies had joined
the tiny household, and Gus moved them to a larger, though no
grander farmhouse on another Potomac property he owned farther
upstream. By 1738, however, the family again outgrew its quarters. Twenty-year-old Lawrence had returned from England, and
Mary had borne two more children and was pregnant with a sixth.

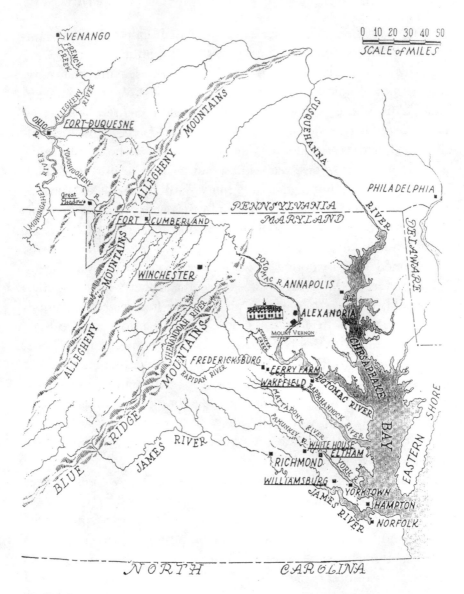

Washington's Virginia: The sites most closely associated with Washington in his native state were Mount Vernon, Ferry Farm (one of his childhood homes), Wakefield (his birthplace), White House (Martha Custis's home and site of her wedding to George), Eltham (homes of many Custis relatives), Williamsburg (colonial capital), Richmond (state capital), Winchester (site of three GW farms and seat of Frederick County, which GW represented as a burgess), Fort Cumberland (haven for GW troops after Braddock massacre), Great Meadows (site of GW humiliation at Fort Necessity), and Fort Du Quesne (target of British attacks and future site of Fort Pitt and Pittsburgh).

Gus left Lawrence to run the Potomac River property and moved six-year-old George and the rest of his family to a third, still larger farmhouse on "Ferry Farm," the site of a profitable iron-ore mine near the ferry at Fredericksburg.

Washington says nothing about ever having attended school. In fact, the sparsely populated South had few schools. The wealthy hired tutors for their youngest and sent their older boys to board with ministers until they were old enough to attend boarding academies in the more heavily populated North or in England. Like sons of "middling" planters, Washington acquired much of his basic reading, writing, and calculating skills by endless copying, motivated at times by an itinerant tutor's or his father's whipping stick.

When George turned eight, Britain went to war with Spain, and Lawrence joined the Virginia expeditionary force as a captain under Admiral Edward Vernon, who sent nine thousand men to slaughter on the beach at Cartagena. Lawrence Washington never left his ship, but he and other survivors returned as heroes, and he won appointment as Virginia's adjutant general. As tall as his father, Lawrence Washington's "grace, bearing and manners" transfixed young George. In a world of coarse, mud-stained linen and woolen homespuns—and nagging mothers—an officer's brilliant uniform and sparkling scabbard and sword seemed a certain escape to glory— and independence.

George elevated Lawrence to heroic heights, marching behind him, standing as straight and tall as he could in what he imagined was military attention. For Lawrence, the boy's attentions were endearing, often in sharp contrast to his stepmother's cold indignation at his intrusion into her crowded household. Lawrence drew closer to his wide-eyed little half brother, tutored him, and took him on hikes and horseback rides that converted ten-year-old George's affection into veneration and a resolve to become a soldier.

When George was eleven, Gus Washington died suddenly, ending all prospects for George's further education. As executor of his father's estate, Lawrence assumed a paternal role in his younger brother's upbringing, but had no resources for sending George to an academy. Their father's will left the 260-acre Ferry Farm and its ten slaves to George when he reached age twenty-one, with tenancy granted to George's mother, Mary, until then. Lawrence inherited the 2,500-acre upcountry Potomac River farm and replaced the austere, one-story farmhouse with a proper Virginia manor of more than twice the size—almost thirteen hundred square feet on the ground floor, topped by a half-story attic and more bedrooms. Set on a bluff overlooking the Potomac River Valley, it was typically Virginian, with a rectangular ground floor bisected by a wide central passage that opened at both ends for breezes and light to flow through in summer and cool the interior. Two rooms on both sides of the hall served as parlors or bedrooms, while a staircase along one wall of the hall led to the attic. Lawrence Washington named the estate for his commander in the Cartagena campaign, Vice Admiral Edward Vernon.

Two months later, Lawrence married Ann Fairfax of the storied Fairfax family, whose titular head—Lord Fairfax—owned the 4.5-million-acre royal land grant stretching along Virginia's Northern Neck up and over the Blue Ridge Mountains. It was a marriage that elevated Lawrence, and with him young George, to the pinnacle of Virginia society. George was determined to remain there.

Ann was the daughter of William Fairfax, a cousin of Lord Fairfax and superintendent of His Lordship's vast Virginia properties. A colonel in the Virginia militia and a burgess, Colonel Fairfax lived four miles downriver from Mount Vernon, at "Belvoir," a palatial, two-story brick mansion on a bluff overlooking the Potomac.[2]

Enthralled by the luxurious elegance of Virginia's high society, George rode off with increasing frequency to Mount Vernon, where bright silks and gilded fixtures shone in sharp contrast with the dull gray whitewash of Ferry Farm—and where the solace of Lawrence and Ann were welcome relief from his mother's snarls. Eager for their love, yet unobtrusive and ingratiating, he grew ever closer to them as they lost their own newborns—a girl in 1744, a boy in 1747, and a girl in 1748. For Lawrence, George became the only "son" he would ever have, and he outfitted him with fashionable clothes and tutored him, while Ann taught him music and dance and drew him into the bosom of the Fairfax family at Belvoir. In contrast with the silence at Ferry Farm, music, song, and gaiety filled the air at Belvoir. Young and old danced to popular minuets and gavottes on festive

Lawrence Washington, George
Washington's older half brother
and surrogate father, died of
tuberculosis at thirty-four and
bequeathed his Mount Vernon
property to George.

holiday evenings and staged droll plays of their own devising. Washington would always recall that "the happiest moments of my life were spent there. . . . I could not trace a room in the house that did not bring to mind the recollection of pleasing scenes." Reproducing those scenes in his own home would become one of his life's driving ambitions.[3]

Ann's father, Colonel Fairfax, gave George the run of his huge library and taught him about the art and fine furnishings that filled the mansion. Washington absorbed it all. When Fairfax's son George William returned from school in England, he and George began what would be a long-lasting friendship—despite a seven-year age gap.

By the time George Washington was fifteen, he had grown into a tall, handsome, pleasing young man with more than adequate manners in the salon and grace on the dance floor. At the hunt, his horsemanship amazed fellow riders as he left their mounts staggering in his dust. Like a centaur, at one with the horse, he guided the giant animal with imperceptible impulses from the sinews of his powerful legs; he had only to glance ahead to send his horse flying right, left— or over obstacles so tall that other horses veered to the side or staggered to a stop.

Like his father and forefathers, George dreamed of acquiring land and expanding the modest farm he had inherited into a vast estate like Mount Vernon or Belvoir. With help from a tutor, he mastered the mathematics of surveying and took up his father's surveying instruments to practice the craft on his family's farm. In October 1747 he coaxed a local surveyor to hire him as a helper and earned a tidy £3 2s., or about $235 in today's currency,[4] in a single month. Exulted, he recorded not only every inch of land he surveyed, but every penny he earned, spent, loaned, or borrowed—a habit he would retain the rest of his life.

When Washington turned sixteen, the sixth Lord Fairfax arrived at Belvoir from England, intent on having his hundreds of thousands of acres surveyed and divided into profitable leaseholds. Colonel Fairfax hired the region's most prominent surveyor to lead the expedition and sent his son George William, twenty-three, as agent for Lord Fairfax, with power of attorney to sell leaseholds. The younger Fairfax asked George to accompany him, and, on March 11, 1748, Washington set out on his first adventure into the wilderness. That evening he began a diary he would maintain for much of his life: "A Journal of my Journey over the Mountains" began "Fryday the 11th. of March 1747/1748." (The two dates refer to "New Style" [Gregorian calendar] and "Old Style" [Julian calendar] dating, both of which were then in use. Old-style dating set the beginning of the new year on March 25. England ended the confusion in 1752 by adopting the New Style Gregorian calendar.) His first day's entry, though, was less than revealing: "Began my Journey in Company with George Fairfax, Esqr.; we travell'd this day 40 Miles to Mr. George Neavels in Prince William County."[5]

. . . and the future father of his country fell asleep.

Four days later, he discovered the realities of frontier life. Instead of the hardworking, God-fearing pioneers he had expected, he found "a parcel of barbarians . . . an uncouth set of people . . . man, wife and children, like a parcel of dogs or cats, and happy's he that gets the berth nearest the fire."[6] After supper at one frontier cabin, he "went in to the Bed as they call'd it when to my Surprize I found it to be nothing but a Little Straw—Matted together without sheets or any thing else but only one Thread Bear [sic] blanket with double its

Weight of Vermin such as Lice Fleas &c. I made a Promise . . . from that time forward . . . to sleep in the Open Air before a fire as will Appear hereafter." After incessant scratching the next day, he and his friends reached an inn and "cleaned ourselves (to get Rid of the Game we had catched the Night before) & . . . had a good Dinner prepar'd for us Wine & Rum & a good Feather Bed with clean Sheets which was a very agreeable regale."[7]

Although Washington started his journey an immature, apprentice surveyor, he returned to Mount Vernon a professional, with a profound knowledge of the frontier, its people, and its vegetation—and a deft hand at cards acquired at the campfire. His journey also transformed him from an adolescent farm boy to a confident, self-sufficient frontiersman, as his diary reveals: "swum our Horses over [the creek] got over ourselves in a Canoe . . . shot two Wild Turkeys . . . a much more blostering night . . . had our Tent Carried Quite of[f] with the Wind and was obliged to Lie the Latter part of the Night without covering . . . Killed a Wild Turkey that weight 20 Pounds . . . Every[one] was his own Cook. Our Spits was Forked Sticks our Plates was a Large Chip as for Dishes we had none . . . travelld over Hills and Mountains . . . about 40 miles."

Along the way, too, his conversations with young Fairfax added gentlemanly polish to his speech and manners, and when he returned to the salons of the Northern Neck for the winter social season, he easily won over Virginia's aristocracy. At six feet, three inches, he towered over them, commanding attention by forcing them to look up at him. But what they saw was a gentle, endearing face that spoke softly and listened intently to what they had to say and won their favor.

In December 1748 Lawrence developed a serious respiratory illness. George was so devoted to Lawrence that he left Ferry Farm to winter at Mount Vernon and help care for his brother. He arrived in time to attend some of the holiday festivities at nearby Belvoir, using money from the sale of a small property he had inherited to buy a fashionable wardrobe that included nine shirts, seven waistcoats, and other accoutrements—and his first razor. He paid a dancing master for lessons before attending a series of Christmas balls, where he fell in love with two young ladies—his first conquest a "Low Land

Beauty" and his second, simply, "Very Agreeable." One of the two—
or perhaps a third—inspired one of the future president's few ventures in poetry:

> Oh Ye Gods why should my Poor Resistless Heart
> > Stand to oppose thy might and Power
> At Last surrender to cupids feather'd Dart
> > and now lays Bleeding every Hour
> For her that's Pityless of my grief and Woes
> > And will not on me Pity take.

He was fortunate to have learned surveying as a means of earning his
living.

In the fall of 1749, Lord Fairfax appointed George to survey
more properties on the great Fairfax land grant. Speed was essential
for surveying the wilderness, where thick foliage blocked sight lines
for all but a month each in spring and fall and deep snows barred
access in winter. George left immediately for the Shenandoah Valley,
and within a month he had run more than fifteen surveys. He was
efficient, swift, and, above all, shrewd in his work, collecting a max-
imum of fees in the least amount of time by surveying contiguous
properties when possible, to permit one survey on as many common
boundaries as possible. In this way he could survey three, sometimes
four or five properties a day. From 1749 to 1752 he conducted about
a hundred surveys, working only a few months a year, and became
financially self-sufficient.

He accumulated enough money and confidence in his knowledge of land and land values to buy three farms, two of which he leased
to tenant farmers to create a steady flow of rental income to add to
his surveying revenues. Within four years he accumulated seven
income-producing farms totaling more than twenty-three hundred
acres in the Shenandoah Valley near Winchester, thus matching the
acreage if not the opulence of Lawrence's property at Mount Vernon.

When he returned from surveying in the spring of 1750, Lawrence
was suffering from severe respiratory problems, and by the fall of 1751,
doctors warned that another Virginia winter would kill him. They
urged him to winter in Barbados, where the climate had become a
haven for patients with lung disease. With Ann needed at home to
care for her babies, George sacrificed his successful surveying busi-

ness and all but carried his ailing older brother onto a ship bound for the Caribbean and sailed to Barbados. Within days of their arrival, however, George developed a high fever, searing pains throughout his body, and the telltale red spots of smallpox on his skin. After three weeks of agony, he gradually recovered. Although pitlike scars would dot his face and entire body the rest of his life, he acquired a valuable immunity to a disease that claimed tens of thousands of lives in the New World each year.

As George regained his health, Lawrence grew worse and insisted that his younger brother return home. Lawrence wrote to Colonel Fairfax, asking that he see to George's future. Six months later, in June 1652, Lawrence returned to Virginia—to die. With no sons to inherit his estate, he left Mount Vernon to his two-year-old daughter and ultimately to her male issue. In the event she died childless, Mount Vernon would go to George—"in consideration of the Natural Love & affection which he hath and Doth bear unto his Loving Brother George Washington."[8]

George struggled to hide his grief over the loss of his brother and instinctively turned to Lawrence's father-in-law, Colonel Fairfax, who reached out to him generously. He asked Virginia governor Dinwiddie to appoint George to succeed Lawrence as the colony's adjutant general, with responsibility for recruiting and training the state's militia. The governor thought George too young, but divided the colony into four districts and appointed George adjutant for one of them with the rank of major. Fairfax gave him Lawrence's military training manuals—and his sword—and guided him into the Freemasons, whose members included Virginia's most powerful men. George also resumed surveying and assumed some of Lawrence's responsibilities as a director of the Ohio Company, a speculative land venture with the Lees and other prominent Virginians. Together with his brother Austin, Lawrence Washington had owned 6 percent of the two-hundred-thousand-acre Ohio Company land grant—twelve thousand acres, near the confluence of the Allegheny, Monongahela, and Ohio rivers.

Although Ohio Company lands were an English royal grant, France claimed sovereignty over the same territory, and in the summer of 1752, fifteen hundred French troops attacked a British trading post in what would mark the beginning of a brutal seven-year war for global economic and military supremacy across four continents. Governor Dinwiddie prepared a warning to the French to leave Ohio or face military retaliation. With Colonel Fairfax's approval, Washington volunteered to carry the warning to the French, reasoning that he would be protecting the Fairfax and Washington investments in Ohio while gaining influence in Virginia's political establishment by winning the governor's patronage. Convinced that Washington's wilderness experiences made him the perfect (and perhaps *only*) candidate for the mission, Governor Dinwiddie sent twenty-one-year-old Major George Washington west on October 30, 1753, to deliver an ultimatum to the French.

Washington's first steps into public life proved a harrowing, two-and-a-half-month ordeal that took him through uncharted wilderness across northern Virginia into Pennsylvania to the southern shores of Lake Erie, where the French commander greeted him with a brusque rejection and ordered him to return to Virginia.

Over the next two days, Washington and his guide floated downstream, traveling nearly thirty miles until ice blocked their passage. "I took my necessary papers," Washington noted in his diary, "pull'd off my Cloths; tied My Self up in a Match Coat [a long cloak of fur skins used by Indians]; and with my Pack at my back, with my Papers & Provisions in it, & a Gun, set out [on foot] on Wednesday the 26th [December]."[9] After traveling eighteen miles, "a Party of French Indians . . . laid in wait for us, one of them fired . . . not 15 steps, but fortunately missed. . . . [We] walked all the remaining Part of the Night . . . that we might . . . be out of the reach of their Pursuit next Day. . . ."[10] Exhausted at sunrise, Washington nonetheless pushed on through the snow, reaching the west bank of the Allegheny River after dark that evening.[11]

"The Ice was driving in vast Quantities," Washington recalled. "There was no way for us to get over but upon a raft, which we set about with but one poor hatchet. We got it launch'd . . . & sett off; but before we got half over, we were jamed in the Ice in such a Manner, that we expected every Moment our Raft wou'd sink, & we perish; I put out my seting Pole to try to stop the Raft, that the Ice might pass by, when the Rapidity of the Stream through [sic] it with so much Violence against the Pole, that it Jirk'd me into 10 Feet Water, but I fortunately saved my Self by catching hold of one of the Raft Logs."[12]

Far from both shores, and spinning uncontrollably downstream, Washington and his guide swam to an island, where they huddled together through the bitter night. "The cold was so severe," Washington lamented, "that Mr. Gist got all his fingers & some of his Toes Froze."[13] By morning the river froze enough for them to cross on foot and continue their trek home to Virginia. On January 11, 1754, Washington reached Belvoir, and, after resting a day, he went to Williamsburg to report to the governor, presenting a terse, self-effacing account of his mission. His guide, however, sent the governor a detailed description of Washington's resourcefulness and courage, for which Washington earned a promotion to lieutenant colonel and the full confidence of the governor.

As reports of further French incursions in the Ohio Valley reached Williamsburg, Governor Dinwiddie ordered each of his adjutants to recruit a company of a hundred volunteers to go "to the Fork of the Ohio . . . to finish and compleat . . . the Fort w'ch I expect is there already begun" and "to make prisoners of or kill and destroy . . . any Persons [who] obstruct the Works or interrupt our Settlem'ts."[14]

Washington managed to recruit only seventy-five men, but with French troops on the move, Dinwiddie ordered him "to march what Soldiers You have enlisted immediately to the Ohio." He promised to send additional recruits and aid. Dinwiddie signed his letter with a warm, personal wish: "Pray God preserve You & grant Success to our just Designs. I am most Sincerely Sr Yr Friend & hble Servt."[15]

In mid-May, Washington and his undermanned, underequipped force reached the Youghiogheny River, sixty miles south of the French fortification at the Fork of the Ohio (see map on page 12). He made camp at Great Meadows, an all-but-suicidal position he called "Fort Necessity," a hollow between two ridges, on the edge of a marsh (see maps on pages 12 and 22). On May 27, a scout reported fifty French troops only six miles away, and Washington set out to attack with forty troops and a contingent of friendly Indians.

"We were advanced pretty near to them . . . when they discovered us; whereupon I ordered my Company to fire . . . [we] received the

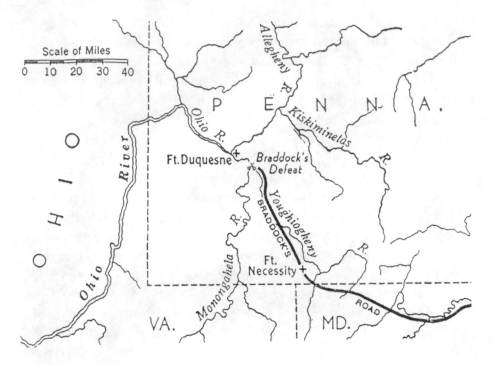

Sites of Washington's early battles, first, at Fort Necessity, where he surrendered to the French, then with Braddock's force, which the French all but annihilated in the Battle of the Wilderness, July 9, 1755.

whole Fire of the *French*, during the greatest Part of the Action, which only lasted a Quarter of an Hour, before the Enemy was routed. We killed . . . the Commander of the Party, as also nine others. . . . The Indians *scalped* the dead and took away Part of their Arms."[16]

He embellished his triumph for his adoring eighteen-year-old brother John Augustine. Without mentioning that he had lost his first tooth, he adopted a matter-of-fact tone that he thought appropriate for a hero-warrior:

D[ea]r John

Since my last . . . 3 days agoe we had an engagement with the French that is, between a party of theirs & Ours; Most of our men were out upon other detachments, so that I had scarcely 40 men under my Command, and about 10 or a doz. Indians, nevertheless we obtained a most signal Victory. . . . We had but one man killed, 2 or 3 wounded and a great many more within an Inch of being shott.

I fortunately escaped without a wound, tho' the right Wing where I stood was exposed to & received all the Enemy's fire and was the part where the man was killed & the rest wounded. I can with truth assure you, I heard Bulletts whistle and believe me there was something charming in the sound. [Often misinterpreted, "charming" here connotes bewitching or supernatural rather than pleasant.]

We expect every Hour to be attacked by a superior Force, but . . . some reinforcements . . . will enable us to exert our Noble Courage with Spirit. I am Yr affe[ctionate] Bro[the]r.

Geo. Washington[17]

Nor did he forget the adoring ladies at Belvoir's festive balls. Washington's letter to Sarah Carlyle provoked her tender concerns about "the many Risques you run" and fervent prayers that "your good Constitution and a kind protector will bring you out of them all as it has in the last Ingagement preserved you from harm."[18]

Washington's triumph earned him accolades: "Your victory over the French," wrote the master of his Masonic lodge, "gave me & your other friends such satisfaction as is only felt by those who have hearts full of Mutual affections & friendship. . . . I hope this is only a prelude to your future Conquests."[19]

Dinwiddie was ecstatic and sent Washington a medal and a generous portion "of my private Store [of] rum . . . Pray God preserve You in all Yr proceedings & grant Success to our Arms."[20]

Instead of retreating to the safety of Fort Cumberland to await reinforcements and supplies, Washington allowed bravado to govern his intellect by remaining at Fort Necessity—knowing that the French had eleven hundred men at Fort Du Quesne. "If the whole detach't of French behave with no more Resolution than this chosen Party did," he boasted to Dinwiddie, "I flatter myself we shall have no g't trouble in driving them to . . . Montreal."[21] Although his conceit knew no bounds, his knowledge of military fortifications did. He envisioned the ridges at Fort Necessity as protection for his troops instead of perches for attackers; he saw the marsh as a barrier to attack from the rear rather than as a barrier to his own retreat; he called the gullies on the fourth side of the meadow "natural entrenchments" from which his men could fire at oncoming enemy troops rather than the muddy traps they would become. Washington pulled out his surveying instruments and ordered his men to build a circular stockade that proved attractive fencing, but useless as fortification.

At dawn on July 3, the crack of a musket shot pierced the chatter of heavy rain, followed by the cry of a wounded sentry. As echoes of shot and cry resounded across the encampment, Washington's troops grabbed their arms and raced to the trenches, only to stare into an opaque screen of rainfall. By morning's end, the deluge had engulfed the trenches and transformed the ill-chosen ground into a mire that sucked soldiers' legs so deep they could only extricate themselves by surrendering shoes and boots to the mud. As noon approached, Indian war whoops heralded the emergence of three columns of French troops on the ridges—"from every little rising, tree, stump, Stone and bush . . . [they] kept up a constant galding [galling] fire upon us."[22] They raked the entire camp with musket fire, slaughtering livestock as well as troops. By the end of the day the French had stripped the Virginians of sustenance and transport: every horse, cow, and other animal in camp lay dead, and what Washington called "the most tremendous rain that [could] be conceived" had soaked his men's cartridge boxes and powder and rendered them impotent. With 30 men dead and 70 wounded, Washington's force had shrunk to 165 mud-encrusted caricatures of soldiers, clinging to useless weapons without ammunition. Washington had little choice but to accept French demands that he surrender all his arms in exchange for safe passage home for him and his troops.

After his return east, Washington resigned and resumed life as a private citizen, smarting from his humiliation at Fort Necessity but still craving wealth, influence, and position among Virginia's landed aristocracy. He would acquire all three far sooner than he anticipated. Lawrence's infant daughter had died, and his widow, Ann, had remarried and was now living with her new husband in Westmoreland County. Although Ann had inherited lifetime tenancy rights to Mount Vernon, George would now inherit the property, and, with the house vacant and deteriorating, Ann and her new husband sold George her life tenancy. On December 17, 1754, only two months shy of his twenty-third birthday, George Washington became master of Mount Vernon, a twenty-three-hundred-acre plantation with its lovely thirteen-hundred-square-foot house and five-bedroom attic—and contingent of slaves and servants.

When, however, a British convoy sailed into Chesapeake Bay with troops to drive the French from the Ohio Valley, Washington could not resist writing to British commanding general Edward Braddock, offering "to serve my King & Country . . . as a Volunteer."[23] Despite British contempt for Washington's military skills, they could not ignore his experience in the wilderness, and Braddock's chief aide replied: "The General . . . has orderd me to acquaint you that he will be very glad of your Company in his Family . . . [and] I shall think myself very happy to form an acquaintance with a person so universally esteem'd."[24]

From the first, however, everything that could go wrong for Braddock did. Maryland failed to send wagons to carry supplies; Pennsylvania failed to send horses; and Maryland, Pennsylvania, and Virginia all failed to raise their complements of troops to supplement British regulars. Even the Indians who had pledged to support the English failed to appear.

"I am almost in despair," Braddock lamented, "from the . . . sloth and ignorance . . . of the people and the disunion of the several Colonies."[25]

Nonetheless, he set off to war against the French and Indians in the West, and Washington pledged to follow as soon as he trained his brother Jack to oversee Mount Vernon and protect his private interests. He also took care to further his political ambitions by informing the state's most influential men of his bold resolve to serve Virginia.

"I am now preparing for, and shall in a few days sett off, to serve in the ensueing Campaigne," he wrote to one burgess. "If I can gain any credit . . . it must be from service to my Country with out fee or rewd, for I can truely say I have no expectation of either."[26] To another he penned: "I am just ready to embark a 2d time in the Service of my country, to merit whose approbation & esteem is the sole motive that enduces me to make this Campaign; for I can truly say

I have no views of profitting by it or rising in the Service I go as a Volunteer without Pay."[27] And to the House Speaker and treasurer he wrote disingenuously that "the sole motive wch envites me to the Field, is, the laudable desire of servg my Country; & not for the gratification of any ambitious or lucrative plans; this, I flatter myself, will manifestly appear by my going as a Volunteer, without expectation of reward, or prospect of attaining a Command. . . . I have been importuned to make this Campaigne by Gnl Braddock, conceiving, I suppose, that the small knowledge I have of the Country, Indians &ca was worthy of his notice and I might be useful to him in the progress of this Expedition."[28]

Before leaving, Washington asked his brother "to sound the pulses" of influential figures in Fairfax County to determine "if they were inclinable to promote my Interest." Although eager for a seat among the colony's political and social elite in the House of Burgesses, he did not want to risk the humiliation of failure. "If . . . you find them more inclind to favour some other," he told his brother, "I wd have the Affair entirely dropped."[29]

When Washington reached Braddock's camp at Fort Cumberland, Braddock's army set off for Great Meadows—the site of Washington's disastrous encounter with the French the previous year. Washington warned "the gen'l and principal Officers . . . to the mode of attack which, more than probably, he would experience from the *Canadian* French, and their Indians . . . but so prepossessed were they in favr. of *regularity* and *discipline* and in such absolute contempt were *these people held*, that the admonition was suggested in vain."[30]

On July 9, Braddock's troops crossed the Monongahela River (see maps on pages 12 and 22) and advanced on Fort Du Quesne, "confident they would never be attacked."[31] Suddenly, crackling shots and blood-curdling whoops engulfed the woods. A mob of half-naked French and Indians materialized among the trees above the British right column, fired a staccato of shots, then disappeared into the forest. Dozens of British troops fell dead and wounded. Before stunned survivors could re-form their lines to return fire, the French and Indians had vanished. The British fired at trees, only to hear war whoops build to a deafening crescendo at the rear. Before they could turn, another band of savages had emerged, fired, and vanished.

In and out they sprang, left, right, front, rear . . . appearing, disappearing, reappearing. They were everywhere, nowhere, never forming lines to fight by European rules of linear warfare.

Confusion and terror gripped the British ranks. Officers on horseback charged back and forth, their mounts shifting to the right, the left, whinnying in blood-curdling dissonance with Indian war cries. All-too-easy targets on the open ground, troops, officers, and horses toppled like toys. Conspicuously tall in his saddle, Washington felt musket balls slice through his hat and uniform as he tried in vain to rally troops; shots felled two of his horses but left him uninjured, and he remounted horses of dead riders. Braddock was less fortunate. A ball shattered his arm, smashed through his rib cage, and lodged in one of his lungs. One by one other officers fell onto the blood-soaked ground as they tried to rally troops. The slaughter lasted three hours; 977 of the 1,459 British troops lay dead or wounded; 26 of the 86 officers were killed; 37 others lay wounded. French casualties amounted to 17 dead or wounded; the Indians lost about 100 warriors.

As they ran out of ammunition, British survivors dropped their weapons, ran to the river, and thrashed their way to safety on the opposite bank. Instead of pursuing, the Indians remained on the battleground, hopping about the dead and wounded like vultures, plundering wagons and bodies, methodically scalping, ignoring shrieks of the wounded as they sliced and ripped hides off living heads as well as dead.[32]

"The dead, the dying, the groans, lamentation, and cryes . . . of the wounded for help," Washington recalled, "were enough to pierce the heart of adamant."[33]

British general Edward Braddock died four days later, near Great Meadows. Washington ordered the general's body buried in an unmarked grave in the middle of the road at the head of the column. Then, after a brief ceremony, the column began the march eastward, trampling over the grave to erase all traces that might allow Indians to find and desecrate the general's body.

Astonished that he had survived the slaughter, Washington managed to find a germ of humor to relieve his despair. "Dear Jack," he wrote his younger brother. "As I have heard . . . a circumstantial acct of my death and dying Speech, I take this early oppertunity of contradicting the first and of assuring you that I have not as yet composed the latter. But by the all powerful dispensation of Providence, I have been protected beyond all human probability & expectation for I had 4 bullets through my Coat, and 2 Horses shot under me yet escaped unhurt, although death was leveling my companions on every side of me."[34]

On July 26, Washington rode into Mount Vernon and collapsed into his brother's arms. He sent servants with the joyful news of his arrival to the Fairfaxes at Belvoir and invited them to Mount Vernon the following day. The servants returned with letters from the entire family. "Your safe Return," wrote Colonel Fairfax, "gives an uncommon Joy to Us and will no Doubt be sympathiz'd by all true Lovers of Heroick Virtue. From our first inexpressible affecting Intelligence . . . of the total Defeat of our Forces . . . We have been in torturing Suspence, Each One for their best belovd. Now You are by a kind Providence preserv'd and return'd to Us, We can say the Catastrophy might have been worse."[35]

The colonel's daughter-in-law—George William Fairfax's wife, Sally—and the other young ladies at Belvoir decided that a bit of flirting might lift young Washington's spirits, and she wrote this note for inclusion with her father-in-law's letter:

> Dear Sir—After thanking Heaven for your safe return I must accuse you of great unkindness in refusing us the pleasure of seeing you this night I do assure you nothing but our being satisfied that our company would be disagreeable should prevent us from trying if our Legs would not carry us to Mount Virnon [sic] this Night but if you will not come to us tomorrow Morning very early we shall be at Mount Virnon.
>
> S. Fairfax
Ann Spearing
Elizth Dent[36]

After a week's rest, Washington regained his strength, but seethed at what he considered "our shameful defeat," which, he realized, stemmed from failure to adapt to unconventional, "Indian-style" warfare. It was clear to him that a handful of individuals firing from behind trees and rocks had a clear advantage in the wilderness over large columns of troops firing from upright positions in traditional, European, linear-style warfare. He also learned the dangers of relying on even the most well-meaning promises of civilian political leaders. Washington reported Braddock's every blunder to Colonel Fairfax during the campaign, and Fairfax, in turn, had circulated Washington's analyses to every burgess and made him the only logical choice to command the Virginia regiment.

"Dear Washington," wrote a burgess from Williamsburg, "I most heartily congratulate your safe return from so many Dangers & Fatigues & by this Time I hope you are well enough recovered to give us the pleasure of seeing you here which all your Friends are extremely desirous of. In Conversation with the Govr . . . I said . . . I suppose his Honour would give the Command . . . to Col. Washington for I thought he deserved every thing his Country cou'd do for him. The Govr made a reply much in yr Favour."[37]

"I am just come from Wmsburgh," another burgess assured him, "every one of my acquaintance profess a fondness for your having the command."[38]

Virginia governor Dinwiddie agreed and, in early September 1755, appointed twenty-three-year-old George Washington "Colonel of the Virginia Regiment and Commander in Chief of all the Forces . . . for the Defence of H[is] Majesty's Colony; & for repellg the unjust & hostile Invasions of the Fr. & their Ind Allies—And You are hereby charg'd with full Power and Authority to act defensively & Offensively as You shall think for the good & Wellfare of the Service."[39]

Washington tried to convert the humiliation of Braddock's army into a personal triumph by imposing his authority with pomp and ceremony on a grand tour of regimental installations. "I think it my duty, Gentlemen," he warned his officers, "to give this friendly admonition . . . I am determined . . . to observe the strictest discipline . . . you may as certainly depend upon having the strictest justice administered to all: and that I shall make it the most agreeable part of my duty, to study merit, and reward the brave, and deserving. I assure you, Gentlemen, that partiality shall never biass my conduct."[40]

His declaration fell on deaf ears, however—indeed, on almost no ears. Only ten officers and twenty recruits appeared on the parade

Colonel George Washington,
commander in chief of the
Virginia regiment that defended
his colony's wilderness areas west
of the Blue Ridge Mountains
against attacks by French and
Indian forces. Portrait by Charles
Willson Peale.

ground in Alexandria, where Washington was to review the Virginia
regiment. It was evident that he was commander in chief of nothing
and almost no one. Making matters worse, the ever-present friction
between colonies all but sparked open warfare when Maryland militiamen seized Fort Cumberland, which Virginia had long claimed as
its own. Recognizing the absurdity of intercolonial warfare in the
face of common Indian and French enemies, Washington responded
diplomatically and went to Boston to appeal to Massachusetts governor William Shirley, who was acting commander in chief of His
Majesty's forces in America.

The trip worked wonders for Washington's career, extending his
renown into the centers of power in the North and broadening his
knowledge of political and social thinking in areas he had never
before visited. He spent nearly five days in Philadelphia, meeting the
city's notables, shopping for fashionable clothes at the city's fine
clothiers and hatters, and attending society dinners and dances.
From Philadelphia they rode to Perth Amboy, boarded the boat for
Flat Bush, then New York City, where "the curiosity to see a person

so renowned for his bravery and miraculous escape at Braddock's defeat, procured for him much notice."[41] As in Philadelphia, he could not resist the city's fashionable clothing stores—or the social life. Introduced into the salons of the city's elite, he attended several gatherings, where he lost a few shillings at cards, but met the city's most eligible young ladies and escorted two of them to "entertaining exhibitions—twice."

After visits to New London and Newport, he reached Boston on February 27. The *Boston Gazette* characterized him in mixed terms as "a gentleman who has deservedly a high reputation for military skill and valor, though success has not always attended his undertakings."[42] Washington met with Shirley, then went to enjoy himself while awaiting the governor's decision on the territorial dispute. He lost £4 at cards and spent £200 for gloves, hats, and shirts at the tailor's and hatter's, carefully recording every pound, shilling, and ha'penny spent in his little diary. He attended receptions with the city's social and political celebrities, including one at Governor's House.

On March 5, 1756, Governor Shirley ordered Maryland to restore sovereignty over Fort Cumberland to Virginia, and he reasserted Washington's full authority as commander in chief in the West, thus ensuring the young Virginian's celebrity across the colonies.

With the French and Indians threatening to overrun her North American colonies, Britain declared war against France on May 17, 1756, and ordered an expeditionary force to sail to North America. In September, the French and Indians renewed their raids in the Shenandoah, and the *Virginia Gazette* blamed Washington. "When raw Novices . . . who have never been used to command . . . are honored with Commissions in the Army," the editorial asked, "how wretchedly helpless must a Nation be?"[43]

Infuriated by the attack, Washington threatened to resign. "I only want to make the country sensible how ardently I have studied to promote her cause," he protested to Dinwiddie, "and wish very sincerely my successor may fill my place more to their satisfaction. . . . I flatter myself the country will . . . be convinced I have no sinister views, no vain motives of commanding."[44] His threat to resign provoked the House of Burgesses to rally about him, and in the end, even those who resented his swift accession to power recognized that he had made himself indispensable. He had mastered the art of acquiring power by feigning disdain for public life and threatening to shed powers he already held. The House of Burgesses—friends and enemies alike—pleaded with him to remain at his post. At Colonel Fairfax's urging, Washington's half brother Augustine—"Austin," a burgess—pleaded that "your country never stood more in need of yr assistance. . . . [If] you resign, what will be the consequences, all the officers . . . will follow your example, & the common soldiers will all desert, our Country then left defenceless to a barbarous & savage Enemy & . . . I am sensible you will be blamed by your Country more for that than every other action of yr life."[45]

Washington returned to Winchester at the end of May and found his troops deserting. He responded with uncharacteristic fury: "I have a gallows near forty foot high erected," he railed. "I am determined . . . to hang two or three on it, as an example to others."[46] On July 29 he sentenced fourteen deserters to death, five others to fifteen hundred lashes, and two to a thousand lashes. An unbearable silence gripped the town as the day of reckoning approached.

In the end, he couldn't go through with all of it. He pardoned all but two: one had deserted twice before, and the other he called "one of the greatest villains upon the continent." He ordered them hanged in particularly gruesome fashion—raised by the neck to strangle slowly and convulse instead of dropping to their deaths quickly. He ordered the lashings carried out. "Your honor will, I hope," he wrote to Governor Dinwiddie, who had sent him sixteen blank death warrants, "excuse my hanging instead of shooting them. It conveyed much more terror to others; and it was for example sake we did it."[47]

In early September, Washington's longtime benefactor Colonel Fairfax died. Washington attended the funeral at Belvoir, then returned to his post at Winchester, where he suffered an attack of "bloody flux," as dysentery was called. After writhing in pain for a week, he collapsed, and his physicians warned him to return home on indefinite leave to rest—or face death.

2

An Agreeable Consort for Life

IN GEORGE'S ABSENCE, Jack Washington had married, and he and his wife were waiting to care for George when he arrived home at Mount Vernon in mid-November. For the next month, George slipped in and out of feverish sleep. Sick as he was, he—and his brother and sister-in-law—longed for company, and in mid-February, he wrote to Sally Fairfax, his friend George William Fairfax's wife, who, with her husband, had sent Washington warm letters of support during the Braddock campaign.

Although George William had gone to London, Washington nonetheless asked Sally to come to Mount Vernon—"When you are at leizure to favour us with a visit." He made certain to add that "My Brother & Sister[-in-law] join me in their Compliments to you."[1] Her visit remained indelibly etched in his mind—and, to some degree, his heart. To comfort him, she promised to continue writing to him when he returned to the frontier.

By early March he showed no improvement and, believing that he faced a slow descent into death if he did nothing, he went to Williamsburg, where Virginia's leading physicians practiced on the colony's leading planters. To minimize his discomfort, he traveled in slow stages, taking twelve days to make the four-day ride. He stopped at his mother's at Fredericksburg, then at the House Speaker's home in King and Queen County, and finally the capital, where Dr. John

Amson, the colony's authority on "bloody flux," prescribed appropriate powders and assured him he was actually recovering and should return home for more rest. His spirits reassured and revived, he skipped the usual amusements of Williamsburg to begin the journey home—but having heard that the beautiful widow of Daniel Parke Custis, Martha Dandridge Custis, was receiving suitors, he decided to pay his respects at her home, the "White House," in New Kent County, about twenty-five miles out of Williamsburg. At twenty-seven, she was a few months older than George, a foot shorter, but with a pleasant face that exuded warmth and a simple, unaffected beauty. "The complacency of her manners speaks at once the benevolence of her heart," one of her friends would write later, "and her affability, candor and gentleness qualify her to soften the hours of private life, or to sweeten the cares of a hero, and smooth the rugged pains of war."[2]

She was also very rich.

Her husband had left an estate worth more than £23,000—about $1.75 million today[3]—and nearly 18,000 acres of land and more than 250 slaves. Two of her four children from her first marriage had died in early childhood, and she doted over the two survivors, all but smothering them with maternal care, lavish clothes, and playthings. John Parke ("Jacky"), almost four, and Martha Parke ("Patcy"), nearly two years younger, were almost as rich as their mother, each having inherited about a third of their father's estate.

After years in the wilderness, alone or among rough, filthy, foul-mouthed men, Washington found Martha, the children, and the warm family setting—and perhaps her money and social standing—the realization of a lonely soldier's fantasy. After a day and a half, Washington returned home for a week, then rode back to the White House and asked for Martha's hand. When he left for a brief visit to the capital, she had pledged to marry him. A few days later, he was on his way back to his post at Winchester, where he ordered wedding clothes from England: "As much of the best superfine Blue Cotton Velvet as will make a Coat Waistcoat & Breeches for a Tall Man with a fine Silk button to suit it & all other necessary Trimmings and Linings together with Garters for the Breeches . . . Six pr of the very neatest Shoes (viz.) 2 pr double Channel pumps—2 pair turned Ditto & 2 pr Stitched Shoes."[4]

After he returned home from the frontier, he ordered carpenters to transform his one-and-a-half-story house into nothing less than a mansion by building a second-story addition he designed. By raising the roof, he would add four new, full-sized rooms upstairs, with a half-story attic above for storage space. He ordered elegant touches in reception rooms to mimic the beauty he so admired at Belvoir; to give the exterior walls the look of a stately stone mansion, he ordered them "rusticated"—a process of beveling the edges of wood blocks and covering them with a sand-laced paint that makes them all but indistinguishable from stone blocks. He also ordered construction of what he called "two houses in the Front of my House . . . and running Walls for the Pallisades to them . . . from the Great House to the Wash House and Kitchen also." He installed the kitchen and laundry in separate outbuildings to prevent any accidental fires from spreading to the mansion. He also began beautifying the grounds immediately adjacent to the mansion.[5]

Just as transformation of his house was under way, he learned that English brigadier general John Forbes was preparing to lead a powerful army of fifteen hundred British regulars and two thousand-man regiments of Virginians against the French at Fort Du Quesne.

Restored to near-perfect health—as much by the promise of Martha's affections as Dr. Amson's powders—Washington could not resist renewing his quest for military glory, asking for a command "distinguished in some measure from the *common run* of provincial Officers."[6]

Forbes gave him a brigade, and, leaving the work at Mount Vernon in his brother's hands, Colonel George Washington left for Winchester at the beginning of April—with a slight detour to reaffirm his affections for Martha Custis and preen a bit in his handsome uniform.

Washington found Winchester preparing to elect a new burgess for Frederick County, where he owned twenty-three hundred acres of farmland. Although he would have to leave for Fort Cumberland three weeks before election, the prestige of membership in the House of Burgesses was too much to resist, and he asked the officers assigned to defend Winchester to campaign for him while he went off to battle. In accordance with custom, they, in turn, drenched voters and

Evolution of the Mansion at Mount Vernon, from the time George Washington became master in 1754 to the expansion of 1758–1759 and its final transformation, by 1787, into the structure we know today.

their families with forty gallons of rum, twenty-six gallons of rum punch, thirty-four gallons of wine, and forty-three gallons of beer on election day, and ensured George Washington's seat in the House of Burgesses. His final cost was about half a gallon of spirits per vote.

"I am extremely thankful; to you & my other friends," Washington exulted to Colonel James Wood, Winchester's founder, "for entertaining the Freeholders in my name . . . my only fear is that you spent with too sparing a hand."[7]

Washington received good news from Mount Vernon as well: "You have some of the finest Tobacco & Corn I have seen this Year," his friend George William Fairfax wrote, "and a pritty full Crop of both, which I believe is more than any in this or the next County can say."[8] George's wife, Sally, also sent him encouragement on the eve of battle with a reminder of "the animating prospect of possess-

ing Mrs. Custis." Two and a half centuries later, his cryptic reply continues to provoke debate among historians:

> Tis true, I profess a Votary to Love—I acknowledge that a Lady is
> in the Case—and further confess, that this Lady is known to
> you.—Yes Madam, as well as she is to one, who is too sensible of
> her Charms to deny the Power, whose Influence he feels and must
> ever Submit to. I feel the force of her amiable beauties in the rec-
> ollection of a thousand tender passages that I could wish to oblit-
> erate, till I am bid to revive them.—but experience alas! sadly
> reminds me how Impossible this is.
>
> You have drawn me my dear Madam, or rather I have drawn
> myself, into an honest confession of a Simple Fact—misconstrue
> not my meaning—'tis obvious—doubt it not, nor expose it,—the
> World has no business to know the object of my Love, declared in
> this manner to—you when I want to conceal it. . . . but adieu to
> this, till happier times, if I ever shall see them.—I cant expect to
> hear from my Friends more than this once, before the Fate of the
> Expedition will, some how or other be determined.[9]

Historians have analyzed and debated *ad absurdum* the meaning
of Washington's letters to Sally Fairfax—some insisting he was
deeply in love, others calling his relationship an adolescent "crush."
His letters, however, might simply be those of the roguish flirt he
reveled playing in drawing rooms, dining rooms, and ballrooms. His
letters later in life to a woman he never met—Lafayette's wife, Adrienne—are equally suggestive. There is little doubt he loved Sally, as
he loved all his closest friends. And he no doubt found her beautiful.
But he was also a loyal friend, and it is absurd to suggest that he would
jeopardize—indeed, violate—his friendship with *both* the Fairfaxes
and with his patron, George William's father, Colonel Fairfax, by
having a sexual liaison with Sally. Nor is there any documentary evidence to suggest his having done so.

On September 9, 1758, Forbes sent an advanced detachment of
more than 750 troops to attack Fort Du Quesne. As they inched
closer to the fort, an explosion of musket fire erupted from the woods
around them. Before they could respond, the fort gates opened, and
French troops and Indians poured out firing. Within minutes, three
hundred British soldiers and officers lay dead, with the rest fleeing in

agony from painful wounds or shock. As he watched survivors limp into camp, Washington shook his head at the folly of pitting lines of regular troops standing abreast in woodland warfare against the French and Indians.

"So miserably has the Expedition been managd," he wrote to Sally Fairfax, "that I expect after a Months further Tryal, and the loss of many more Men by the Sword, Cold and Perhaps Famine, we shall give the Expedition over as Impracticable this Season and retire to the Inhabitants, condemnd by the World and derided by our Friend[s]."

He prefaced his letter, however, by asking, "Do we still misunderstand the true meaning of each others Letters? I think it must appear so, thô I woud feign hope the contrary as I cannot speak plainer without—but I'll say no more, and leave you to guess the rest." As he ended, he added, "One thing more and then have done. you ask if I am not tird at the length of your Letter? No Madam I am not, nor never can be."[10]

Again, the historians! Some cite this letter as proof of his love for Sally. But others who have been to war recognize the words of a lonely soldier on the eve of battle, homesick for friendships and pleasures of home, despairing over the course of a campaign in which, expecting glory, he found nothing but death, defeat, and humiliation—with worse yet to come. Although affianced to Martha Custis, Washington did not yet know her well enough to confide the fears he could share with his friends the Fairfaxes.

In early November, a courier raced into Washington's camp warning of imminent attack by a column of French troops. Determined to entrap the oncoming enemy, Washington waited until sundown, then sent Lieutenant Colonel George Mercer with five hundred men around the enemy's right flank while he led an equal force around the opposite flank. In the dark, three miles out of camp, amid an enveloping mist, shots rang out; the two companies mistook each other for the enemy and fired. While the French vanished into the night without loss, forty Virginia troops fell dead or wounded by their compatriots, with Washington barely escaping with his life. Washington would not mention his humiliation for thirty years, by which time he had kneaded his memory into believing that Mercer's troops rather than his own had "commenced a heavy fire."[11]

On November 17, Forbes led his army to Fort Du Quesne—only to find that the French had anticipated his move and vanished. Nothing but smoldering embers remained. Five years had elapsed since Washington had warned the French to leave the fork of the Ohio River, and they finally had done so.

The capture of Fort Du Quesne reopened the West to English settlers, and with Fort Pitt rising over the ashes of the former French bastion, twenty-seven-year-old Colonel George Washington resigned his commission and retired from the military. He returned to Mount Vernon with the aura of a great military leader despite his failures in battle. He had suffered a shameful defeat at Fort Necessity and displayed questionable leadership in the suicidal exchange of fire with another Virginia company on the eve of the capture of Fort Du Quesne. Although he had set out to "attain a small degree of knowledge in the military art"—and he did learn the futility of regular warfare in the wilderness—he remained relatively inexperienced in warfare, had led no armies into battle or designed any grand military strategies. He nonetheless returned home a hero.

Although he had displayed great personal courage, it was his uncanny political instinct as much as his battlefield exploits that created his legend as a great commander by establishing close ties to political leaders from Boston to Williamsburg and feeding them his interpretation of events. By the time the western campaign ended, Virginia and five other states believed he had directed the campaign and all but single handedly driven the French out. Washington was also careful to form friendships among subordinate officers from prominent Virginia families. Accordingly, twenty-seven of them saluted his resignation from the military with a letter of farewell expressing "great Concern, at the disagreeable News . . . of your Determination to resign the Command . . . you took us under your Tuition, train'd us up in the Practice of that Discipline which alone can constitute good Troops. . . . Judge then, how sensibly we must be Affected with the loss of such an excellent Commander, such a sincere Friend, and so affable a Companion."[12]

Washington thought carefully about his response, finally finishing it on January 10, 1759:

> That I have for some years . . . been able to conduct myself so much to your satisfaction, affords the greatest pleasure I am capable of feeling . . . if I have acquired any reputation, it is from you I derive it. I thank you also for the love & regard you have all along shewn me. It is in this, I am rewarded. It is herein I glory.[13]

Washington sent copies of the correspondence to the governor with the request that he show it to the council.

Although the Seven Years War raged in Europe for six more years, the North American phase, or French and Indian War, ended the following year with British expulsion of the French from upper New York and Canada. George Washington returned to Mount Vernon in December 1757, and slightly more than a year later, on January 6, 1759, he arrived at the Custis "White House" to marry his "Patcy," as he spelled the common nickname then for Martha.

With his marriage, he assumed responsibility over Martha's share of her late husband's estate, as well as the shares that each of her children had inherited. In effect, Washington now controlled five plantations totaling 17,438 acres, more than 250 slaves, £27,854 in cash and securities (worth more than $2 million in today's dollars), and huge numbers of livestock, farm equipment, carriages, household goods, and furnishings, and a library of more than 450 titles. Together with his own 2,300-acre plantations in the Shenandoah and 2,400 acres at Mount Vernon (22 slaves), he would have to oversee more than 22,000 acres spread across the state. Although he fully intended stepping off the public stage, his vast wealth, his position as a burgess, and his reputation—deserved or not—as a great military commander made him one of the most prominent men in Virginia. Whether he knew it or not, his every whisper reverberated far beyond the confines of Mount Vernon.

Because Martha's husband had left no will, the court named Washington to administer the estate, which meant dividing lands, slaves, and thousands of household items and farm implements among Martha and the two children. From the first, Washington took his obligations most seriously, saying that a guardian had to be far more careful handling a child's affairs than "a natural parent who, is only accountable to his own conscience."[14]

After a honeymoon of sorts at the Custis "White House"—shared with the two children and the customary throng of guests—the Washingtons went to Williamsburg for the festive opening of the new session of the House of Burgesses. In addition to her home in New Kent County, Martha had inherited a magnificent house in Williamsburg, with a four-acre park whose resplendent gardens drew almost every visitor in the capital to its gate to stare.

On February 22, 1759, Washington's twenty-seventh birthday, he took his seat among Virginia's landed aristocracy for the first time. No longer a second-tier freeholder, Colonel Washington emerged among the First Families of Virginia—the Lees, Randolphs, and Masons, if not the Fairfaxes of British nobility. On the fourth day of the session, a burgess proposed "that the Thanks of the House be given to *George Washington*, Esq., a Member of this House, late Colonel of the First Virginia Regiment, for his faithful services to his Majesty, and this Colony, and for his brave and steady Behaviour, from the first Encroachments and Hostilities of the *French* and their *Indians*, to his Resignation, after the happy Reduction of Fort *Du Quesne*."[15]

The House passed the resolution with a unanimous voice vote that welcomed Washington into Virginia's power elite and fulfilled his long-standing ambitions for honor and social status. He and Martha entertained and were entertained every night, and all heads turned as they arrived at the magnificent Capital Ball, where, at six feet, three inches and almost two hundred pounds, he towered over others—more than a foot above his petite lady. She was barely five feet tall—a fragile bird in a titan's arms. He was unique, with "a pleasing and benevolent . . . commanding countenance . . . his movements and gestures are all graceful, his walk majestic."[16] She was no less graceful in a gold and purple damask dress, trimmed with lace. Pearls streamed through her hair. Together they were perfection as they toed the minuet, shifting feet with precision, in a classical mating dance, wooing with only their eyes—never a touch. A tender silence followed every minuet—usually broken quite suddenly by the crashing introduction of an allemande, a rousing courtship dance that George and Martha loved dearly. As the dance began, the man strutted and swaggered like a cockerel about his intended, then spun her around beneath and between his arms before stepping out with her in a hop and a turn in three-quarter time. Others stepped back to marvel at his grace—she, like a feather, floating in his gentle arms. The dance left Martha breathless and giddy, George thoroughly enchanted, and both of them laughing and madly in love.

On Sundays, the Washingtons joined other burgesses and their wives at church—an important social as well as religious event. Although Martha was deeply religious and prayed for an hour each morning, George was less so and, unlike Martha, he never took communion. Although he thoroughly enjoyed church services and believed deeply in God, he rejected rituals that excluded nonmembers—both at church and Masonic lodges. The open door that welcomed all was, to him, one of the beauties of the Anglican Church—and communion seemed to close that door.

By mid-March, however, a profusion of spring blooms drew Washington's thoughts away from political affairs to the bare fields yawning for seeds at Mount Vernon. On April 2 he set out for Mount Vernon. Martha and his stepchildren rode in a gracious coach, while he rode his horse alongside, shepherding his new family and a small wagon train northward. Martha brought twelve skilled household slaves with her, among them her maid, seamstress, laundress, cook, waiter, and carpenters, along with Jacky's and Patcy's maids and two juveniles—a boy and a girl—to wait on and play with Jacky and Patcy. The wagons that followed carried stacks of Martha's household possessions—six beds, a desk, chests of drawers, and other furniture in one wagon; bedroom and dining-room linens, bedding, flatware, crystal, china—two sets—and endless numbers of dishes and kitchenware filled another. Then came the food; despite her husband's bulk, she had no idea what to expect in a bachelor soldier's larder. So she ordered her servants to fill the wagons with hams, cheeses, sugar, wine (120 bottles), a cask of rum, another of brandy, and more.

George now realized how inadequately he had prepared Mount Vernon for his new family. Despite its commanding view, his house was, after all, a Spartan bachelor soldier's home. When he reached his mother's home in Fredericksburg, he sent an urgent note to his

Martha Dandridge Custis, by
John Wollaston, 1757, two years
before her marriage to George
Washington.

overseer to rectify matters: "You must have the House very well
cleaned . . . make Fires in the Rooms . . . get two of the best Bedsteads put up . . . and have beds made. You must also get out the
Chairs and Tables, & have them very well rubd & Cleand—the Stair
case ought also to be polishd in order to make it look well. Enquire
abt in the Neighbourhood, & get some Egg's and Chickens, and prepare in the best manner you can for our coming."[17]

The closer they got to Mount Vernon, the more anxious he grew
about the appearance of his home in comparison to the sumptuous
mansions of Williamsburg. Martha and George came from similar
stock and reveled in luxurious surroundings—to compensate for the
rather "middling" plantation homes they had known as children.
Born Martha Dandridge, she was the oldest of eight children of a
second-tier planter, who needed the few slaves he owned to work the
fields and raise food for the family. His wife and children saw to most
household chores themselves. Martha and the other Dandridge children learned to clean house, cook and preserve foods, make and
repair clothes and linens, and perform every imaginable task.

Martha's well-trained eyes saw at a glance what needed to be
done at Mount Vernon, and she immediately made endless lists for

Robert Cary & Co., the most prominent British merchant bank in the Virginia trade. Martha's late husband and other wealthy plantation owners had long conducted their trade with Cary, routinely shipping their tobacco to him to sell in Britain after each harvest. Cary, in turn, credited each planter's cash account with the proceeds, then tapped the accounts to fill their orders for everything from fine clothes and furnishings to farm equipment and other products unavailable in America.

At Martha's behest, Washington enclosed an order that included a complete bedroom set—a seven-and-a-half-foot-tall "Tester Bedstead [canopied bed], with fashionable blew [blue] or blew and white Curtains to suit a Room lind wt. the Incld paper[.] Window Curtains of the same for two Windows . . . 1 Bed Coverlid to match the Curtains 4 Chair bottoms of the same . . . in order to make the whole furniture of this Room uniformly handsome and genteel."[18]

Washington also ordered housewares that Martha needed, shoes that he needed, dolls and toys the children thought they needed, and a supply of grass and clover seed for a broad, sweeping lawn east of the house, overlooking the Potomac and the rolling Maryland hills across the river. He ordered the "newest, and most approvd Treatise of Agriculture"—which, at the time, meant such works as *A New System of Agriculture; Plain, Easy, and Demonstrative Method of speedily growing Rich* (London, 1755), *The Principles of Agriculture and Vegetation* (Edinburgh, 1757), and *New Principles of Gardening, or the Laying Out and Planting Parterres* (London, 1728).

Nor did he forget family hygiene. By then he had lost several more teeth, and he ended his order with a request for two dozen toothbrushes and "Six Bottles of Greenhows Tincture" for cleaning teeth and soothing toothaches.

And a "pipe of the best old wine [about 126.1 U.S. gallons] from the best House in Madeira."[19]

As he ordered more from Cary, his purchases from his own, far smaller merchant Richard Washington declined, but he continued sending him small orders and maintained a polite correspondence: "I am now I believe fixd at this Seat with an agreeable Consort for Life," he wrote, "and hope to find more happiness in retirement than I ever experiencd amidst a wide and bustling World."[20]

Washington managed his accounts and plantation with military precision, but was frustrated not knowing in advance how much his tobacco would earn in England (or how much would be lost at sea or stolen) and how much he was actually spending to refurbish his home and properties. Like other planters, he relied on the English merchant to get the best market price for his tobacco in the London market and buy the best-quality goods for the money at the lowest possible price. Even the most respected London merchants, however, took full advantage of their positions, tacking on hidden charges to raise their commissions on tobacco sales and on the goods they purchased on behalf of colonists.

To try to outmaneuver the London tobacco market, Washington improved the quality of his tobacco, but the war with France had raised insurance rates to levels that, with freight, duties, and taxes, absorbed as much as 70 percent of the gross price. American planters were fortunate to reap 25 percent of the final London price for their tobacco—from which they then had to pay production costs.

Washington spent late spring and summer riding across his properties, ordering outbuildings repaired, stables and other animal quarters cleaned, and unplanted fields cleared for the 1760 season. He doubled the number of tenant farmers to eighteen, increased rents (payable in tobacco) more than 35 percent, and began charging them for blacksmith and other services that his slaves provided. Rather than allowing slaves to roam from field to field, he reorganized them into military-style units, assigning each to a specific tract under an overseer and recording the productivity of each unit. He tested his system by personally taking charge of six slaves and supervising the crop on one tract.

In November he went to the wharves on the James and York rivers, where tobacco from the Custis and Mount Vernon plantations was accumulating for shipment to England. Like most planters, he tried minimizing losses at sea by dividing shipments on as many ships as possible. Although he tried to run his business efficiently, lessons learned in books were as inadequate for economic combat as they had been for military combat. One ship sailed away and left four hogsheads of tobacco—about twenty-six bushels—on the wharf. Some tobacco he expected from his Shenandoah farms near Winchester never arrived. He later found that two hogsheads (about thirteen bushels) had been left in Alexandria "in an open shed with the ends of the H[ogs]h[ea]ds out and in very bad order."[21]

Washington tried to compensate for the vagaries of elements beyond his control by focusing on elements he could control. He supervised every aspect of plantation work, including slaughtering hogs for winter meat, cutting wood for kitchens and fireplaces in the mansion, filling cider bottles from barrels, and repairing fences and outbuildings. Even in mid-February, he was up by 4:00 A.M., riding about the plantation by daybreak. "Brought home 4003 lbs. of Hay," reads his diary in mid-February. "Landed 65 Barrels of Corn. Began Plowing the Field by the Stable and Quarter for Oats and Clover . . . had the Fence put up . . . round my Peach Orchard . . . Bottled 35 dozn. of Cyder . . . Finished Grubbing [plowing under, clearing] the Field by the Garden . . . Bought 3000 Shingles."[22]

Washington sought to develop new sources of profit by diversifying his crops. He experimented with different soil samples to learn what would or would not grow in each. Like other tobacco growers, he knew that tobacco absorbed soil nutrients quickly. By planting different types of grass in empty fields—in varying depths and densities—Washington discovered ways to revitalize soil and, without realizing it, he was becoming one of America's leading agriculturalists. Apart from making fields productive, he also looked for ways to reduce his dependence on a single crop. Winter wheat had become Virginia's second most important product, filling otherwise empty tobacco fields after the fall harvest and producing a cash crop in spring to pay for seeds and other supplies for the summer planting season. He decided to conduct experiments with different types of seed in different soils—at first in the fields, then in small laboratory-style containers.

"Sowed my fallow field with Oats today, and harrowed them in," he wrote in his diary. "Got several Composts and laid them to dry in order to mix with the Earth . . . Sowd abt. one Bushl. of Barley . . . Harrowd & cross Harrowd the Ground in the Field intended for Lucerne [alfalfa]." In mid-April 1760 his experiments grew more complex:

> Mixd my Composts in a box with ten Apartments [small containers] in the following manner viz.—in No. 1 is three pecks of Earth

brought from below the Hill . . . in No. 2 is two pecks of the said
Earth and one of Marle [sandy soil] from the said Field. . . .
3. Has a Peck of said Earth and 1 of Riverside Sand.
4. Has a Peck of Horse Dung.
5. Has Mud taken out of the Creek.
6. Has Cow Dung.
7. Marle from the Gullys on the Hill side . . .
8. Sheep Dung.
9. Black Mould [from a marsh] . . .
10. Clay got just below the Garden.
All mixd with the same quantity & sort of Earth in the most effec-
tual manner by reducing the whole to a tolerable degree of fineness
& ju[m]bling them all together. . . . In each of these divisions were
planted three Grains of Wheat 3 of Oats & as many of Barley, all
at equal distances in Rows & of equal depth. . . . Two or three
hours after sowing them in this manner, and about an hour before
Sun set I watered them all equally alike with Water that had been
standing in a Tub abt. two hours exposed to the Sun."[23]

In addition to new crops, Washington looked to nearby waters to
reduce his dependence on tobacco. He developed a fishery on the
banks of the Potomac, using rowboats to stretch nets across the river
to catch saltwater fish swimming upstream to spawn in freshwater.
Slaves cleaned and packed hundreds of thousands of herring, shad,
and other fish with salt in barrels—enough to feed everyone at
Mount Vernon and leave a surplus to sell in other markets. Instinctively, he was on his way to becoming one of America's leading
entrepreneurs. His success with the fishery encouraged him to further diversify, and before spring ended, he added a flock of sheep to
produce wool and a stallion and several mares for horse breeding. In
adding sheep and horses, he also added a rich source of manure to
fertilize his fields.

With his newly acquired wealth, Washington's lust for land grew
insatiable, and on February 26, four days after his twenty-eighth
birthday, he bought 1,806 acres for £1,150 ($70,000 today[24]), nearly
doubling his acreage at Mount Vernon, to about 4,600—and he had
every intention of doubling it again.

While Washington supervised the plantation, Martha supervised
the children's education. Although she hired a tutor to teach the
basics of reading, writing, arithmetic, and music, she kept an eagle

eye over her nestlings to ensure their progress. The Washingtons spared no expense on the children's musical education, ordering the finest English spinet made by the renowned John Plenius for six-year-old Patcy and a "good violin" and flute for Jacky. Knowing that English instrument makers reserved their finest instruments for local clients and shipped defective ones to the colonies, Washington "begged as a favor" that Cary "would bespeak this instrument as for himself or a friend and not let it be known that it is intended for exportation." He also ordered "a good assortment of spare strings."[25] To facilitate the children's musical education, the Washingtons hired one of the many itinerant music teachers who stopped for three or four days each month at the wealthiest homes to teach children and, as often, their parents. Martha proved an eager participant in the children's music lessons. George couldn't carry a tune, however, and despite the legend that he played the flute, he never learned to play an instrument or sing.

In addition to supervising the children's early education, Martha converted what they now called the Mansion into a delightful desti-nation for relatives, friends, acquaintances, Williamsburg notables, and George's former military comrades. Washington always trotted home to the Mansion in time to change clothes and powder his hair for dinner at three, but he was never sure whom he would find at the dinner table when he came in from the fields each day: "Some young woman whose name was unknown to any Body in the family din'd here," he puzzled over his diary one evening.[26]

George William Fairfax and Sally joined them with ever-increasing frequency as Martha and Sally became close friends, often horseback riding together (sidesaddle) or with their husbands before or after din-ner. Late afternoon tea became a ritual at the Washingtons—on the lawn overlooking the Potomac. Evenings were a delight at Mount Vernon. Many nights saw guests join the Washingtons in conversa-tion, but just as often the men and women separated in different rooms—the women to chat, the men to play cards or backgammon. Often they all joined in song or dance. A dancing master stopped at Mount Vernon each month to put the youngsters through their paces early in the day, then stage a splendid "assembly" for the adults. Fam-ilies came from nearby plantations to enroll their children in classes with Jacky and Patcy Custis, then join Martha and George for a joyful evening of dance—beginning with elegant minuets, but as wine and spirits took effect, breaking into high-spirited country reels and jigs and laughter.

Late in spring, the ugly realities of the tobacco trade began to beset the master of Mount Vernon. The *Deliverance*, carrying twenty hogsheads (just over one hundred thirty bushels) of tobacco, had been lost at sea, and insurance covered only half its market value. To make matters worse, London market prices collapsed, and Washington's tobacco was selling at less than half the price it had commanded a year earlier. Still worse: the Cary & Co. bill for the first Washington order of household furnishings added up to an unexpectedly high £353 15s 9d. (about $21,600 today). Washington lost his temper: "I cannot forbear ushering in a Complaint," he wrote to Cary & Co., "of the exorbitant prices of my Goods this year all of which are come to hand. . . . For many Years I have Imported Goods from London as well as other Ports of Britain and can truely say I never had such a penny worth before—It woud be a needless Task to innumerate every Article that I have cause to except against, let it suffice to say that Woolens, Linnens, Nails &ca are mean in quality but not in price, for in this they excel indeed, far above any I have ever had—It has always been a Custom with me . . . to estimate the Charge . . . for my own satisfaction, to know whether I am too fast or not, and I seldom vary much from the real prices . . . but the amount of your Invoice exceeds my calculations above 25 prCt."

Despite his annoyance, Washington did nothing to curtail his and Martha's spending. In the same letter, he told Cary he had issued checks for nearly £670 (about $51,000 today) "for a valuable purchase I had just made of abt 2000 Acres of Land adjoining this Seat. There are more payments yet to make, and possibly I may have occasion to draw upon you for a further Sum. . . . I hope their will be no danger of my Bills returning. I mention this rather for a matter of Information . . . than as a thing I ever expect to happen—for my own aversion to running in Debt will always secure me against a Step of this Nature, unless a manifest advantage is likely to be the result of it.

"Since writing the foregoing I have added to my Landed purchase, and shall have occasion in a few days to draw upon you to the amount of about £250 [$19,000 today]."[27]

Before sending his letter, Washington did some calculations and recognized that his and Martha's unrestrained spending had far exceeded their current and projected income. To prevent embarrassing overdrafts, he sent Cary a money order for £1,650 ($100,000) drawn on the Bank of England from the Custis estate—then placed another huge order for clothes for Martha and himself. There seemed no way to satisfy her needs; each increase in her wardrobe only spurred a desire for more—ten yards of lace, six of satin, two pairs of "sattin" shoes, six pairs of white kid gloves, six pairs of black kid gloves, a velvet cape.

Whatever she demanded, however, Washington dutifully, lovingly provided. He gave her everything but the one thing she wanted most: another child. She had borne four by her first husband, but George was incapable of providing her with another. For whatever reason, he was either sterile or impotent. Nonetheless, Martha always referred to George as "Poppa" to the children, and, to his deep satisfaction, both children grew up calling him that. Little Patcy grew particularly affectionate, and he responded as warmly as he knew how. George often despaired, however, of Jacky's ever bonding with him—as he, George, had bonded with Lawrence—sharing the vigorous outdoor life, galloping across fields, leaping fences, following the hounds. He loved Jacky, and Jacky's need for a father developed into a sincere affection for his "Poppa." But neither saw himself—his face, his instincts—in the other. Jacky liked to *play* soldier; George loved *being* one. Work and sacrifice were paramount to George; play, an afterthought. For Jacky, play came first, work second, and because Martha had never taught him the word, sacrifice had no meaning and never would, because of his almost unlimited financial resources.

Martha's overindulgence shaped the boy into an eight-year-old effete. She simply couldn't let go. "I think it is impossible for me to leave him," she confessed to her sister after gentle pressure from George had convinced her to try. "I carried my little Pat with me and left Jackie at home for a trial to see how well I could stay without him. . . . I was quite impatient to get home. If I at any time heard the dogs bark or a noise out, I thought there was a person sent for me. I often fancied he was sick or some accident happened to him."[28]

Martha was not unusual. She had, after all, lost two of her four infant children during her first marriage. In an age of high infant mortality, inadequate interior climate control, and few effective medicines, even an ordinary cold could kill a perfectly healthy child. Accepting the inevitable, George embraced the children as they were and joined Martha in buying them every imaginable article of dress or plaything. A stepfather's duties, he reasoned, were to be "generous and attentive."[29] Accordingly, he and Martha ordered lavishly appointed clothes and accessories for seven-year-old Jacky and a suit of livery for his fourteen-year-old black servant and playmate.

"Note," Washington added to his London merchant, "let the Livery be suited to the Arms of the Custis Family."

For little Patcy, who was more frail than her brother, he ordered a Bible, a psalter, a "persian quilt coat made of fashionable silk," "one fash-dressed Doll to cost a Guinea" (about $170 today), and "a Box Ginger Br'd Toys and Sugr. Imags. and Comfits."[30]As with everything else he ordered from London, he had no idea of costs—and would not learn what he had spent until months later, long after Cary & Co. had put them aboard ship with the bills.

Washington's own obsession with luxuries from London was no more manageable than his wife's. He ordered as many clothes for himself as for her, along with ever richer sets of equipment for his horses, sixty gallons of ale, a mahogany liquor stand to hold sixteen decanters, a pair of backgammon tables, two dozen packs of playing cards.

And something for the entire family: "1 dozn Stone Chamber Pots."[31]

By early October 1760 many of the magnificent furnishings the Washingtons had ordered from England the previous spring had arrived, and when they left for the autumn session of the House of Burgesses, they did so in a magnificent coach-and-six that matched any in America or England. It signaled to all that Washington had reached the pinnacle of wealth and influence in Virginia. Dressed in the finest English silks and velvets, George and Martha dazzled Williamsburg society, drawing admiring stares when they appeared in elegant salons or as they rode through town and stepped into or out of their coach. Although he appeared regularly in the House, he spent much of his time with Martha, attending theater and social galas. She adored dance and theater as much as he. Washington's favorite play was Addison's enormously popular tragedy *Cato*, in which the Roman statesman expresses noble sentiments that Washington and other American patriots would later cherish as their own during the Revolution, when Nathan Hale's words would echo those of Cato. "What pity is it that we can die but once to serve our country," Cato declares, all but addressing American colonists as he exhorts his fellow Romans to

Remember, O my friends, the laws, the rights
The gen'rous plan of power delivered down
From age to age, by your renowned forefathers,
(So dearly bought, the price of so much blood)
O let it never perish in your hands!
But piously transmit it to your children.
Do thou, great liberty, inspire our souls,
And make our lives in thy possession happy,
Or our deaths glorious in thy just defense. [III, v]

Cato also summarized Washington's religious beliefs by declaring Providence inscrutable and uncontrollable. Although Washington agreed with Cato that Providence left man relatively free to choose his own destiny, Washington believed prayer might sway the Almighty.

Despite bad weather, Washington's skills in agricultural science produced bigger and better tobacco crops, but London prices—and his net receipts—kept falling. Dissatisfied with the returns, Washington stepped up his experiments with alternative crops and the effects on seed and plant growth of various types of soils and fertilizers. Always in character, he kept careful records of his increasingly complex projects:

For an Experimt.
   Take 7 Pots (Earthen) or 7 Boxes of equal size and number them.
   Then put in No. 1 pld. Earth taken out of the Field below, which is intend. for Wheat—in No. 2, 3, 4, 5, 6 and 7 equal pro-

portion's of the same Earth—to No. 2 put Cow dung—to No. 3 Marle, 4 (with) Mud from the Marshes (& bottoms) adjoining the [illegible] Field, to 5 Mud [tak]en out of the River immediately, to 6 the same Mud lain to Mellow sum time, and to 7 the Mud taken from the Shoreside at low Water where it appears to be unmixd with Clay. Of each an equal quantity—and at the proper Season of Sowing Oats put in each of these Pots or Boxes 6 Grains of the largest and heaviest Oats planted at proper distances—and watch their growth and different changes till Harvest.[32]

In mid-September Washington engaged a full-time tutor for the children and ordered appropriate Bibles, English and Latin grammar books, and other texts, along with such usual luxuries as dolls for Patcy and two "handsome suits," a silver-laced hat, and a pair of silver shoe and knee buckles for Jacky.[33]

Favorable weather produced a record 1761 tobacco crop. With England still warring with France, Washington sent his London merchant Christmas wishes that "a stop would soon be put to the Effusion of Human Blood."[34] Washington started the new year by helping to organize a new horse racing establishment in Alexandria. The first "Alexandria Annual Purse" was held at the end of May. Although Washington failed to note how his horses fared in the race, he set out to improve his breed by paying more than £2 (about $120 today) the next day to have his bay and sorrel "covered by Mr. Rozers Traveller," a five-year-old horse "full Sixteen Hands and an Inch high." On the second day after the race, he paid £3 to another owner for "the use of your Horse to 4 Mares."[35]

In February 1762 George Washington turned thirty, only to face the grim news that his other half brother, Augustine—"Austin"— had died of tuberculosis at age forty-two. The loss all but confirmed his anxiety—intensified by his own recent pulmonary illness—that he would follow his Washington forebears to a premature death of tuberculosis. "How long can I have left?" he asked himself. Lawrence had died at thirty-four, his father at forty-nine, and now Austin at forty-two.

He took his mind off the macabre by immersing himself in more agricultural experiments, grafting new, hardier varieties of fruit trees with each other—about a dozen each of cherry, peach, and apricot trees. Developing hardy fruit became so important an element of

Washington's enormous household gardens that he hired a full-time "kitchen gardener" to "employ himself in Grafting, Budding, & pruning of Fruit Trees and Vines—likewise in Saving, at proper Seasons, and due order, Seeds of all Kinds." And, of course, he continued expanding his Mount Vernon estate, adding another 135 acres to bring the total acreage to more than 5,100 acres.

In addition to his lust for land, he satiated his own and Martha's lust for luxuries with a colossal order equal to nearly $25,000 in today's currency. He included some essentials—plows, augers, chisels, sheep shears, and other tools, and housewares such as brooms. But he bought more than £55 ($3,400 today) of silks and linens, "satten" pumps and kid gloves; he bought a leather hunting saddle "with a Silver embroidered border"; and, without knowing the price, he ordered "One very full and complt Sett of Table China, 2 dozn Table Knives & 2 dozn Forks with China handles to suit ditto 2 dozn small desert Knives & 2 dozn Forks to Ditto 2 dozn small Dessert Silver Spoons with my Crest, as Inclosed."[36] He ordered a "pipe" (126 gallons) of his favorite Madeira wine, which he drank regularly at dinner—about three to four glasses a sitting.

Although he loved Madeira and had no intention of cutting his consumption or spending for it, he was annoyed by the amount he was spending on brandy—a costly spirit purchased largely for guests, many of them uninvited! He decided to turn an unwanted expense into a profit by distilling his own. For what he was spending for imported brandy each year, he could buy a still and related equipment to fill his own needs for brandy and other spirits—and profit from the sale of surplus production to neighbors. He was the ultimate entrepreneur.

Late in November he went to the House of Burgesses in Williamsburg, but rushed home to Mount Vernon when he learned that Martha might be ill. Martha was fine, but Patcy was not. Always somewhat taciturn, she had occasionally drifted off to sleep at odd moments—a habit the Washingtons had attributed to fatigue. Now she had drifted off and suffered convulsions: she was epileptic. Washington tried his best to cheer the little girl and comfort her mother. Seldom able to express himself or communicate his true feelings at such moments, he could only place his hand on Martha's shoulder, hold her to him, and then withdraw, grim-faced, to his study to busy himself with his ledgers.

In closing his books for 1762, Washington found to his dismay that his and Martha's spending had all but decimated her fortune, reducing their cash balance to less than 6 percent of what Martha had inherited. With London commodity prices falling precipitously, some major planters were left bankrupt, and the Washingtons themselves now faced financial "complications" for the first time. In colonial Virginia, "complications" were often a long way from "ruin," however. Although profligacy and poor management plunged some larger plantations into bankruptcy, smaller freeholders were most subject to outright ruin in a barter economy, where every one bought and sold on trade—pledging either their own labor or portions of future crops or livestock or the output of their stills. With huge crops in the tens of thousands of pounds annually and more than ten thousand pounds of hogs sent to slaughter each winter, great landowners like Washington routinely accumulated and maintained mountains of credit as well as debt—and they lived in luxury until their deaths, when estate administrators would try to untangle their impossibly complicated affairs. Washington had built his plantation into a major agricultural enterprise, shipping tons of commodities and buying enormous amounts of equipment, supplies, and merchandise. He accumulated and depleted substantial cash balances and routinely drew from his account at his London merchant bank against future shipments. As a major planter, he loaned funds to local freeholders—and to all his relatives—against receipt of future goods and services. For tradesmen and small farmers, Washington and his like were merchant bankers as well as processors, lending money or feedstock in expectation of repayment in kind or equivalent goods or services—with interest—just as they purchased goods from English merchants with the proceeds from the sale of their tobacco or grain in British markets.

American planters such as Washington, therefore, greeted the end of the Seven Years War in 1763 somewhat differently from Europeans. While Europe mourned the deaths of 1 million civilians and more than 850,000 soldiers, Washington and other Virginia planters "rejoiced at the prospect of Peace which 'tis hoped will be . . . introductors of mutual advantages to the Mercht & Planter, as the Trade to this Colony will flow in a more easy and regular Chanl than it has done for a considerable time past." In the same letter, Washington asked his English merchant to ship "a Pipe of Wine" (126 gallons) for himself and added, "Mrs. Washington begs to have 4 Yds of Silk sent according the Inclosed pattern."[37]

3

"Fox Hunting . . . but Catchd Nothing"

THE END OF THE SEVEN YEARS WAR—and expulsion of the French from continental North America—opened the Ohio and parts of the Mississippi Valley to English settlers and land speculators. In June 1763 Washington, his younger brother Jack, and fifty other Virginians, including the Lee brothers—Thomas, Richard Henry, Francis Lightfoot, and William—formed the Mississippi Land Company and petitioned the king for "two million five hundred thousand acres of Land on the Mississippi & its waters." With each participant claiming at least fifty thousand acres, company lands would stretch from the Appalachian Mountains to the Mississippi River and blanket Ohio from the Great Lakes southward for two hundred miles. Not satisfied with owning most of the Ohio Territory, Washington and ten others formed the Dismal Swamp Land Company to exploit forty thousand acres of marshland in southeastern Virginia into North Carolina. Washington and his partners planned to harvest the timber, drain swamps, and turn the area into farmland. To carry crops to market, they planned building a canal across the barrier island separating Albemarle Sound from the Atlantic Ocean. By year's end, 148 people—including Washington's brothers, cousins, and neighbors—had subscribed to at least a thousand acres each.

Washington gave no indication of how he intended paying for his vast new holdings. By the spring of 1763 he had accumulated

9,381 acres of his own—apart from Custis properties—but he ran out of cash. Lack of cash, however, did not interfere in his land speculations—or deter him and Martha from mad shopping sprees for his treasured Madeira and her treasured silks. In early 1764, their British merchant grew concerned at the precipitous decline of the Washington-Custis cash position to a negative balance. Washington's embarrassment was evident in his disingenuous reply: "I am at a loss to conceive how my ballance can possibly be as much as £1811.1.1 in your favour, or Master Custis's so little as £1407.14.7 in his. . . . As to my own debt, I shall have no objection to allowing you Interest upon it untill it is discharged . . . but had my Tobacco sold as I expected and the Bills paid according to promise I was in hopes to have fallen very little in arrears."[1]

By August he whined like a child—but still failed to curtail his spending:

> Mischances rather than Misconduct . . . have caused me to fall so much in arrears to you. . . . For it was a misfortune that Seasons and chance shoud prevent my making even tolerable Crops in this part of the Country for three years successively and it was a misfortune likewise when they were made that I shoud get little or nothing for them—It may also be looked upon, as unlucky at least, that the Debts which I thought I had collected, and actually did remit to you should be paid in Bills void of credit, and as things have turned out . . . it is unlucky likewise that I made some purchases of Lands & Slaves in this Country since it obliged me to apply more of the . . . money . . . towards the payment thereof than I expected and of consequence . . .[2]

He rambled on like any profligate in debt, page after page, denying all personal responsibility for his arrears; his purchases were unavoidable—"trifling things"—and it was not his fault that his debtors were insolvent and their checks not negotiable.

In England, however, Washington's merchant, and every other commercial house, were buckling under an avalanche of tax increases. The Seven Years War had sent England's national debt soaring to £130 million (nearly $8 billion today), and, by raising taxes to cover the debt, Parliament had inadvertently forced forty thousand Englishmen into debtor's prisons and provoked antitax riots. Threatened with national rebellion, Parliament rescinded some taxes at home but compensated by imposing new taxes on America's imports and exports, including molasses and Madeira wine—Washington's favorite beverage. Military garrisons in North America were costing nearly £700,000 a year, and Parliament—and most Englishmen—believed Americans should pay for their own military protection. When Chancellor of the Exchequer George Grenville proposed extending the stamp tax to the colonies, Washington evaluated it as a businessman. In a letter to his British merchant, he called it "an ill Judgd measure" and predicted that "the advantages accruing to the Mother Country will fall far short of the expectation's of the Ministry."

He continued,

> all Taxes which contribute to lessen our Importation of British Goods must be hurtful to the Manufacturers of them, and to the Common Weal . . . many of the Luxuries which we have heretofore lavished our Substance to Great Britain for can well be dispensed with. . . . Great Britain may then load her Exports with as Heavy Taxes as She pleases but where will the consumption be? . . . who is to suffer most in this event—the [English] Merchant, or the [Virginia] Planter.[3]

Of more concern to Washington than the stamp tax, however, was the price Cary had paid for the last shipment of tobacco. Calling it "pitifully low" and "worse than many of my Acquaintance upon this river," Washington asked Cary, "Can it be otherwise than a little mortifying to find that we, who . . . contribute so largely to the dispatch of your Ships in this country shoud meet with such unprofitable return? Surely I may answer NO! . . . purchasing of Our Goods upon the best Terms, are matters of the utmost consequence to our well being, it behooves me to be plain and sincere on these points . . . that I may stand acquitted of ficklness if I am at last forced to a discontinuance of my corrispondance with your House."[4]

Rather than submit to Cary's unpredictable tobacco prices, Washington decided to replace tobacco in some fields with wheat and other hardy grains that commanded more stable prices. When the British Board of Trade offered bounties to encourage hemp and flax production, he planted a crop of each. He began growing turnips—

a winter crop in great demand in England for feeding livestock. He expanded spirits production at his still and operations at his mill and smithy. He ordered construction of a schooner, and an appropriately large wharf and loading area, to expand his fishery. He also cut his lavish personal spending by more than half, limiting his winter order to Cary & Co. to £168.14.0 (just over $10,000 today).

Hard as he tried, however, new and unpredictable expenses kept presenting themselves. Neither he nor Martha ever stinted on their children. They lavished the children with luxuries that only stimulated their demands for more. They filled each of the children's rooms with treasures: a magnificent miniature coach-and-six for Jacky, with a little stable that housed six additional horses—and a gilt-handled toy whip (gold plate!); Patcy's tea set—cups, saucers, dishes—was nothing less than fine bone china, with silver-plated spoons. She sported silk dresses as elegant as her mother's, and wore the most fashionable coats.

As plantation enterprises and administrative chores grew in number and complexity, Washington looked for a knowledgeable manager. To his delight he found a distant cousin, twenty-eight-year-old Lund Washington, a skilled, hardworking agriculturalist who had served as an estate manager in Westmoreland County. Lund proved so successful that Washington would later give his younger cousin a small farm of his own on which to live and a share of all crops grown on the plantations he managed.

Other Virginians were far more outspoken than Washington about the stamp tax. By the end of the year, the Virginia House of Burgesses—led by the fiery Richard Henry Lee—protested that "the people are not subject to any taxes but such as are laid on them by their own consent."[5] Like-minded leaders in eight other colonies—Connecticut, Delaware, Maryland, New Jersey, New York, Rhode Island, Pennsylvania, and South Carolina—met in New York and issued a "Declaration of Rights and Grievances of the Colonists in America" that provoked mob action across the colonies to prevent distribution of stamps. As Washington had warned, English merchants suffered harsh consequences. Americans cut purchases of English goods, and British exports fell 14 percent. As goods piled up in British warehouses, British merchants besieged Parliament to repeal the Stamp Act. On March 18, 1766—or four and a half months after the act had gone into effect—Parliament repealed it without a single stamp having been affixed to a colonial document.

In 1767, tobacco prices continued slumping, and Washington converted more fields to wheat and corn. To further stabilize crop production and income, he planted different varieties of wheat, with each ripening at a different time of year—a progression that kept his mill functioning year-round. When prices of English cloth began to climb, Washington set up a weaving plant to convert his flax crop into homespun textiles that clothed his slaves and many servants all but cost-free. Construction of his schooner was completed in time for the spring herring and shad runs, and he arranged to charter it to planters and shipmasters for the rest of the year and produce still another stream of income.

With his plantation humming smoothly, Washington went to Williamsburg for the spring session of the House of Burgesses, a visit notable only for his receiving one of two known surviving letters to him from Martha—a brief note with little historic significance that she penned at the bottom of a letter Lund Washington was sending:

> My Dearest   [Mount Vernon, March 30, 1767]
>
> It was with very great pleasure I see in your letter th[at] you got safely down we are all very well at this time but it still [is] rainney and wett I am sorry you will not be home soon as I expe[ct]ed you I had reather my sister woud not come up so soon, as May woud be much plasenter time than April we wrote to you las[t] post as I have nothing new to tell you I must conclude my self your most Affcetionate
>
> Martha Washington[6]

After overseeing the harvest of the last summer wheat, he, Martha, George William, and Sally Fairfax left for an extended vacation in Berkeley Springs, whose facilities had expanded with the growth in demand for the benefits of its warm waters. The Washingtons took their own cook from Mount Vernon and rented a proper cottage, where they dined on freshly baked bread, fresh vegetables, veal, mutton, venison, and other foods available from local tradesmen. It was the first time Martha had ever left both her children, however, and she was terrified. With infant mortality so integral a part of family life, Martha felt a need to hover over her two surviving children to protect them. Before leaving Mount Vernon, she and George instructed Lund Washington repeatedly to report on the children's health *at least* once a week. Patcy's fits had increased in frequency and severity, and Martha had become distraught.

"The children are very well & were Yesterday at Alexandria Church," Lund Washington wrote obediently the day after they left.

"My compliments to Mrs. Washington," he wrote again, "& let her know that her children are as well as I ever saw them & have been dureing her absence. They desire their Compliments to Colo. Fairfax & his Lady, & their Love and affection to Mrs. Washington & you."

And again: "The children are very well & have been during your absence, they desire their Love to their Mama & you, I am very glad to hear Mrs. Washington has reap'd much Benefit by the Springs."[7]

Washington's visit west coincided with a three-year-old project of British surveyors Charles Mason and Jeremiah Dixon to determine the Maryland-Pennsylvania boundary, just north of Berkeley Springs. Boundary disputes between the two colonies had left would-be settlers uncertain that their claims were valid. The Mason-Dixon line would create a permanent boundary and ensure the location of each claim. Sensing that huge profits awaited the first claimants, Washington wrote to Captain William Crawford, a surveyor who had been one of his officers in the campaign at Fort Du Quesne. Crawford had settled on the Youghiogheny River, near the site of Braddock's defeat (see maps on pages 12 and 22), where Washington wanted

> a Tract of about 1500, 2000 or more acres . . . somewhere on those Waters. Ordinary, or even middling Land woud never answer my purpose . . . No: A Tract to please me must be rich. . . . I shall . . . let some few of my friends . . . also partake of the advantages . . . my Plan is to secure a good deal of Land. You will consequently come in for a very handsome quantity . . . without any Costs. . . . Any Person . . . who neglects the present oppertunity of hunting ou[t] good Lands . . . will never again regain it.
>
> I woud recommend it to you to keep this whole matter a profound secret . . . if the Scheme I am now proposing to you was

known it might give the alarm to others & by putting them upon a Plan of the same nature.[8]

Crawford eventually secured 2,650 acres on the Youghiogheny, which Washington would later turn into a plantation with a mill.

Back in Mount Vernon, the conversion from tobacco to wheat gave Washington so much leisure time that in late autumn he took up fox hunting with neighborhood friends. Although he continued supervising his plantation, his diary focused on his new avocation, which he described with his usual succinctness:

"Fox hunting . . . but catchd nothing."

"Fox hunting . . . but catchd nothing."

"Started a fox. Run him four hours & then lost him."

Then, at last: "Fox hunting. . . . Catchd two foxes."[9]

Washington broke his routine only to go "a ducking"—hide by a nearby creek to shoot ducks ("2 Mallards & 5 bald faces")—or walk the fields firing at quail, pheasant, or any other bird that dared fly from cover. Martha, meanwhile, filled the Mansion with friends who joined Washington's own business guests in consuming all his game, drinking all his ale and wine, and wearing out every deck of cards. In reordering Madeira he complained that "there was a good deal of ullage"—unfilled space in the cask—in his previous shipment—"and what I disliked still more was, a large Tap in the head of the Cask which left me in doubt whether it was done on the Passage (which occasiond the deficiency) or was in the Cask before Shipping of it (as the Sailors, who deliverd it to me, affirmd)."[10]

Before 1767 ended, Parliament retaliated against the colonists for their opposition to the Stamp Act by imposing duties on a variety of staples from England—paints, glass, paper, tea, etc. Although the new duties caused controversy in Boston, Washington seemed oblivious to events beyond the Northern Neck. He was far more concerned with Patcy's health. Now approaching twelve, she had a serious crisis in mid-February 1768, prompting the Washingtons to call in English surgeon Dr. William Rumney. He prescribed 12 "powders," "a vial of Nervous drops," and a package of the herbal drug valerian.

On March 4 Rumney did double duty, treating Washington for a relapse of his dysentery. He spent a week "mending . . . at home," and by midmonth felt well enough to take short rides on his horse,

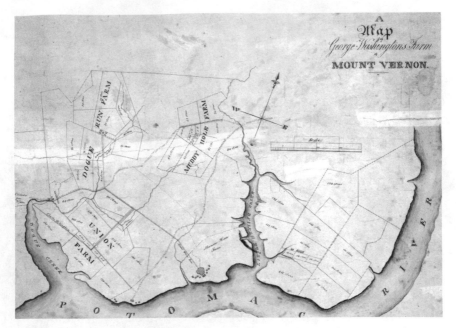

George Washington's five farms totaling nearly eight thousand acres in and about Mount Vernon, with the Mansion Farm situated in the center, bottom, overlooking the Potomac River, between the Union Farm on the left and River Farm on the Right. The Dogue Farm is on the upper left, separated by a forest from the Muddy Hole Farm.

usually just far enough to see the progress on a road he ordered cut through the forests to connect all five farms that now made up the Mount Vernon complex. In addition to the original plantation surrounding the Mansion, he had bought four adjacent farms over the years: River Farm (1,207 acres) to the east, Muddy Hole Farm (476 acres) to the northeast, Dogue Farm (649 acres) to the northwest, and Union Farm (928 acres) to the west.

After Jacky's tutor left for England, Washington watched the boy wander about the house listlessly, his mind festering. Although young Custis would inherit a fortune, he would have to manage a large, complex estate, and Washington wanted him to obtain a formal education, which Washington believed essential to assumption of the position and power Jacky would hold. With Patcy ailing, Martha had less time to dote on her son, and Washington convinced her to let him send Jacky to board with Jonathan Boucher, a minister who had opened a school for boys in his home near Fredericksburg. In his letter to Boucher, Washington described his "son in law & Ward" as

> a boy of good genius . . . untainted in his Morals, & of innocent Manners. Two yrs and upwards he has been reading of Virgil, and was . . . entered upon the Greek Testament, tho I presume he has grown not a little rusty in both; having had no benefit of his Tutor. . . .
>
> If he comes, he will have a boy [slave] and two horses, to furnish him with the means of getting to Church, and elsewhere as you may permit. . . . [Jacky] is a promising boy—the last of his family—& will possess a very large Fortune—add to this my anxiety to make him fit for more useful purposes, than a horse Racer & ca.[11]

As Washington assumed, Boucher jumped at the chance to teach a student of "very large Fortune." Boucher replied with effusive praises for the colonel's recognition of "the vast importance of a good education . . . and . . . ardent desire . . . for the cultivation of his moral as well as his intellectual powers."[12]

Washington and Martha went to Williamsburg for the spring session of the House of Burgesses, where the growing conflict with England over Parliament's right to tax colonists dominated discussion. Although Washington listened intently, he said little or nothing, and, indeed, was undecided about his own position. So when the gavel signaled adjournment, he eagerly rushed to join Martha. They had a grand time together—shopping, fashionable dinners, theater, dancing assemblies, and sometimes simple strolls. They saw five plays in the six nights at Williamsburg. After dropping Martha off at her sister's home, he visited the various Custis plantations, "dragging for Sturgeon" one afternoon, "gunning" on another, and "hair [hare] hunting on a third." His diary entries, which almost never dealt with politics, report only that "the hound Bitch Mopsey brought 8 puppies, distinguishd by the following Names—viz.—Tarter—Jupiter—Trueman—& Tipler (being Dogs)—and Truelove, Juno, Dutchess, & Lady being the Bitches—in all eight."[13]

On June 28 Washington left Mount Vernon with Jacky and Jacky's servant, two horses, trunks, and other luggage to enroll the boy at school. Martha was frantic as they left and rushed into the Mansion to embrace Patcy—who promptly went into convulsions.

Although the doctor came to treat the little girl, Martha enhanced the treatment with gifts, and when Washington returned, he eased Martha's anxiety in similar fashion, ordering his wife "a new handsome Chariot, made of best Materials, handsomely carvd . . . lined wt. green Morocco Leather trimmed with Cuffey Lace . . . a large Trunk under the Seat . . . Plate Glass diamd cut . . . Body gilt, handsome scrowl, shields Ornamentd wt. flowers all over the Panls . . . 4 Venetian Patt. Blinds with Mahy frames." As he did with many items he ordered, Washington sent a sketch to ensure precision. The summer's bill from Cary & Co. came to £315.13.6 (nearly $20,000 today).[14]

A month after Jacky enrolled at school, Jacky's schoolmaster reported the boy as "insufferably spoiled, lazy and demanding." He urged the Washingtons to pay "more vigilant Attenn to the Propriety & Decorum of his Bhavr, & the restraing Him fm any Indulgences."[15] Washington not only ignored Boucher's criticism, he also told the schoolmaster to send the boy home for an unscheduled two-week vacation—which George and Martha stretched into two months: to visit the families of George's two brothers, Samuel and Jack; to sail and fish aboard the new Washington schooner in the lower Potomac; and to attend theater in Alexandria.

When Washington returned home, he decided to forgo campaigning for the House of Burgesses in far-off Frederick County and run, instead, in his native Fairfax County, where he could campaign and return to his own hearth each night. He won election on December 1 and spent the rest of December and much of January hunting. Toward the end of January, however, Patcy took a turn for the worse: her fits increased in frequency and intensity. Washington called in Rumney and another doctor for several days; both agreed to give the little girl a combination of mercurial pills, purging pills, and Rumney's own "ingredients for a decoction," to extract bodily poisons doctors believed caused the disease. All Patcy's treatments are now known to have been poisonous, and, indeed, they worsened her condition. The Washingtons, desperate to ease little Patcy's horrors, turned to a fourteenth-century English folk remedy for epileptic convulsions: "cramp rings." Made with differing designs and metallic compositions for each patient, the finger rings carried specific blessings and inscriptions to relieve or cure epileptic convulsions. Washington sent for blacksmith Joshua Evans, who practiced the "secret art" and put an "Iron Ring upon Patcy."

In mid-March Washington's continuing obsession with land took him west to survey 2,682 acres he had bought near Winchester. After dividing his property into 18 lots of about 100 acres each, he spent a week honing his newer skills as an entrepreneur, leasing his lands to local farmers for shares of their crops, while cleverly retaining timber and mineral rights and the "Priviledge of hunting and fowling." Refreshed—and richer—he returned to Mount Vernon after two weeks and resumed chasing foxes and entertaining Virginia gentlemen and their ladies. His love of the hunt educed a passion for producing a perfect hunting dog, and his adventures in dog breeding filled the pages of his diary.

> [March] 24. Returned home from . . . Frederick &ca. and found that the Hound Bitch Maiden had taken Dog promiscuously. That the Bitch Lady was in Heat & had been promiscuously lined [copulated]. . . . Dutchess was shut up, and had been lin[e]d twice by Drunkard . . . that Truelove was also in the House—as was Mopsy likewise (who had been lin[e]d to Pilot before she was shut up).
>
> 26. The Bitch Musick brought five puppies one of which being thought not true was drownd immediately. The others being somewhat like the Dog (Rockwood of Mr. Fairfaxs) which got them were saved.
>
> 27. The Hound Bitch Countess brought 7 puppies. . . . Began about the 28th. to Plow behind the Quarter for oats & grass seeds.[16]

As spring arrived in 1769, his routine remained as constant as it had been the previous month—until April 3, when he received "a letter and sundry papers" that would change his and Martha's lives forever.

4

A Death in the Family

THE LETTER TO WASHINGTON urged Virginia planters to boycott British imports taxed by Parliament. Washington liked the idea and wrote to his neighbor George Mason, whose magnificent home, Gunston Hall, sat, like Washington's, on a hillside cape overlooking the Potomac, just downriver beyond Belvoir.

> At a time when our lordly Masters in Great Britain will be satisfied with nothing less than the deprivation of American freedom, it seems highly necessary that something shou'd be done. . . .
>
> That no man shou'd scruple, or hesitate a moment to use a—ms [arms] in defence of so valuable a blessing . . . is clearly my opinion; Yet A—ms . . . should be the last resource. . . . Addresses to the Throne, and remonstrances to parliament, we have already, it is said, proved the inefficacy of; how far then their attention to our rights & priviledges is to be awakened or alarmed by starving their Trade & manufactures, remains to be tryed.
>
> The northern Colonies, it appears, are endeavouring to adopt this scheme—In my opinion it is a good one. . . . The more I consider a Scheme of this sort, the more ardently I wish success to it.[1]

On April 30, 1769, Washington arrived in Williamsburg for the opening session of the House of Burgesses. The governor arrived in a splendid chariot and dress that bespoke his station as a baron; his speech was warm and conciliatory: "I have nothing to ask, but that you consider well, and follow exactly, without passion or prejudice the real interests of those you have the honor to represent; they are most certainly consistent with the prosperity of Great Britain."[2] That evening he hosted a magnificent gala dinner at his palace for the burgesses and their wives.

Within days, however, the burgesses forgot the governor's hospitality, denounced Parliament, and reaffirmed their exclusive right to tax themselves. The governor's response was quick and decisive: "Mr. Speaker, and Gentlemen of the House of burgesses, I have heard your resolves, and augur ill of their effect: You have made it my duty to dissolve you; and you are dissolved accordingly."[3]

While Martha went to her sister and brother-in-law in Eltham (see map on page 12), Washington and eighty-six other burgesses reassembled at Raleigh Tavern and adopted a resolution to boycott British imports, effective September 1. Washington bought a copy of *Letters from a Farmer in Pennsylvania to the Inhabitants of the British Colonies*—a series of twelve stirring essays by John Dickinson, a brilliant, London-educated lawyer in Philadelphia. Dickinson called for nothing less than economic independence from England. "If Britain can order us to come to her for necessities," Dickinson wrote, "and can order us to pay what taxes she pleases before we take them away or when we land them here, we are . . . slaves."[4]

Despite the ill feeling engendered by dissolution, the Washingtons and other burgesses and their wives flocked to the governor's "splendid ball and entertainment at the Palace" to celebrate the queen's birthday on May 19. The Washingtons left for home the next day, with no intent to found a new nation. What they needed most was money.

Reasoning that the boycott of British goods would force planters to become more self-sufficient, Washington made plans to expand flax, hemp, and wool production and his weaving operation to produce more clothes for his slaves and servants. Martha agreed to train and supervise spinners, seamstresses, and knitters, and he would hire additional weavers. With British ironwork banned, he would enlarge his smithy and produce hand tools that he and other planters had been importing from England. He would expand his fisheries and export salted herring and whitefish to the West Indies. And, with his improved wheat crop yielding more than six thousand bushels a year, he would build a new, larger mill to convert wheat to flour and eliminate grain wholesalers and millers from his revenue chain and reap their profits himself.

The Washingtons returned to Mount Vernon ebullient. George rejoiced at finding "my Wheat much better . . . than ever it was at this Season before." His animal breeding had also yielded fine results: "Mopsy the Hound Bitch and Truelove another Hound brought 12 puppies—that is Mopsy had five and the other seven."[5] When the time came to order goods from England, he reduced his purchases to less than 25 percent of his usual amount and stipulated that "if there are any Articles . . . which are Taxd by Act of Parliament for the purpose of Raising a Revenue in America, it is my express desire and request, that they may not be sent, as I have very heartily enterd into an Association . . . not to import any Article which now is, or hereafter shall be Taxed for this purpose until the said Act or Acts are repeal[d]."[6]

When Washington returned to Williamsburg for the autumn session, the governor drew cheers with news that Parliament had removed duties on all exports to America except tea. With tensions eased, Washington dined with His Lordship, and each enjoyed the other so much that the governor eagerly granted Washington's request to open the two hundred thousand acres of Ohio River Valley lands that former governor Dinwiddie had promised the three hundred volunteers of the 1754 campaign against Fort Du Quesne. Entitled by rank to fifteen thousand acres, Washington intended to be first to claim the richest lands for himself. He would then try to buy rights to other claims from widows of dead veterans, poor veterans in need of money, and veterans who had moved back to England with no intention of returning to America.

Before returning to Mount Vernon for Christmas, Washington advertised in the *Virginia Gazette* for "every officer or soldier, or their representatives" to "exhibit their respective claims" to Ohio Valley lands "before the 10th day of *October* next."[7] Few if any veterans would ever see the ad in England, and the poorest veterans in America were largely illiterate. As for the dead ones . . .

Washington asked his youngest brother, Charles, to contact former soldiers "who may be in want of a little ready cash . . . in a joking way, rather than in earnest at first, see what value they seem to set upon their Lands, and if you can buy the rights . . . at the rate of five, Six or Seven pounds a thousand acres I shall be obligd to you, & will pay the money upon demand. . . . If you should make any purchases, let it be done in your name. . . . In the whole of your transaction . . . do not let it be kn[own that] I have any concern therein."[8]

Washington's interest in western bounty lands took on new urgency when John Semple, the Scottish owner of a big iron furnace and gristmill ten miles south of Mount Vernon, submitted a proposal to build a canal to bypass the Great Falls of the Potomac River and open the river to navigation from Fort Cumberland to the deep-water estuary near Alexandria. He proposed raising funds for the project by selling 5 percent ownership shares to twenty "gentlemen" for £250 (nearly $20,000 today) each. Ultimately he envisioned tying the Potomac to the Youghiogheny, Monongahela, and Ohio rivers, thus opening an inland water route between Chesapeake Bay, the Ohio, Mississippi, and Missouri rivers, the Great Lakes, and the Gulf of Mexico. The waterway would allow the wealth of the continent—furs, ore, timber—to travel swiftly, easily, and inexpensively to Atlantic ports for transport to England.

Anticipating an end to the boycott, Washington resumed buying luxuries from England, including "A Man's very best Riding Sadle of Hogskin . . . A Fashe and handsome small Sword wt. Belt Swivels . . . A Neat Sword Belt with Swivels &ca for GW . . . A Topaz or some other handsome Stone fixd in the gold Sckt Sent, wt the Washington Arms neatly engravd thereon . . . Another Stone fixd in the other gold Socket with the Washington Crest . . . 3 dozn fashe Wine Glasses." Washington also ordered 400 to 500 bookplates with the Washington arms and, inevitably, "6 Stone Chamberpots."[9]

Washington's appetite for western lands did not dissuade him from buying every property he could near Mount Vernon. In 1769 he acquired 300 acres and raised his total acreage on the Potomac to 5,790, and in February 1770 his men began building a new, larger, industrial-size mill on Dogue Creek, which bisected his property and flowed into the Potomac. Washington's plan for the 40-foot-by-50-foot mill was ingenious: Dogue Creek flowed into the Potomac tidal basin, thus allowing flat-bottom boats to sail up to the mill with grain with the rising tide and float out with flour as the tide ebbed.

The mill was to be two and a half stories high, with a 16-foot diameter breast wheel and two sets of millstones, one for merchant work, the other grinding for local farmers, from whom Washington would collect one-eighth of their grain as his milling fee. Eager to finish the project before the summer harvests, Washington rode out to the mill almost every day—often with his pack of hunting dogs bounding along beside him, yelping at full throat. Impatient with the rate of progress, he offered the ditchers an 18-pence-a-rod bonus "if they would be brisk and stick to it."[10]

In the spring of 1770, Rev. Boucher was installed as rector of a church in Annapolis, Maryland, and closed his school near Fredericksburg. Both the Washingtons wanted Jacky, now seventeen, to continue his education, but the English minister had despaired of ever educating or disciplining Jacky. In fact, Boucher had lost all control of the boy, who came and went as he pleased and saw no purpose in learning, knowing how rich he would be when he reached the age of majority and gained control of his enormous estate. Rather than lose so important a connection and source of income, Boucher agreed to continue trying to instruct him in Annapolis.

With Jacky's education apparently settled, Washington turned to the August harvest and the festive social life that followed it. He went to visit his mother, attended a barbecue, then visited his brother Charles, and called on a succession of friends. He and Martha went fishing several times. Patcy's fits, however, caused him and Martha enormous concern. They increased in severity and frequency, racking her frail little body once every third day—often twice a day, according to Washington's meticulous records. Her worst attack ended in her collapse on July 31. After a severe fit, she fell ill with "ague [recurring chills and sweating] and fever," and Washington's doctor rushed to Mount Vernon to bleed the girl and try a variety of the latest medicines and treatments. After nine days he found that after sniffing ether, she suffered fewer fits, but sank into lethargy. Washington nonetheless ordered a supply and continued the treatments, cradling the child in his embrace as she inhaled the dizzying fumes.

When the leaves began to fall and forest sight lines cleared enough for surveying, Washington rode west to claim the two hundred thousand acres in veterans' lands in the Ohio River Valley. He was eager to reach the area before settlers and speculators arrived to stake out the richest ground. "The greatest estates we have in this Colony were made," he knew, "by taking up and purchasing at very low rates the rich back lands which were thought nothing of in those days, but are now the most valuable lands that we possess."[11]

Washington retraced much of the route he had traveled in the French and Indian War—Winchester, Fort Cumberland, and Great Meadows. Twelve days after leaving Mount Vernon, he reached Fort Pitt and the ruins of Fort Du Quesne. On his way, he crossed the Youghiogheny River and saw the 2,600 acres that his surveyor, Captain William Crawford, had claimed for him after establishment of the Mason-Dixon Line. Washington was ecstatic, saying the tract "includes some as fine land as ever I saw, a great deal of rich meadow, and, in general, is leveller than the country about it."[12] He asked Crawford to find 15,000 acres more and to try to buy the 234-acre tract at Great Meadows that he had named Fort Necessity before his humiliating surrender to the French. By owning it himself, he would preclude public exploitation of his disaster.

Over the next month, Washington traveled, by his count, 1,164 miles by canoe or on foot along and about the Ohio River, marking boundary trees delineating some 200,000 acres of land east of the Ohio River, bounded by the "Great Bend" (or "Big Bend") of the Ohio and the Great Kanawha River. "This is a good Neck of Land the soil being generally good; & in places very rich,"[13] Washington noted in his diary. He still knew how to evaluate land, but he worried that the Indians who lived on the Ohio "view the Settlement of the People upon this River with an uneasy & jealous Eye, & do not scruple to say that they must be compensated for their Right if the People settle thereon."[14]

Nine weeks after he had left, Washington rode along the familiar forest lanes to Mount Vernon—exhausted, but exhilarated by the certainty that he had scored a major financial coup in marking and setting aside the lands of the Ohio for himself and his veterans in advance of oncoming settlers and speculators. He looked forward to a quiet, prosperous Christmas at home with Martha and Patcy.

The Big Bend of the Ohio and Kanawha rivers—center of the two hundred thousand acres of "Bounty Lands" that Virginia (lieutenant) governor Robert Dinwiddie offered veterans of Fort Necessity. GW surveyed the area in 1769 and claimed more than twenty-four thousand acres for himself.

Three days later, however, Jacky turned up unexpectedly, complaining that he felt too restricted at Boucher's. A letter from Boucher followed, saying he was on the verge of abandoning young Custis. "I must confess to you," he wrote to Washington,

> I never did in my Life know a Youth so exceedingly indolent, or so surprizingly voluptuous; one wd suppose Nature had intended Him for some Asian Prince. . . . It is, possibly, a Misfortune to Him, that every where much Notice is taken of Him. Whether This may be owing to his Family, his Fortune, his Manners, or his Connexions, or all together, I will not now enquire. He has many Invitations to Visits, Balls, & other Scenes of Pleasure. . . . He has contriv'd to learn a great Deal of Idleness & Dissipation. . . . There is another Particular too which perhaps Discretion wou'd bid Me suppress . . . Jack has a Propensity to the Sex. . . . He does not much like Books. . . . I still hope & believe He will turn out, if not very

clever, what is much better, a good Man. That He may, I shall not cease to use my best Endeavours, as well as my fervent Prayers.[15]

Although Martha dismissed Boucher's assessment, the boy was clearly incorrigible. Washington still believed education held the answer to everything, and he clung to a faint hope that a little more formal schooling would change his stepson. "I should have thought . . . his study of the Greek Language . . . no bad acquisition," he had written to Boucher. But the minister-schoolmaster insisted the only way to control the boy would be to keep his horses at Mount Vernon and restrict him to Boucher's house. Martha grew incensed, saying she would keep the boy with her rather than see him deprived or punished. On January 2 Washington wrote to Boucher that "Jack's return has been delayd . . . from a desire of gratifying him in his favourite amusement of Hunting." Washington said that "Jack"—at seventeen he insisted he be called Jack instead of Jacky—that "Jack" had pledged to return to school "with a determination of applying close to his Studies; and I confide entirely in your promise of making him do so."[16]

Despite problems with his stepson, Washington's year ended on a triumphant note. He had added tens of thousands of acres in the West to his holdings, including the site of Fort Necessity. At Mount Vernon, the few fields that still sprouted tobacco had produced the biggest crops in six years to complement record crops of corn and wheat. His fishery had trapped and packed nearly 700,000 herring and 8,000 shad. His and Martha's spinners and weavers had produced huge quantities of thread and wool and cotton textiles, including striped and plaid woolens, broadcloth, dimity and other fabrics— enough to clothe all their slaves and servants at no cost. And his gristmill was nearing completion. He had hired a skilled miller and expanded Mount Vernon acreage to nearly 6,100 acres—enough land to supply six such mills with wheat each year. By early 1771 his mill was producing huge quantities of flour in three grades—"fine" (finely ground and relatively free of bran and impurities), "middlings" (medium-grade, containing some bran), and "shipstuff," the lowest-quality flour, with considerable bran. One local company—a baker and exporter—bought more than 10,000 pounds of Washington's flour in May, then, after sampling it, increased his order to 125,000 pounds in June. Washington's mills struggled to keep up with demand. Two Norfolk merchants—one a baker, the other a West Indies trader—bought nearly 40,000 pounds of Washington's flour.

In the spring of 1771, ten days of heavy rains drenched inland mountains and sent a 40-foot-high wall of water over the banks of Virginia's low-lying rivers, carrying away houses, outbuildings, and, farther downstream, tobacco warehouses bulging with the previous year's harvest—and the fortunes of hundreds of planters, large and small. James River planters alone lost 2.3 million pounds of warehoused tobacco, and when the waters receded, most were left penniless, searching for missing children and other family members and family retainers. Hundreds died; thousands of livestock vanished; tens of thousands of acres of spring plantings and topsoil flowed away into the maelstrom, leaving direct losses estimated at £2 million (more than $150 million) today.

While the floods devastated the lowlands, they spared planters along the Potomac, whose towering walls guided angry waters harmlessly downstream into Chesapeake Bay. With Washington's plantations untouched amid the mass destruction, his crops soared in value and left many Virginians shaking their heads in disbelief at his apparent immunity to ill fortune. Just as Providence had spared his life at the epic slaughter on Braddock's field, it had spared his life and fortune—indeed increased his fortune—amid the devastation of a biblical flood.

Early in September, Washington moved his mother from his childhood home at Ferry Farm to a house of her choice in Fredericksburg, near her daughter Betty and within easy reach of shops and other services she needed. At sixty-three, his mother had grown too old to live alone on an isolated plantation. Washington had never failed to stop to see his mother, but it was never pleasant. She grumbled incessantly of her children having abandoned her, of her imminent death and probable burial in an unmarked grave, and always, always, of her paucity of funds. Washington invariably left her £10, £20, or £50 ($75, $150, $375 today) to quiet her, then went to spend his night in the warmth of his sister Betty's house, where he enjoyed the love and friendship of her husband and children.

The Mansion at Mount Vernon overflowed with guests when George returned—mostly Washingtons, Dandridges, Bassetts, Lewises, and Fairfaxes, who, with the Washingtons, spent a festive October, sometimes dining at home, other times at Belvoir. The men hunted by day and played cards and sipped wine after dinner. As Washington put it in his diary, life, like the weather during the rest of 1771, was "exceeding pleasant, being quite clear and Calm."[17] It was a good year to be a rich, successful Virginia planter—even if his teeth were deteriorating and giving him almost constant pain.

The new year—and the fortieth anniversary of Washington's birth—began with what he described as "the deepest snow . . . the oldest man living ever remembers to have seen in this country . . . the snow being up to the breast of a Tall Horse."[18] The Washingtons were housebound for nearly two weeks, and when the snows cleared, it was time for George to make his way to Williamsburg for the spring meeting of the House of Burgesses to win government approval for the Potomac River waterway. At his urging, the burgesses approved the sale of twenty thousand shares to pay for construction of the canal and collection of public tolls to pay for management and maintenance. Virginia needed only the approval of the Maryland government to go ahead with the project. Washington wrote to Maryland governor Sir Robert Eden and other influential Marylanders he knew from the campaign of 1754, assuring them that "the opening of the Potomack will . . . end in amazing advantages to these two Colonies [Maryland and Virginia]."[19]

Before returning home, Washington went to see Dr. John Baker, an English surgeon-dentist who was one of the first qualified dentists to practice in America. Washington's irregular teeth had been inflicting increasing pain—sometimes excruciating when he chewed. Baker extracted the most severely decayed.

Teeth or no teeth, when he returned to Mount Vernon, Martha insisted that her husband sit for his portrait. All prominent Virginians were doing it, she said, and she wanted his portrait. She left him little choice in the matter, having already invited Charles Willson Peale to the Mansion to paint the entire family. Peale had studied under Benjamin West of London and was building a career touring Virginia, Maryland, and Pennsylvania, painting America's *faux noblesse*.

Martha insisted on Washington's posing in his 1st Virginia Regiment uniform, with his sword and rifle. Though he towered over her, he had little choice but to do as she said when "His Lady" made up her mind.

"I am now, contrary to all expectation under the hands of Mr Peale," Washington lamented to the Rev. Boucher, who had recommended Peale. "Posing puts me in a sullen Mood—and now and then under the influence of Morpheus, when some critical strokes are making."[20] Peale stayed at Mount Vernon two days, finishing the Washington portrait and miniatures of Martha, Jacky, and Patcy.

Washington spent the summer of 1772 increasing his wealth and landholdings, and by the end of the year he owned more than 6,500 acres at Mount Vernon alone and needed more slaves to do all the work. When he sent a load of premium-priced "Superfine Flour" to Barbados, he instructed the captain to use the proceeds from the sale to buy

> Negroes, if choice ones can be had under Forty pounds Sterl. [about $2,500]; if not, then in Rum and Sugar. . . .
>
> If the Return's are in Slaves, let there be two thirds of them Males, the other third Females—The former not exceeding . . . 20 yrs of age—the latter 16—All of them to be strait Limb'd, & in every respect strong & likely, with good Teeth & good Countenances—to be sufficiently provided with Cloaths.
>
> I have also to request the favour of you to bring me the following Articles.
>
> A Cask of about 50 or 60 Gallns of the best old Spirits especially from Barbadoes
>
> A Barrel of best Oranges
>
> A Ditto of Lemon's or Lymes. . . .
>
> Some Pine apples & a dozn or two of Coco Nuts
>
> Wishing you a pleasant and prosperous Voyage I remain Sir Yr Most Obedt Servt.
>
> Go: Washington[21]

In March 1773 Washington took Martha and Patcy to Williamsburg for the spring session of the House of Burgesses. Although Patrick Henry, Tom Jefferson, and younger burgesses talked boisterously of a Committee of Correspondence to link with other colonies in confronting the British, Washington, as always, thought about land, and when he dined at the governor's palace, he found the Scottish peer's

John Parke ("Jacky") Custis, Martha's son by her first marriage, at eighteen, by Charles Willson Peale, 1772.

Martha Parke ("Patcy") Custis, Martha's daughter by her first marriage, at sixteen, by Charles Willson Peale, 1772.

appetite for land as voracious as his own. The two formed a partnership that other speculators could only envy—an English lord who governed the colony and its western territories partnering with a wealthy Virginia planter who knew good soil when he saw it and had explored every inch of those territories. Dunmore and Washington gleefully agreed to prospect for western lands together that summer. To seal the deal, His Lordship opened the way for Washington to claim twenty-five thousand acres in western Florida.

The resolution to establish a Committee of Correspondence passed, with Washington voting in favor, but making it clear he would not participate because of the distance of his home from the capital, where the committee would have to conduct business.

When the Washingtons returned to Mount Vernon, a letter from Jacky awaited them. Martha shrieked; George's face turned to stone: Jacky had become engaged without asking their permission. His intended was a perfectly lovely girl from a prominent and exceptional family, but that wasn't the point: at nineteen, Jacky was still a minor, undisciplined, uneducated, footloose, fickle, not ready for marriage. In any case, he did not have the moral, let alone legal, right to contemplate such a step without permission from his parents. The

Washingtons fretted through the night: the first step was to bring Jacky home to Mount Vernon, then respond appropriately to the family of the injured girl.

Two weeks later, Jacky completely outmaneuvered his mother and stepfather. He returned, as ordered, to Mount Vernon—but with his future father-in-law, Benedict Calvert, in tow—*and* . . .

Sir Robert Eden, the governor of Maryland.

Eden and Calvert were close friends, and the governor had come to discuss Washington's cherished Potomac River navigation project. Washington seethed with anger and embarrassment, but waited until all but Jacky had left to discuss the boy's engagement. It was a one-way discussion. Two weeks later, Martha agreed to let Washington send Jacky to King's College (now Columbia) in New York—far enough from his betrothed to prevent the accidents of continued intimacy. He wrote to the girl's father accordingly, reading the final draft to Martha:

Dear Sir,   Mount Vernon, April 3d 1773

I am now set down to write you on a Subject of Importance, & of no small embarassment to me. My Son in Law, Mr Custis, has, as I have been informed, paid his Addresses to your Second Daughter, & having made some progress in her Affections required her in Marriage—How far a union of this Sort may be agreeable to you, you best can tell, but I should think myself wanting in Candour was I not to acknowledge, that Miss Nellys amiable qualification's stands confess'd at all hands; and that an alliance with your Family, will be pleasing to his.

This acknowledgement being made, you must permit me to add Sir, that . . . his youth, inexperience, and unripened Education is, & will be unsuperable obstacles in my eye, to the completion of the Marriage—As his Guardian, I conceive it to be my indispensible duty (to endeavour) to carry him through a regular course of Education. . . . I do not conceive that he is capable of bestowing that due attention to the Important consequences, of a Marriage State . . . & of course am unwilling that he should do it till he is. . . .

Delivering my Sentiments thus, will not, I hope, lead you into a belief that I am desirous of breaking of the Match—to postpone it, is all I have in view; for I shall recommend it to the young Gen-

tleman with the warmth that becomes a Man of honour (notwithstanding he did not vouchsafe to consult either his Mother, or
me . . .) to consider himself as much engagd to your Daughter as if
the indissoluble Knot was tied; and as the surest means of effecting
this, to stick close to his Studies (in which I flatter myself you will
join me). . . .

It may be expected of me perhaps, to say something of Fortune . . . In General therefore I shall inform you, that, Mr Custis's
Estate consists of abt 15,000 Acres of Land . . . between two &
three hundd Negroes; and about Eight or ten thousd Pounds [about
$600,000 to $750,000 today]—this Estate he now holds indepen-
dant of his Mothers Dower . . . I should hope, & expect . . . that you
would also be willing to do something genteel by your Daughter.

At all times when you, Mrs Calvert, or the young Ladies can
make it convenient to favour us with a visit we should be happy in
seeing you at this place. Mrs. Washington & Miss Custiss join me
in respectful Compliments, and I am Dr Sir Yr Most Obedt Servt.

Go: Washington[22]

Benedict Calvert, to whom Washington had written this difficult letter, was the illegitimate son of Charles Calvert, the fifth Lord
Baltimore, a rake of the first magnitude, but nonetheless lord propri-
etor of Maryland. Far from disowning his illegitimate offspring, he
left them rather well off: Benedict won appointment to the state
Council (equivalent to Virginia's burgesses) and married the daughter of the Maryland governor at the time. A close friend of the current governor, Sir Robert Eden, Calvert had met Washington at
Annapolis social functions, and neither Washington nor any of the
Virginia or Maryland landed gentry held Calvert in disrepute
because of his illegitimacy. Few Americans of wealth dared trace
their own ancestry too carefully, so they naturally ignored Calvert's
origins. After Jacky Custis delivered Washington's letter, Calvert
sent Jacky back to Mount Vernon with his reply, in which he made
clear that, with ten daughters, he would not be able to give any of
them dowries of any consequence. After thanking Washington for
approving Jacky's marriage to his daughter, he agreed "intirely . . .
that it is, as yet, too early in life for Mr Custis to enter upon the mat-
rimonial State, and hope his being placed at New York [college]—

may be attended with every advantage to him which, you and Mrs Washington can, at present, desire . . . Permit me at the same time to hope with you, that this Separation will only delay, not break off, the intended Match."[23]

Early in May, Martha and George let Jacky go to Mount Airy, Maryland, to say good-bye to Nelly, and two days later, George arrived to take him to New York to enroll at King's College. After a night at the Calverts, however, Washington spent several days at Governor Eden's home before he, the governor, and Jacky boarded the governor's family ship *Annapolis* to sail to Philadelphia, where they all dined with Governor Richard Penn, grandson of William Penn. After a night at the governor's mansion, Penn took them to festivities at the Jockey Club, of which he was president and official host of the Philadelphia Assemblies, the oldest, most fashionable society ball in the Americas. Washington's stay turned into a five-day bacchanal—at the races each day, at the governor's for dinner, cards at night, two balls, and two nights of drinking at the Jockey Club.

It was heady company for Jacky, who had not realized until then the full extent of his stepfather's renown and political connections. With the race meeting over, they left for New Jersey and a dinner with Governor William Franklin, son of Benjamin, before visiting New Jersey College, at Princeton, where Washington's two nephews, the sons of his sister Betty Washington Lewis, were studying. More than two weeks after they had left Mount Vernon, Washington and Jacky finally reached New York—only to begin a new round of entertainments. By coincidence, they had arrived in time for an enormous celebration and farewell banquet for General Thomas Gage, the commander of British troops in North America. Washington and Gage had fought together in the ill-fated Braddock expedition, with Gage then a lieutenant colonel in a regiment of British regulars. In addition to the public farewell dinner, Washington, Gage, and other high-ranking officers shared a private dinner two nights later. After taking Jacky to two plays—including *Hamlet*—Washington remembered to enroll Custis at King's College, and, to Jacky's continuing amazement, the president of the college—the renowned Reverend Myles Cooper—was there to greet them both.

"My dear Momma," Jacky wrote to his mother, "I believe I may say without vanity that I am look'd upon in a particular Light by them all [the faculty].

> There is as much Distinction made between me, & the other Students as can be expected. I dine with them [the professors] (A liberty that is not allow'd any but myself) associate & pertake of all their recreations & their Attention to my Education keeps pace with their other good offices . . . I have a large parlour with two Studies or closets, each large enough to contain a bed, trunk, & couple of chairs, one I sleep in, & the other Joe [his servant] calls his.[24]

Washington returned to Mount Vernon on June 8 to find the usual complement of family and friends at the Mansion—including his brother Jack, his wife, and their two children, and, to Washington's surprise, Miss Nelly Calvert, whom Martha had invited and embraced warmly. Ten days later, however, the joy reigning over the Mansion suddenly vanished.

"[At] About five oclock, poor Patcy Custis Died Suddenly,"[25] Washington wrote in his diary. Martha sobbed quietly, uncontrollably, and George did what he could to comfort her, holding her to him, as tears streamed down both their faces. He had loved Martha's "little Pat" as much as she. The rest of the family sat in the parlor below in silence, not knowing what to do or say—no one more than Nelly Calvert, who still treaded unsteadily on the fringes of the family.

The minister arrived the following day to hold services, after which Washington wrote to Martha's beloved sister "Nancy" (Anna Maria) and her husband, Burwell Bassett, to whom George had grown especially close:

> It is an easier matter to conceive, than to describe, the distress of this Family, especially that of the unhappy Parent of our Dear Patcy Custis, when I inform you that yesterday removd the Sweet Innocent Girl into a more happy, & peaceful abode than any she has met with in the afflicted Path she hitherto has trod. She rose from Dinner about four Oclock, in better health and spirits than she appeared to have been in for some time; soon after which she

was siezd with one of her usual Fits, & expired in it, in less than two Minutes without uttering a Word, a groan, or scarce a sigh. This Sudden, and unexpected blow, I scarce need add has almost reduced my poor wife to the lowest ebb of Misery; which is encreas'd by the absence of her Son . . . and want of the balmy Consolation of her Relations.[26]

Jacky waited a week to send a letter of consolation to his mother and stepfather, not quite knowing how to broach the subject. Self-gratification had so dominated his being that even in his own genuine grief, he began his letter to Washington pretentiously:

> It gives me pleasure that I now have in my Power to inform you how agreeably every thing is settled. there has nothing been omitted by my good Friend [King's College president] Doctor Cooper which was necessary to my contentment in this Place, and Gratitude as well as Truth oblidges me to say, that the other Professors are not the least remiss in their Duty but give all the assistance they can consistant with the Duty, they owe to the other students. . . . I Hope the Progress I make . . . will redown not only to my own Credit, but to the Credit of those who have been instrumental in placeing me here, & in particular render you some compensation & Satisfaction for the parental Care and Attention you have always & upon all occasions manifested towards me, & which demand my most grateful thanks & returns.[27]

In the mournful days that followed, the Fairfaxes came daily, George's brother Jack and Jack's family—and Nelly Calvert—remained to console Martha and George as much as they could. The Calverts paid a consolation call a week later and took their daughter home. Ten days passed before George could convince Martha to leave the Mansion to dine with the Fairfaxes at Belvoir, and a few days later George took Martha riding to various parts of the plantation. Washington plunged into his business affairs for the rest of the summer, never wandering too far from Martha or the Mansion.

On July 8 the Fairfaxes added to the gloom at Mount Vernon by announcing they were leaving for an indefinite stay in England. Fairfax gave George power of attorney over his affairs in Virginia, including Belvoir. All four sensed it was the last time they would ever see each other.

Recognizing that he could not leave his inconsolable wife by herself, Washington canceled his western trip with Governor Dunmore. He also abandoned plans to develop a plantation on the twenty-four thousand acres in veterans' lands he had claimed in the Ohio River Valley, opting instead to advertise for tenant farmers to settle the area.

Nelly and her sisters visited the Washingtons regularly and proved a genuine consolation to both Washingtons. Nelly was Patcy's age and helped fill the void that Patcy had left in Martha's world. Early in September, Nelly and her parents showed up with Maryland governor Eden and several other guests, who, together, helped revive the normally festive atmosphere at the Mansion. At Martha's urging, Washington made plans to attend the races at Annapolis at the end of the month. Leaving Martha at home— at her insistence—he left for the Maryland capital on September 26, where he "spent the evening & lodged at the Governors." He spent the next five days attending the races, theater, and formal assemblies, or balls, where, as usual, he played cards after a few courtesy turns on the ballroom floor with the governor's wife. To Washington's astonishment, Jacky Custis appeared for what he claimed was a vacation of four or five weeks.

When Washington and his stepson returned to Mount Vernon, Jacky convinced Martha to let him quit college and marry Nelly Calvert. Martha had already embraced Nelly as her own in the days following Patcy's death, and she longed to have her "children" home again. Washington recognized the futility of insisting that Jacky complete his education, and he wrote to King's College president Myles Cooper admitting defeat. "I have yielded, contrary to my judgement, & much against my wishes, to his quitting College . . . having his own inclination—the desires of his mother—& the acquiescence of almost all his relatives, to encounter, I did not care, as he is the last of the family, to push my opposition too far; & therefore have submitted to a Kind of necessity."[28]

Adding to Washington's distress was a letter from William Crawford in western Pennsylvania warning that squatters "about 10 or 12 in number has gon on your Cherter Land within this few days and there is no geting them of[f] without by Force of Arms."[29]

Washington often responded to adversity by spending his way out of despondency. He found a contractor to begin a lavish expansion at both ends of the Mansion at Mount Vernon, with a library on the south end and a bedroom above it, and a two-story banquet room at the north end. He would realize his ambition to transform his home into a mansion as stately as Belvoir.

5

The Glorious Cause

ON THE EVENING OF DECEMBER 16, 1773, a mob disguised as Indians dumped 342 chests of tea worth about $1.5 million in today's currency into Boston Harbor. While Boston lawyer John Adams called the act nothing less than "an Epocha in History,"[1] Virginia planters like Washington deplored it as vandalism. Virginians had not only abandoned anti-British boycotts, they had also consumed 80,000 pounds of tea in 1773 and planned on drinking more in '74. Bostonians, Washington concluded, were mad; Virginia had no intention of letting New England disturb the calm, quiet ways of the South.

Although the Washingtons spent Christmas Day of '73 alone, Jacky Custis and some young friends, including portraitist Peale, descended on the Mansion three days later and set it aglow with laughter, song, and games. "One afternoon," Charles Willson Peale recalled, "several young gentlemen visitors at Mount Vernon and myself were . . . pitching the bar . . . when suddenly the colonel appeared among us.

> He requested to be shown the pegs that marked the bounds of our efforts; then, smiling, and without putting off his coat, held out his hand for the missile. No sooner . . . did the heavy iron bar feel the grasp of his mighty hand than it lost the power of gravitation, striking the ground far . . . beyond our utmost limits. We were indeed amazed, as we stood around, all stripped to the buff . . . having thought ourselves very clever fellows, while the colonel, on retir-

ing, pleasantly observed, "When you beat my pitch, young gentlemen, I'll try again."[2]

On February 3, Washington went to the Calverts in Mount Airy,
Maryland, to celebrate the wedding of his stepson, Jacky Custis, to
Nelly Calvert. After the ceremony, he gave Nelly a letter (long since
lost) from Martha, who was still grieving Patcy's death and did not
want to insinuate her sadness or mourning dress on the marriage
festivities.

"My dear Nelly," she is said to have written:

> God took from Me a Daughter. . . . He has now given me another
> daughter about her Age . . . to warm my Heart again. I am as
> Happy as One so Afflicted and so Blest can be. Pray receive my
> Benediction and a Wish that you may long live the Loving Wife of
> my happy Son, and a Loving Daughter of
>
> > Your Affectionate Mother
> > M. Washington.[3]

Martha hoped, in her heart, that Jacky and Nelly would make
their home at Mount Vernon while they built their new home; but
despite urgings from Washington, they remained at Mount Airy.

As the winter of 1774 progressed, the Mansion at Mount Vernon
grew lonely—especially for Martha, who missed the back-and-forth
visits with the Fairfaxes at nearby Belvoir; she missed the sounds of
Patcy, Jacky, and Nelly. All sorts of men streamed in and out to keep
George entertained—making deals, hunting, showing off his property, his mill, and his other accomplishments. Old soldiers stopped to
claim veterans' lands, ask for help or money, and exchange war stories; political leaders of all persuasions stopped to pay their respects;
business associates and acquaintances came to deal in land, commodities, and dreams. Washington cheered Martha by staying as
close to home as possible and taking her with him on some of his
morning rides. As the first buds heralded the coming spring, the
entire Calvert family, including Jacky, Nelly, and nine unmarried
daughters, descended on the Mansion for a week's visit, and the
spring blossoms that followed brought the renewal of other family
visits. Few homes in America matched the beauty of Mount Vernon
in bloom and its sweeping panorama of the Potomac River Valley

and Maryland hills on the horizon. The Bassetts and their children came for two weeks; then the Washingtons went to visit the Calverts at Mount Airy, Maryland—only to see their sumptuous carriage roll off the ferry into the muddy river. It cost him 18 shillings to have the carriage pulled onshore and cleaned.

In early May, the Custises returned to Mount Vernon, and the Washingtons took them to a boat race on the Rappahannock, where they watched two longboats "each with a captain and five or six Negro hands row a mile out 'round a Boat lying at anchor and then back to shore." The Washingtons and Custises picnicked on the shore with other spectators. Martha had ordered her cooks to prepare an elaborate dinner, with hams, cheeses, and a variety of other foods, and Washington ordered forty-eight bottles of claret to wash them down. He preferred having too much on hand to having too little.

Washington was to leave for Williamsburg and the spring session of the House of Burgesses when he received devastating news from the West: civil war had broken out, with Virginia militiamen seizing Fort Pitt from the Pennsylvania militia and renaming it Fort Dunmore. Adding to the turmoil, Indians had taken advantage of the situation by attacking white settlers along the Ohio River on land owned by Washington and other veterans of '54. After Washington's advertisements had failed to attract tenant farmers for his western properties, he had sent a land manager—William Crawford's brother Valentine—with a team of twenty laborers to develop at least one farm—a legal requirement under Virginia law to ensure proprietorship of claimed lands. He had purchased four convicts, four indentured servants, and an indentured couple to go with Crawford and hoped that if they succeeded, their example would lure tenant farmers to the area.

"I am Sorrey to Enform you the disturbence betwen the white people and the Indens has pervented My going down the River as all the Jentlemen that went down is Returnd and Chefly Lost all there bagege," Valentine Crawford wrote.

> I got My Canews and all My provisions Redy and Should have Set of[f] in 2 or 3 days but for this aruption braking out which I bleve wase as much the White people falt as the Indens. . . . I thought it dengerous to goe down with So Much of your property and So

View of the Mansion at Mount Vernon—one of America's most beautiful homes. This view of the west (front entrance), attributed to Edward Savage, may have been painted in 1797.

Came to a Resulution to Send my Son down to you to know what I must doe with your Sarvants and goods.[4]

A second letter arrived the next day:

I am Sorrey to Enform you the Indens have Stopt all the J[e]ntlemen from going down the River.

In the first place the Indens Kild one Murfey a trader and wounded and a Nother and Robed the Canews which Elarmed the Jentlemen verey Much . . . [a] partey of Men . . . way Laid Som Canews that was going down the River and Shot two Endins out of them and Scalped them and Emedently Raised a party and tuck Canews and forlowed a party of Endens . . . and Kild three and wounded Severell the Endens wounded three one of which wase vere Bad he wase Shot through and the other two but Slighty and on Saterday Last . . . about 20 men fell on a party of Endens . . . and Kild 10 of them and brought away one Child a prisoner which is now att my Brother william Crawfords all this Alarming Surcomstances has put it out of My power to Excute your bisness I therefore Come to a Reselution to Send My Son down to you to Let you Know of this Desogreeable desopoinment . . . an allso to

Know what I must doe with your Carpenters and Sarvents and goods.[5]

Washington packed Martha into the coach and set off for Williamsburg, less interested in attending the House of Burgesses than in confronting the governor for triggering hostilities in the West and threatening the enormous veterans' land project in which Washington held so large a stake. Washington dropped Martha off at the home of her sister Nancy Bassett in Eltham, then went to the governor's palace. To his dismay, he learned that when Dunmore had traveled west the previous summer—without Washington—His Lordship concluded it would be easier for troops to seize lands he wanted than to negotiate their purchase. The Scotsman calmed Washington with assurances that Virginia's troops would protect Washington's Ohio River Valley holdings.

With the rest of the Burgesses staunchly in favor of Dunmore's War, they had planned to debate nothing more important than ways to prevent hogs, goats, and geese from running at large in the streets of the capital. Events in London, however, radically changed the complexion of their discussions.

Parliament had been raging over the Boston Tea Party through the winter months, and on March 25 it decided to punish the perpetrators by ordering the port of Boston closed to all shipping beginning June 1. On that date, the British army and navy would seal Boston off from the world and starve its inhabitants until they submitted unconditionally to parliamentary sovereignty by compensating the East India Company for its losses and demonstrating "that peace and obedience to the laws shall be so far restored . . . that the trade of Great Britain may be safely carried on there, and his Majesty's customs duly collected."

News of the Boston Port Bill provoked some "upstart" burgesses in Williamsburg—Thomas Jefferson, Patrick Henry, and Richard Henry Lee—to name June 1 "a day of fasting, humiliation, and prayer."[6] Although most burgesses pompously out-Britished British aristocrats whenever they could, almost all were planters and merchants who recognized that if Parliament could shut the port of Boston with impunity, it could shut every American port. Even Washington could not tolerate that kind of government intervention in his business affairs. With the other burgesses, he voted for the day of fasting and prayer, and, again like the others, sent a note to church pastors in his home county to ask parishioners to participate.

Governor Dunmore was furious, but postponed his response to confer with Washington at the governor's farm outside town. In a careful political dance, Washington suggested ceding Fort Pitt back to Pennsylvania and sending the Virginia militia to quell the Indians on the Ohio River. Dunmore, in turn, asked Washington to convince the burgesses to rescind the resolution for a day of fasting and prayer. Each thought he had an understanding with the other as they rode into town the next day. Washington voted with the majority of burgesses for resolutions asking "royal interposition" to reverse Parliament's measures. Lord Dunmore responded by dissolving the House of Burgesses. As they had before, the burgesses—all of them angry commoners now—reconvened at Raleigh Tavern. Led by Washington, they agreed that "an attack, made on one of our Sister Colonies . . . is an attack made on all British America" and recommended that "deputies from the several Colonies of British America . . . meet in general congress . . . to deliberate on those general measures which the united interests of America may from time to time require."[7] They named Washington, among others, to represent Virginia.

The following evening, however, Washington, Martha, and the other burgesses and their wives donned their English silks and velvets to attend the festive ball in honor of Lady Dunmore, the governor's wife. Virginia's "aristocracy" were, for the moment, still British.

On June 1, Washington and the others went to church and fasted the entire day.

After a few days of relaxation with Martha at the Bassetts, Washington returned to Williamsburg for a rump session of burgesses at Raleigh Tavern. They debated endlessly over wording a resolution to support the people of Boston without provoking Parliament into closing Virginia's ports. Washington was as indecisive as his colleagues, however, believing, on the one hand, that Americans should "never be tax'd without their own consent" and that "the cause of Boston . . . [is] the cause of America." On the other hand, he strongly disapproved of the Boston mob's "cond[uc]t in destroyg the Tea" and disavowed all schemes to suspend all trade with Britain, which he said would only bankrupt planters and destroy Virginia's economy. Then news arrived from London that Parliament was about to pass what colonists would soon call the "Intolerable" or "Coercive" Acts. Evidently not content with economic reprisals, Parliament was ready to exact political reprisals on American colonists by giving the king the right to appoint all members of the provincial council, or upper house, of the Massachusetts legislature—hitherto an elected body. Still worse, Parliament gave colonial governors power to send persons accused of treason to England for trial, thus stripping colonists of the right to trial by a jury of their peers. And a third act extended Canada's boundaries to the Ohio River, effectively expropriating western territories of Virginia, Pennsylvania, Connecticut, and Massachusetts—and the properties of Washington and other landowners.

That was too much!

For Washington and his insatiable appetite for land, the right to redress for government property seizures was inviolable. Washington's friend Bryan Fairfax—George William Fairfax's brother—urged giving Parliament "a fair Opportunity" to reverse itself by sending "a petition unaccompanied with any Threats [of a boycott]," but Washington responded abruptly: "Have we not tried this already? Have we not addressed the Lords, and remonstrated to the Commons? And to what end?"[8]

When Washington returned to Mount Vernon, nothing but frightful news awaited: "Endens Murdred one famely Concisting of Six and tuck two boys preseners," wrote Valentine Crawford from western Pennsylvania, "and att another place the[y] Kild 3 which makes in the hole Nine and two preseners . . . we have att this time att least 300 Men out after Indens."[9]

As Indians were overrunning his Ohio River Valley lands, Washington received a letter from George William Fairfax that he and Sally would remain in England permanently, and he asked his friend from boyhood to sell Belvoir and its contents. Washington had no choice. Perhaps they were right to abandon Virginia, he replied to Fairfax. "God only knows what is to become of us, threatned as we are with so many hoverg evils as hang over us at present . . . there is a confederacy of the Western, & Southern Indian's formed against us and our Settlemt over the Alligany Mountains . . . a general war is inevitable whilst those from whom we have a right to Seek protection are endeavouring by every piece of Art & despotism to fix the Shackles of Slavry upon us."[10]

In mid-August Washington went to preside over the huge, sad auction to strip Belvoir of the beautiful furnishings he had known and loved since boyhood. He could not resist bidding and spent large sums for a variety of furniture and furnishings that had special meanings to him, among them a mahogany tallboy, or two-tiered chest of drawers, a mahogany sideboard, a set of dining room chairs, and a large gilt-framed mirror.

Washington had no sooner carted the last of his purchases from Belvoir than the youthful lawyer Patrick Henry and the aging Virginia justice Edmund Pendleton appeared at the Mansion door. They spent the night and, after dining early the next afternoon, they and George said their farewells to Martha. "Mrs. Washington talked like a Spartan to her son on his going to battle," Pendleton wrote to a friend. "'I hope you will all stand firm,' she said. 'I know George will.'"[11]

They reached Philadelphia on September 4 and, as in the House of Burgesses, Washington listened, said nothing, won no committee appointments—and slipped out to shop for clothing (and three bedsteads) that he had promised Martha. Washington was an outspoken—indeed, a gifted—debater and orator one on one, but he despised standing before an assemblage; he felt self-conscious and lost his voice. He was happiest in a room of card players. Then he could talk! "I think the Parliament of Great Britain," he scolded Bryan Fairfax, "hath no more right to put their hands in my pocket, without my consent, than I have to put my hands into your's for money."[12]

Former governor William Penn and other notables he had met the previous year taking Jacky to college invited him to dinner parties to meet other delegates. The city's civic and religious leaders sponsored a major "Entertainment" for the "genteel strangers as happened to be in town. . . . After dinner . . . toasts were drunk, accompanied by musick and a discharge of cannon."[13] It was a perfect site for Washington, who had only to stand upright to be visible across the room and draw a crowd about him. Even those he did not know had heard of his exploits as a soldier and commander in the French and Indian War, as one of Virginia's wealthiest planters and wiliest land speculators, and as a figure of note in Williamsburg political circles. Each repetition invariably embellished the previous tale.

Connecticut delegate Silas Deane wrote to his wife that Washington was "tall," with "a hard . . . contenance; yet . . . a very young look, and an easy, soldier like air and gesture. He does not appear above forty-five [he was forty-two], yet was in the first actions in 1753 and 1754, on the Ohio, and in 1755 was with Braddock, and was the means of saving the remains of that unfortunate army. It is said in the House of Burgesses in Virginia, on hearing of the Boston Port Bill, he offered to raise and arm and lead one thousand men himself at his own expense, for the defence of the country, were there need of it. His fortune is said to be equal to such an undertaking."[14]

South Carolina's Thomas Lynch confided to John Adams that the ever-silent Colonel Washington "had made the most eloquent Speech at the Virginia Convention that ever was made. Says he, 'I will raise 1000 Men, subsist them at my own Expence, and march my self at their Head for the Relief of Boston.'"[15]

Washington dined several times with Adams, and their long, intense conversations proved decisive in Washington's personal thinking. A brilliant attorney, Adams did most of the talking and Washington, true to form, listened—to the intense pleasure of both. The two were an incongruous pair: Adams, five feet, six inches, admittedly "short, thick, fat,"[16] tilting his head back to bark at the huge, soft-spoken Virginian, who looked down quizzically. Onlookers held their breaths, fearing the consequences of disagreement. But both were farmers—avid farmers; skilled and knowledgeable, at ease talking weather, soil, crops—although Adams had some difficulty relating his forty acres to Washington's forty thousand. Both also loved horses, hunting, and "ducking." Washington admired men of learning; Adams had gone to Harvard. Adams admired soldiers, felt guilty that he had not served in the French and Indian War. When the two were done, they were as one, with lawyer Adams's cogent arguments ending Washington's indecision about the use of arms to protect colonist rights and the role he was to play.

The people of Massachusetts, Washington wrote a few days later, "are every day receiving fresh proofs of a Systematic ascertion of an arbitrary power, deeply planned to overturn the Laws & Constitution of their Country, & to violate the most essential & valuable rights of mankind . . . none of them will ever submit to the loss of those valuable rights & priviledges which are essential to the happiness of every free State, and without which, Life, Liberty & property are rendered totally insecure." Washington predicted that if Parliament did not yield, "more blood will be spilt . . . than history has ever yet furnished instances of in the annals of North America."[17]

Until then, the public man and the private Washington had acted in concert, marching on- and offstage filling secondary rolls in such regional theaters as the French and Indian War and the Virginia House of Burgesses. With his appearance at the Continental Congress, the public man now stepped front and center onto the national—indeed, international—stage and relegated the private man to the wings.

Curiously enough, the private Washington and the private Adams had many other common interests: both savored Madeira, and both obsessively noted every ha'penny they spent. The two shared many pleasant experiences in Philadelphia. Although Washington normally attended Anglican services, sheer interest took him to a Quaker service one Sunday, and Adams took him to Presbyterian services. Then, "led by curiosity and good company," Adams and Washington drew stares as they jaunted together to experience "Romish" [Roman Catholic] services.[18]

On September 17, Congress resolved "unanimously that this assembly deeply feels the suffering of their countrymen in the Massachusetts Bay . . . that they most thoroughly approve the wisdom and fortitude, with which opposition to these wicked ministerial measures has hitherto been conducted." The members pledged to continue sending gifts of food and other necessities to ease the plight of besieged Bostonians—but that was all.

"Tedious indeed . . . slow as snails,"[19] John Adams grumbled.

As always, the private Washington eased the public Washington's boredom by shopping—shoes, gloves, a pocketbook for Martha, a "Cloak for my Mother," and a "Chaize for my Mother." With Mount Vernon never far from his thoughts, he explored the produce market for unusual varieties of fruit whose seeds he could propagate when he returned home. He bought a gross of exceptionally sweet peaches and removed the stones to take back to plant. And, of course, Washington always found a card game and a few private moments to pen a letter to Martha, to keep her informed of the proceedings and reiterate his love.

The emerging public man, however, did not ignore the obligations of that role: he bought a stack of "sundry pamphlets" on every political point of view on the Anglo-American crisis. He was, in the end, as well versed as any delegate—if not more so—in the thinking processes generating congressional debates—without having said a word. By mid-October, Washington's grasp of the issues, his ingratiating personality, and the curious oratorical gifts he so easily displayed in small groups earned him "membership" in the exclusive, policymaking Governor's Club, "a select Number of Gentlemen that meet every Night at a certain Tavern, where they pass away a few Hours in the Pleasures of Conversation and a Cheerful Glass."[20]

In October, Congress agreed to ban imports of British and Irish goods and slaves beginning December 1 and to cease exporting to Britain the following year, 1775, beginning in September—unless Parliament redressed colonial grievances before then. Congress urged each colony to select delegates to meet at a second Congress, in May 1775.

On October 27, Washington set off for home, having conversed incessantly with other delegates outside the meeting hall, but not having addressed a single word to "Congress assembled." In his absence, Lord Dunmore's Virginia militiamen had won a decisive victory against the Indians at the junction of the Ohio and Kanawha rivers—on George Washington's property. Although Dunmore's troops pushed the Indians out of the Ohio River Valley, his victory cost Washington a small fortune. During the fighting, all his slaves and indentured workers had fled—taking his implements and supplies.

When he reached Mount Vernon, he found Virginia preparing for war. One hundred of Alexandria's leading citizens had formed a "Fairfax Independent Company" to defend the county against British or Indian attack and, without his knowledge, elected Washington its commander. He would now have to drill the company each week and provide it "with a pair of Colours, two Drums, two Fifes, and two Halberts" (typically, a battle-ax and pike mounted on a six-foot-long handle). Like his officers, he purchased a handsome new blue-and-buff uniform—blue jacket with buff lapels, vest, and pants, and white stockings.

With no time to travel west himself, he bought a new team of indentured workers and slaves and sent them with one of his most trusted overseers to work his Ohio River Valley properties. Fortunately, his Mount Vernon plantations were functioning smoothly under Lund Washington, and when the year ended, Washington balanced his books and found that almost all his enterprises had produced comfortable profits.

In the new year, he turned to one of his favorite pastimes at Mount Vernon—grafting fruit trees. He adored grafting, had learned it from books, was exceptionally skilled at it, and found great comfort writing about it. Grafting kept him focused—far from the realities beyond the orchards that seemed to be pressing closer.

On the 10th of March when the Cherry buds were a good deal Swelled, & the White part of them beginning to appear, I grafted the following Cherries viz.

In the Row next the Quarter & beginning at the end next the grass walk, 13 May Duke & next to those 12 Black May Cherry both from Colo. Masons and cut from the Trees yesterday.

In the Row next to these 6 Coronation, and 6 May Cherry from Colo. Ricd. Lees but I do not know which is first as they were not distinguished.

March 11th. At the head of the Octagon—left hand side—in the first Row, next the gravel walk 5 Peach Kernals fine sort from Philadelphia. In the next 4 Rows to these 130 Peaches also of a fine kind from Phila.—same as Colo. Fairfax white Peach Row next these 25 Mississippi Nuts—something like the Pignut—but longer, thiner shelld & fuller of Meat.[21]

In mid-March he went to Richmond for a meeting of county delegates, who reelected him and his six colleagues to represent Virginia in the Second Continental Congress, in May. With routine business completed, Patrick Henry electrified delegates with his famous cry for "liberty or death" and won passage of a resolution for Virginia's counties to recruit troops. Henry's words inspired Washington enough to write his brother Jack that "it is my full intention to devote my Life & Fortune in the cause we are engag'd in." Jack himself was organizing an independent company, and George expressed "my entire approbation of the laudable pursuit you are [en]gaged in."[22]

When Washington returned to Mount Vernon he discovered the personal costs of opposing the Crown: a curt note from the man who often hosted him in the palace at Williamsburg announced that "the Patents granted for the Lands under the Proclamation of 1754 will . . . be declared Null and void." It was signed "Dunmore."[23] Fortunately, the workers Washington had sent to Ohio had built three houses, ten cabins, and a barn on each of fourteen lots of his property. They had also cleared and tilled twenty-eight acres—two acres on each lot—and planted "large crops of corn, potatoes & turnips."[24] Dunmore might nullify the patents of other veterans of 1754, but under Virginia colonial law, Washington had established indisputable ownership rights to his own property by building homes and settling and tilling the land productively. He believed the twenty-three thousand acres were legally his and counted on their serving him and his family as a refuge if the British army should overrun Mount Vernon and eastern Virginia.

Before Washington could respond to Dunmore's letter, riots broke out in Williamsburg. Under orders from Dunmore, Royal Marines had removed the gunpowder from the ammunition dump and left the militia without firepower to defend against Indian attacks. Townsfolk and militiamen marched on the palace. As troops from nearby counties mobilized to help them, their commanders wrote to Washington to take command of the combined force. Before he could respond, Speaker Peyton Randolph went to the palace and convinced Dunmore to return the powder to the local militia and avoid needless bloodshed.

Just as peace returned to Williamsburg, a group of farmers in Lexington, Massachusetts, fired at British troops and created a crisis atmosphere in Philadelphia for delegates to the impending Second Congress. "Unhappy it is," Washington wrote to George William Fairfax in London, "that a Brother's Sword has been sheathed in a

Brother's breast, and that, the once happy and peaceful plains of America are either to be drenched with Blood, or Inhabited by Slaves. Sad Alternative! But can a virtuous Man hesitate in his choice?"[25]

Mount Vernon was in full bloom when Washington prepared to leave for Philadelphia: spring plowing was complete; large early crops of corn, potatoes, and turnips were sprouting; and the herring catch had reached record levels. Washington turned his financial affairs over to his brother-in-law Fielding Lewis—sister Betty's husband—and placed Lund Washington in full command of Mount Vernon. Lund agreed to send detailed weekly reports on every aspect of plantation activities. Still, Washington hesitated to leave, fearing Dunmore might punish him for participating in the Congress by confiscating his western lands or, worse, declaring him a traitor and sending troops to Mount Vernon. The Massachusetts governor had done just that: he declared John Hancock and Samuel Adams traitors, seized Hancock's magnificent Boston mansion, and sent troops to capture them and carry them back to England for summary execution.

Relatives filled every bed at Mount Vernon the night before Washington's departure—his brother Jack, sister Betty, their spouses, children, cousins. In addition, a swarm of uninvited guests appeared—Major Horatio Gates, Richard Henry Lee, and others—and, to Martha's dismay, they were staying the night. Martha had hoped to spend some time alone with her husband. He had left her for two months during the previous session of Congress. With open warfare under way, the new session would last longer—and if British troops stormed Congress and arrested members for treason . . . ? Now, on their last evening together, she could only mask her disappointment with a gallant smile as visitors stole him from her. In the morning, she gathered her strength and reassumed the Spartan look that had so impressed Edmund Pendleton when Washington had left for the First Congress the previous autumn.

Washington left Mount Vernon dressed in the striking blue-and-buff uniform of the Fairfax County Independent Company. Riding, hunting, and farming had kept the forty-three-year-old Virginian trim. He looked superb. When he reached Baltimore, he reviewed the town militia, then went to a dinner in his honor. Everyone looked at him as their leader. He not only looked the part, he acted it.

He and the other Virginians arrived in Philadelphia on May 9. The Second Continental Congress convened two days later, reelecting Peyton Randolph president. He immediately startled delegates by announcing that Massachusetts had declared independence from Britain, that its militia had laid siege to British-held Boston, and that state leaders had appealed to Congress to provide "a powerful army" from other colonies for support.

As usual, Washington said nothing on the floor of Congress, but his grandeur in uniform sent a message that reverberated across the chamber. "Colonel Washington appears at Congress in his uniform," wrote John Adams, "and, by his experience and abilities in military matters, is of much service to us."[26] Clearly, Washington was dressed for war, and Congress asked him to chair a committee on military policy and defense and another "to consider ways and means to supply these Colonies with ammunition and military stores and to report immediately."[27] He knew all too well, however, that he lacked qualifications for military high command. His only experience had been to lead a few hundred men to disaster in the wilderness against a handful of French and Indians. His only battle experience—with Braddock—had ended in humiliation. The largest force he had ever commanded was a brigade, never a large army, and he had never planned grand strategies or military tactics. He knew little or nothing about artillery, ordinance, or naval warfare, and although he had served under and learned from such top British generals as Forbes and Braddock, he had been the first to deprecate their tactics as inappropriate to warfare in the American wilderness. Ever the believer in education, however, he did what he had done in his gardens and fields at Mount Vernon: he bought books to study—five huge tomes on military organization, procedures, and tactics, and between letters to and from Martha, he studied to be a general.

On June 10, John Adams moved that Congress "adopt" the Massachusetts army surrounding Boston and appoint a commander in chief. Of the four candidates, the titular leader of the Massachusetts militia, John Hancock, had never been a soldier or fired a shot. The other two—Horatio Gates and Charles Lee—were both experienced officers, but were British, and Congress was in no mood to trust Englishmen to resolve their disputes with England. "I had no hesitation to declare that I had but one gentleman in my Mind for that important command," Adams recalled, "and that was a Gentleman from Virginia . . . whose Skill and Experience as an Officer, whose independent fortune, great Talents and excellent universal Character, would command the Approbation of all America, and unite the Exertions of all the Colonies better than any other Person in the Union. . . . Mr Samuel Adams Seconded the Motion."[28]

"Mr President," Washington began his first address to Congress, "Tho' I am truly sensible of the high Honour done me in this Appointment, yet I feel great distress, from a consciousness that my abilities & Military experience may not be equal to the extensive & important Trust: However, as the Congress desire i[t] I will enter upon the momentous duty, & exert every power I Possess In their service & for the Support of the glorious Cause: I beg they will accept my most cordial thanks for this distinguished testimony of their Approbation.

"But lest some unlucky event should happen unfavourable to my reputation, I beg it may be rememberd by every Gentn in the room, that I this day declare with the utmost sincerity, I do not think my self equal to the Command I [am] honoured with.

"As to pay, Sir[s], I beg leave to Assure the Congress that as no pecuniary consideration could have tempted me to have accepted this Arduous emploiment at the expence of my domestk ease & happi[ness] I do not wish to make any proffit from it: I will keep an exact Account of my expences; those I doubt not they will discharge & that is all I desire."[29]

It was vintage Washington, combining poise with disinterest to unite Congress and win almost every member to his side. And it was honest. He had openly admitted his lack of qualifications, although most listeners interpreted his admission as mere modesty. "There is Something charming to me, in the Conduct of Washington," John Adams exulted. "A Gentleman, of one of the first Fortunes, upon the Continent, leaving his delicious Retirement, his Family and Friends, Sacrificing his Ease, hazarding all in the Cause of his Country. His Views are noble and disinterested. He declared when he accepted the mighty Trust, that he would lay before Us, an exact account of his Expenses, and not accept a shilling for Pay."[30]

Three days after his acceptance speech, the president of Congress gave Washington his commission as "GENERAL AND COMMANDER IN CHIEF of the army of the United Colonies and of all the forces raised or to be raised by them. . . . And you are hereby vested with full power and authority to act as you shall think for the good and Welfare of the service."[31]

After an initial rush of exhilaration, a wave of anxiety and remorse enveloped him. On Sunday he went to Anglican services, then to his lodgings to spend the day writing. His huge hands were unsteady as he put pen and ink to paper:

My Dearest,   Philadelphia, June 18th 1775

I am now set down to write you on a subject which fills me with inexpressable concern—and this concern is greatly aggravated and Increased when I reflect on the uneasiness I know it will give you—It has been determined in Congress, that the whole Army raised for the defence of the American Cause shall be put under my care, and that it is necessary for me to proceed immediately to Boston to take upon me the Command of it. You may believe me my dear Patcy, when I assure you, in the most solemn manner, that, so far from seeking this appointment I have used every endeavour in my power to avoid it, not only from my unwillingness to part with you and the Family, but from a consciousness of its being a trust too great for my Capacity and that I should enjoy more real happiness and felicity in one month with you, at home, than I have the most distant prospect of reaping abroad, if my stay was to be Seven times Seven years. But, as it has been a kind of destiny that has thrown me upon this Service, I shall hope that my undertaking of it, is designd to answer some good purpose—You might, and I suppose did perceive, from the Tenor of my letters, that I was apprehensive I could not avoid this appointment, as I did not even pretend [t]o intimate when I should return—that was the case—it was utterly out of my power to refuse this appointment without exposing my Character to such censures as would have reflected dishonour upon myself, and given pain to my friends—this I am sure could not, and ought not to be pleasing to you, & must have lessend me considerably in my own esteem. I shall rely, therefore, confidently, on that Providence which has heretofore preservd, & been bountiful to me, not doubting but that

General George Washington, commander in chief of the
Continental Army, 1780. Portrait by Charles Willson
Peale, 1780.

I shall return safe to you in the fall—I shall feel no pain from the
Toil, or the danger of the Campaign—My unhappiness will flow,
from the uneasiness I know you will feel at being left alone—
I therefore beg of you to summon your whole fortitude & Resolution, and pass your time as agreeably as possible—nothing will give
me so much sincere satisfaction as to hear this, and to hear it from
your own Pen.[32]

Washington suggested that Martha might prefer moving into a
small house he had built for overnight stays in Alexandria—or to her
relatives in the southern part of the state. "In short, my earnest, &
ardent desire is, that you would pursue any Plan that is more likely to
produce content, and a tolerable degree of Tranquility as it must add
greatly to my uneasy feelings to hear that you are dissastisfied, and
complaining at what I really could not avoid." He told her he had

written and signed a new will, which he enclosed. He told her he had provided for payment of all his debts. "The Provision made for you, in cas[e] of my death, will, I hope, be agreeable. . . ."

He had no sooner signed his letter when one from Martha arrived. Tears welled in his eyes as he added a "P.S."—that he had already bought and sent her "two suits of what I was told wa[s] the prettiest Muslin. I wish it may please you."[33]

After a night of fitful anxiety for Martha, Washington rose early to write a series of emotional letters—one, a plea to his friend Burwell Bassett, husband to Martha's favorite sister, Nancy: "I must Intreat you & Mrs Bassett, if possible, to visit at Mt. Vernon as also my Wife's other friends—I could wish you to take her down, as I have no expectations of returning till Winter & feel great uneasiness at her Lonesome Situation."[34] In the back of his mind were fears that Governor Dunmore might burn Mount Vernon and seize Martha as a hostage.

He then wrote to Jacky Custis that "my great concern upon this occasion, is the thought of leaving your Mother under the uneasiness which I know this affair will throw her into;

> I therefore hope, expect, & indeed have no doubt, of your using every means in your power to keep up her Spirits, by doing every thing in your power, to promote her quiet—I have I must confess uneasy feelings on her acct. . . . I hope it is unnecessary for me to say, that I am always pleased with yours & Nelly's abidance at Mount Vernon . . . I think it absolutely necessary for the peace & satisfaction of your Mother; a consideration which I have no doubt will have due weight with you both, & require no arguments to inforce.

Washington also told his stepson, "You must now take upon yourself the entire management of your own Estate, it will no longer be in my power to assist you."[35]

Washington next wrote to John Augustine ("Jack"), the brother he loved and trusted most. He repeated his plea "that my Friends will visit, & endeavour to keep up the Spirits of my Wife as much as they can, as my departure will, I know be a cutting stroke upon her; and on this acct alone, I have many very disagreeable Sensations—

I hope you & my Sister,* (although the distance is great) will ...
spend a little time at Mount Vernon[.] My sincere regards attend
you both as also the little ones and I am Dr Sir Yr most Affecte
Brother."[36]

As he wrote, a courier arrived with word that full-scale war had
erupted in Massachusetts. British troops had overrun American fortifications on Charlestown Peninsula, across the harbor from Boston.
Although one hundred Americans lay dead, the British suffered
more than one thousand casualties—one of the worst single-day
losses in British military history.

When word of Bunker Hill reached Philadelphia, Congress
ordered Washington to assume command of armed forces in Boston
immediately. He asked for a few minutes to return to his lodgings,
where he stepped to his desk and wrote once more to his beloved
wife:

> My dearest,   Phila June 23d 1775
>
>   As I am within a few Minutes of leaving this City, I could not
> think of departing from it without dropping you a line; especially
> as I do not know whether it may be in my power to write again
> till I get to the Camp in Boston—I go fully trusting in that Prov-
> idence, which has been more bountiful to me than I deserve, &
> in full confidence of a happy meeting with you sometime in the
> Fall.

A voice outside his door demanded his attention. Washington
angrily reminded it who was commander in chief and continued his
note to Martha:

>   I have not time to add more, as I am surrounded with Com-
> pany to take leave of me—I retain an unalterable affection for you,
> which neither time or distance can change, my best love to Jack &
> Nelly, & regard for the rest of the Family concludes me with the
> utmost truth & sincerity Yr entire
>
>   Go: Washington[37]

---

*To show affection, it was common practice to refer to in-laws as "brother" or "sister."

A band blared martial music as General Washington mounted a great white steed and members of Congress boarded a train of carriages to escort him to the edge of town, where he slipped off his horse, jumped into a carriage, and joined his aides for the ride to Boston. Two weeks later, Washington arrived outside Boston to take command of the American army. For the next eight years, Washington, the private man, would cede center stage to the public persona in the great drama of war.

6

"The Fate of Unborn Millions"

On july 3, 1775, george washington settled into the president's house at Harvard College in Cambridge, Massachusetts, to take command of American militiamen surrounding British-held Boston. He did his best to surround himself with the most able commanders, specialists, and aides. As on the plantation, some appointees took advantage of his trust; others responded with love and loyalty. A Philadelphia merchant he appointed as quartermaster-general siphoned kickbacks from suppliers until Washington threatened him with public disgrace if he did not repay his illicit profits. But twenty-five-year-old Henry Knox responded to his appointment as colonel of artillery with unswerving lifelong devotion. Like Washington, Knox had been orphaned at twelve, was a voracious reader and was self-taught. At three hundred pounds, he was an unlikely but eager volunteer, an engineer who displayed such exceptional knowledge of artillery—again, self-taught—that he won Washington's deep admiration and friendship.

At the end of August, King George declared American colonists in rebellion and ordered "all our officers . . . to use their utmost endeavours to withstand and suppress such rebellion."[1] Washington feared Virginia's Lord Dunmore would order Martha seized, and he wrote to her that he feared for her safety and wanted her—needed her—by his side in Cambridge.

Martha all but scoffed at her husband's fears, writing that she felt perfectly safe where she was. Lund Washington apparently agreed: "Tis true," he wrote to Washington, "many people have made a stir about Mrs. Washington Continuing at Mt Vernon but I cannot think her in any Sort of danger . . . you may depend I will be watchfull."[2]

In early November, Governor Dunmore imposed martial law in Virginia and organized a loyalist army at Norfolk. By promising freedom to indentured servants and slaves, he raised a Negro regiment but alienated the entire planter establishment, including loyalists. Martha had been with the Bassetts in Eltham, but they grew so frightened of a rumored slave uprising that she yielded to her husband's entreaties and, with Jacky and Nelly Custis in tow, boarded her coach and left for Cambridge. Washington ordered his military aide Joseph Reed to Philadelphia to meet Martha and present her to the wives of influential congressmen.

"I don't doubt but you have see the Figuer [sic] our arrival made in the Philadelphia paper," she wrote to a friend, "and I left it in as great pomp as if I had been a very great somebody."[3]

To Washington's enormous relief, Martha, Jacky, and Nelly arrived safely in Cambridge—and immediately lifted his spirits and those of the men around him. "Every person seems to be cheerfull and happy hear," Martha wrote in her inimitable phonetic spelling that mimicked her measured drawl. "Some days we have a number of cannon and shells from Boston and Bunkers Hill, but it does not seem to surprise any one but me; I confess I shudder every time I hear the sound of a gun."[4]

Martha immediately took charge of her husband's private life, insisting that he move into a larger, more comfortable private mansion, where she could entertain Boston notables in the same style as Mount Vernon. She served dinners at two in the afternoon, but, in a nod to food shortages, limited offerings at other times to wine and fresh fruit. Apart from Washington's military commanders, her guests included political and literary figures such as Massachusetts Speaker James Warren and his wife, Mercy Otis Warren, a poet, dramatist, and historian. After dining with the Washingtons, Mrs. Warren described Martha to Abigail Adams as "among the well

Martha Washington quartered with
her husband and the army in winter
during the Revolutionary War.
Portrait by Charles Willson Peale,
1776.

bred and with the Ease and Cordiality of Friendship. . . . I think the
Complacancy of her Manners speaks at once the Benevolence of her
Heart, and her affability, Candor and Gentleness Quallify her to
soften the hours of private Life or to sweeten the Cares of the Hero
and smooth the Rugged scenes of War."[5]

Amid deadly sounds of war, Martha proved far stronger than
either she or her husband had anticipated. Insisting on remaining at
her husband's side whenever possible, she "took a look at pore
Boston & Charlstown—from prospect Hill Charlstown has only a
few chimneys standing in it, thare seems to be a number of very fine
Buildings in Boston but god knows how long they will stand; they
are pulling up all the wharfs for firewood—to me that never see any
thing of war, the preparations, are very terable indeed, but I endever
to keep my fears to myself as well as I can."[6]

Elated by Martha's presence—and her effusive reports of Lund
Washington's loving care of the estate—Washington wrote to his
cousin to thank him and to "engage [him] for the Year coming, and
the Year following, that your Wages shall be standing and certain,
at the highest amount that any one years Crop has produced to you
yet. . . .

It is the greatest, indeed it is the only comfortable reflection I enjoy . . . to think that my business is in the hands of a person in whose Integrity I have not a doubt, and on whose care I can rely . . . I am perswaded you will do for me as you would for yourself, & more than this I cannot expect.

I observe you mention something, in respect to the removal of my valuable Furniture, but where can you carry it? or what will be done with it? I wish the Wine could be secured, & the Rum in the barn Sold.

Let the Hospitality of the House, with respect to the Poor, be kept up; Let no one go hungry away . . . provided it does not encourage them in Idleness.[7]

As he promised, Lund sent Washington detailed weekly reports, listing, for example, more than 5,000 barrels of corn with which "we fatnd 132 Hogs they with the fatg Beeves Eat 247 Barrels—you will Ask me what we are going to do with so much meat—I cannot tell—when I put it up, I expected Mrs. Washington woud have live'd at Home, if you did not, was I to judge from the past consumption, there woud have been a Use for it—for I believe Mrs. Washingtons Charitable disposition increased in the same proportion with her meat House."[8] A subsequent letter brought cheerful news of a "Dray Colt [that] I suppose you never expected . . . woud be a very handsome Horse.

He is far from it—but as Clumsy as need be, not having more activity in him than your Bull—he is pretty well grown but not so high as mucht be expected (about 14 hands 3 Inches) he was fed all summer and well taken care of all winter is now very fat—when you say Coverg him will hurt him, surely you cannot mean Spoil his Shape, for in my opinion it is immaterial what shape a waggon Horse is of. . . . Whether will you have the Black Colt that came of the Grey mare you purchased at Philadelphia, Cut or not—he is a fine well grown Colt and promises fair to be very large.[9]

It was the kind of report that exhilarated Washington.

Before the end of 1775, a force of nine hundred Virginians and North Carolinians crushed Lord Dunmore's Loyalist force and sent him fleeing to a British gunboat in Chesapeake Bay off Norfolk.

To remind Virginians of British power, however, he burned Norfolk to the ground—every last structure.

In mid-February 1776, Washington's army occupied Dorchester Heights, an all but impregnable position that put Boston and most of the harbor within range of American cannons. Rather than risk useless slaughter, the British sailed off to Halifax, Canada, ceding Boston to Washington and his joyous troops and ensuring Massachusetts independence.

Congress sent Washington its thanks—and a gold medal—but Harvard College topped Congress by awarding him an honorary degree. For one who regretted his lack of formal education as much as Washington, a Harvard degree was worth far more than gold.

Anticipating the British army's next move, Washington ordered his army to New York, while he went to Philadelphia to badger Congress into giving him more arms, ammunition, and troops. Martha insisted on going with him. Inured to the sounds of shells, she no longer even asked his permission, and when she made up her mind, he dared not utter a breath of protest. Though anxious about her safety, George adored having her by his side and was awed by her quiet courage and determination. Nelly, however, was pregnant, and, having lost her first baby a year earlier, she and Jacky returned to the peace of her parents' home in Maryland, after which they planned to move to his estate. Jacky was twenty-one, the age of majority, and George now freed himself of an enormous responsibility as his stepson's guardian.

Before the Washingtons left Philadelphia, Martha stunned her husband by announcing her decision to undergo smallpox inoculation, then a dangerous procedure involving injection of live virus and submission to what patients and doctors could only pray would be a mild case of the deadly disease. By abandoning the isolated woods of Mount Vernon for crowded quarters at camp, however, Martha knew she was putting herself at risk, and she determined to do everything to remain a strong, healthy helpmate to her husband. Her courage—and the success of the procedure—evoked a joyful response from Jacky: "I do with the most filial Affection congratulate you both on this Happy Event," he wrote. "She can now attend to any Part of the Continent with pleasure, unsullied by the Apprehensions of that Disorder . . . your Happiness when together will be much greater than when you are apart."[10]

Washington rejoined his army in New York on June 4, and Martha was to follow two weeks later. Before she could start her journey, a fleet of 110 British ships sailed into New York Harbor, and he wrote urging his wife to return to Mount Vernon because of the imminent arrival of an even larger British fleet and invading army.

"I am still in this town," she wrote to her sister Nancy Bassett from Philadelphia,

> The General is at new york he is very well and wrote to me yesterday and informed me that Lord Dunmore with part of his fleet was come to General Howe at Staten Island, that another devision of the Hessians is expected before they think, the regulars will begen thare attack . . . the army at New York is very large and numbers of men are still going there. . . . I doe my Dear sister most relegiously wish thare was an End to the matter that we might have the pleasure of meeting again. . . . I hope Mr Bassett has got the better of his cough long agoe—please to present my love to him my Brother and sisters my dear Fanny and the Boy & Except the same yourself . . . I am my dear Nancy your ever affectionate sister Martha Washington.[11]

After sealing her letter, Martha ignored her husband's admonitions and left for New York to be at his side. She carried two letters that, for the first time, temporarily eased their anxieties about Jacky's long-standing want of maturity. Having reached the age of majority and assumed full control of his affairs, he seemed genuinely grateful for the care his stepfather had taken to preserve the boy's wealth. "Hon[ore]d Sir," began the letter to George:

> I am extremely desireous . . . to return you Thanks for your parental Care which on all Occasions you have shewn for Me. It pleased the Almighty to deprive me at a very early Period of Life of my Father, but I can not sufficiently adore His Goodness in sending Me so good a Guardian as you Sir; Few have experience'd such Care and Attention from real Parents as I have done. He best deserves the Name of Father who acts the Part of one. I first was taught to call you by that Name, my tender years unsusceptible of the Loss I had sustained knew not the contrary; your Goodness

(if others had not told Me) would always have prevented Me from knowing, I had lost a Parent—I shall always look upon you in this Light, and must intreat you to continue your wholesome Advice and reprimands whenever you see Occasion. I promise you they shall . . . be thankfully receiv'd and strictly attended to. . . . I shall with the greatest Eagerness seize every Opportunity of testifying that sincere regard & Love I bear you; in which Nelly begs Leave to join Me. I am Hond Sir, wishing you Success in all yr Undertakings, your most Affecte & much Oblidged

John Parke Custis[12]

The letter left both Martha and George in each other's arms. It was by far the most beautiful and rewarding letter George had ever received. Jacky's letter to Martha was more informative, but nonetheless loving. Prospective fatherhood had obviously wrought changes in her son: "I do with the truest Affection congratulate You and thank God for your recovery," he wrote. "I propose Leaveing this Place [Mount Airy] for Williamsburg next Tuesday, I shall stay a Day at Mount Vernon and return as soon as I finish my Business, to be present at a certain Occasion which I believe is not far distant, as soon as the Lady recovers I shall carry Her to Virginia, as the Family here is rather too large for the House, and I believe the Province of Maryd will shortly be in a State of the greatest Confusion."[13]

On July 2, Washington's orders of the day warned his troops, "The time is now near at hand which must probably determine whether Americans are to be, Freeman, or Slaves; whether they are to have any property they can call their own. . . . The fate of unborn Millions will now depend, under God, on the Courage and Conduct of this army. . . . We have therefore to resolve to conquer or die. . . . The Eyes of all our Countrymen are now upon us."[14]

Two days later, as Washington prepared for an attack in New York, Congress declared the United Colonies "are, and of Right ought to be, Free and Independent States," and, after two more days, it approved Thomas Jefferson's Declaration of Independence. After greeting independence with "three Huzzahs," Washington's troops gasped in disbelief as the first of a thousand sails began creeping over the horizon. Within days, hundreds of warships and transports surrounded Staten Island, landing more than twenty thousand troops as

Washington watched helplessly from across New York Bay. Concerned that the end was near, he wrote to his brother Jack:

> Whether you wrote me or I to you last, I cannot undertake to say; but . . . as I expect every hour to be engaged in two [too] busy a Scene to allow time for writing private Letters, I will take an oppertunity to . . . address you a few lines. . . .
>
> To begin then—we have a powerful Fleet within full view of us . . . the Enemy's numbers will amount to at least to 25,000 Men. ours to about 15,000 . . . what kind of opposition we shall be able to make time only can shew. . . . I beg of you to present my Love to my Sister[-in-law] and the Children—and Compliments to any enquiring friends & do me the justice to believe that I am Dr Sir Yr most affecte Brother
>
> Go: Washington

Washington underestimated enemy strength. By early August the British force had grown to thirty-two thousand men, including nine thousand German mercenaries. Fearing for Martha's safety, Washington ordered her to return to Mount Vernon. She protested at first, but a letter from Jacky quickly changed her mind.

> My dearest Mamma
>
> I have the extreme happiness at last to inform you, that Nelly was safely delivered this Morning about five oClock of a fine Daughter. . . . I wish you were present You would be much more pleased, if you were to see the strapping Huzze. . . . Her Cloths are already too smal for Her. She is in short as fine a Healthy, fat Baby as ever was born.
>
> Poor Nelly had a very indifferent Time, her Pains were two Hours long & very severe. She is now thank God as well as can be expected and the Pleasure her Daughter gives Her compensates for the Pain. . . . I wrote to the General the last two Posts. I shall write you again next Post, and ask Him to stand with yourself for my little Lady. My Love to Him in which Nelly joins Me. Nelly, the little Lady & Myself write in Love to you
>
> and am dear Mamma your
> most affectionate Son
> John Parke Custis[15]

Recognizing the hopelessness of his situation, Washington distracted himself with visions of Mount Vernon. Natural fencing with appropriate trees and shrubs, he said to himself, would be more pleasing than man-made barriers. "There is no doubt," he wrote to Lund Washington,

> that the Honey locust if you could procure Seed enough, & that seed would come up, will make (if sufficiently thick) a very good hedge—so will the Hawthorn, and if you cannot do better I wish you to try these—but Cedar or any kind of ever Green, would look better . . . no time ought to be lost in rearing of Hedges, not only for Ornament but use. . . . Plant Trees in the room of all dead ones in proper time this Fall, as I mean to have groves of Trees at each end of the dwelling House . . . at the North end, of locusts altogether. & that at the South of all the clever kind of Trees (especially the flowering ones) that can be got, such as Crab apple, Poplar, Dowgwood, Sasafras, Lawrel, Willow (especialy yellow & Weeping Willow) . . . these to be interspersed with ever greens such as Holly, Pine, and Cedar, also Ivy—to these may be added the Wild flowering Shrubs.[16]

On August 22, Howe landed twenty thousand troops in Brooklyn, where Washington could only muster five thousand men. Within a week, the British and Hessians had killed fifteen hundred Americans, captured their commanding generals and a thousand troops and officers, and corraled thousands of cattle on which Washington's army depended for food. Survivors escaped in the dark of night across the East River to New York Island (Manhattan).

On September 15, British troops assaulted New York Island and sent the Americans fleeing northward to Harlem Heights. British buglers took pains to humiliate Washington by sounding the call to hunt instead of customary battle calls. With the enemy "within stone's throw of us," Washington wrote in despair to Lund Washington that "if I were to wish the bitterest curse to an enemy . . . I should put him in my stead . . . I do not know what plan of conduct to pursue. I see the impossibility of serving with reputation . . . yet I am told that if I quit the command inevitable ruin will follow. . . . In confidence I tell you that I never was in such an unhappy, divided state since I was born."[17]

The humiliating defeats continued for the next three months, with British troops capturing more than twenty-eight hundred Americans in New York, then routing Washington's men in White Plains and chasing him and them across the Hudson River to New Jersey and westward to the Delaware River. On December 11, the remnants of the American army—a mere fifty-two hundred—one-third of them too sick or hungry to serve—barely escaped capture by crossing the Delaware River into Pennsylvania. The desperate American commander wrote to his brother that "it is impossible . . . to give you any Idea . . . of my difficulties—& the constant perplexities & mortifications I constantly meet with. . . . God grant you all health & happiness—nothing in this world would contribute to mine as to be once more fixed among you in peaceable enjoymt of my own vine, & fig Tree. Adieu my dear Sir—remember me Affectionat[e]ly to my Sister & the Family & giv my Compliments to those who enqui[re] after Yr Sincerely Affectionate Brother, Go: Washington."[18]

With New York and New Jersey in British hands, Congress fled from Philadelphia to Baltimore on December 12 and all but conceded defeat in the struggle for independence. Some congressmen believed Washington incompetent; he was thinking much the same thing.

In despair, Washington took his mind off his military woes with visions and fantasies of Mount Vernon, reiterating his love to Martha and then writing to Lund Washington: "If you can get some Holly Trees to plant upon the Circular Banks in the manner, or rather thicker than I did a year or two ago I should be glad of it—or if good & well set Holly can not be had then young & strait bodied Pines will do . . . If you can get a good match (and a young horse) for the Stallion, I should like it very well—but let the match be good, & the Horse handsome."[19]

Although most of the British army went to winter quarters in New York, clots of troops remained garrisoned in most major New Jersey towns to prepare for a spring offensive to crush the last vestiges of rebellion. With Congress debating capitulation, Washington conceived a bold move to revive American morale. In the dead of night on Christmas night, he led twenty-four hundred troops across the ice-choked Delaware to storm a Hessian garrison in Trenton, before moving to Princeton to seize a second, British garrison. By mid-January Washington's courageous little army had cleared most of western New Jersey of enemy troops and sent American morale— civilian and military—soaring. Congress returned to Philadelphia.

By spring, Washington grew so lonely for Martha that he yielded to her repeated requests to come to winter quarters in Morristown, New Jersey. She rushed northward by a circuitous route through Pennsylvania and all but fell from the chariot into her husband's embrace. She immediately seized the reins of his household and resumed the daily entertainments that had so enlivened the atmosphere at Mount Vernon. Notables and high-ranking officers and their wives flocked to her dinner table, along with Washington's young aides, whom one visitor described as "polite, social gentlemen who . . . keep the dinner table in constant laugh . . . [and] make the day pass with a great deal of satisfaction to the visitors." After dinner, Washington often led his guests on riding parties where he "throws off the hero and takes on the chatty, agreeable companion."[20]

With Martha at his side again, he wrote with unaccustomed cheer to his brothers, sending Samuel "every Sentiment of regard & love" for "my Sister & the little ones."[21] Similarly, his letter to John Augustine ended with unaccustomed joy: "My love to you all, in which Mrs Washington (who at present is with me) joins."[22]

Martha's arrival coincided with that of twenty-two-year-old Alexander Hamilton, a charming New York artillery captain and hero at Washington's Princeton triumph. At Washington's invitation, Hamilton had joined the general's military staff and quickly became Washington's "principal and most confidential aide."[23] Recommended by Henry Knox, Hamilton, like Knox and Washington, had been orphaned at twelve—a status that automatically won the hearts of both Washingtons, who believed caring for parentless children was their particular calling and obligation. Washington adopted him into his "military family," which George insisted be housed with him to remain in constant touch during every crisis; Martha gave Hamilton a place at the table and a bed of his own in the Washington house. Often calling Hamilton "my boy,"[24] Washington saw him as the ideal soldier-son he had never had—handsome, correct dress and bearing, intelligent, hardworking, responsible, fearless, and brave under fire . . . every inch the soldier Washington had aspired to be as a young man.

At the end of May, Washington prepared to leave Morristown and insisted that Martha return to the safety of Mount Vernon—though she would have stayed and charged into battle with him. In midsummer the British army landed on the north shore of Chesapeake Bay and marched toward the rebel capital at Philadelphia. As Washington prepared to meet the challenge, a nineteen-year-old French officer—yet *another* orphan—joined his staff. The marquis de Lafayette had just arrived from France and offered to serve as an unpaid volunteer—*exactly* as Washington had done. Last in a long line of distinguished soldiers, he had left his château, a vast personal fortune, and a young wife pregnant with their first child, to fight for liberty under Washington. Lafayette was handsome, with the bearing of a soldier, and, at six feet, four inches tall, one of the few who could look Washington straight in the eyes. Both men found it pleasant to keep their necks upright while talking to each other. After examining Lafayette's splendid uniform and his two "squires," Washington told the youngster, "I suppose we ought to be embarrassed to show ourselves to an officer who has just left the French forces." Lafayette snapped to attention and responded without hesitation, "I have come here to learn, *mon général*, not to teach."[25] It was the perfect answer to endear him to Washington.

It was ironic that on the very day he first met Lafayette, Washington received a letter from another young man—twenty-three-year-old John Laurens. Though not an orphan, he was, quite simply, brilliant—schooled in Geneva, Switzerland, trained in the law in London, and the son of a wealthy Charleston, South Carolina, merchant. In a humble but zealous letter to Washington, he offered to serve what Washington called "the cause" in any capacity—again, as an unpaid volunteer. For Washington, the offer was irresistible, and, to his delight, Laurens, Lafayette, and Hamilton developed a deep, brotherly affection for one another, facilitated by Hamilton's and Laurens's fluency in French. Washington's military family lacked only blood ties to distinguish it from a father and his boys. At the time and during the course of the war, other members of Washington's "military family" drew equally close to him; Washington invariably treated them as sons, mentoring them in the arts of war, leadership, and diplomacy. They ate with him (and Martha when she was there), slept near him, and became an integral part of his life.

The Marquis de Lafayette. Fatherless and only nineteen when he volunteered to serve in the American Revolutionary War, he and Washington formed a close father-son relationship, with Lafayette calling Washington "my adoptive father."

He saw them as the sons he had never had, and they responded by emulating him. All were brave, honest, professional soldiers. He genuinely enjoyed their company and trusted them. It was rare for older officers to trust the young, but the death of his own commander in the Ohio wilderness had forced him to assume command as a young man, and he was eager to train a cadre of young officers to succeed him and other older leaders should he or they fall. They adored him for that trust and gave him unqualified loyalty. Like any father, he was often overprotective, often lost his temper unfairly. Only Hamilton railed openly at such treatment—enough to have a shouting match on a stairway one afternoon that left both men deeply hurt.

Ironically, the one "son" who was not at his side was his stepson, whom Martha had so indulged that she crippled the normal boyhood instincts to charge into battle—instincts that fired Hamilton, Laurens, Lafayette, and Washington when they were boys. Washington knew Jacky's importance as Martha's only surviving child and heir, however, and he refused to hurt her by forcing her boy to go to war. Jacky nonetheless participated in his own way. He served in the Virginia General Assembly and bought a £1,000 share in a privateer for himself, his wife, his mother, and his stepfather to profit from goods seized off British merchant ships.

On September 11, British troops routed Washington's army at the Brandywine River, and two weeks later, marched into Philadelphia. Congress fled westward to Lancaster, then York, Pennsylvania. Apart from Washington's humiliating defeat, the Battle of Brandywine left his protégé the marquis de Lafayette with a bullet wound in his upper thigh. As they carried the young nobleman away on a litter, Washington rushed to his side and ordered the surgeon who was dressing Lafayette's wound to "treat him as if he were my son."[26]

As the first snows began falling, Washington's exhausted troops slogged toward improbable winter quarters at Valley Forge, a wooded plateau some twenty miles northwest of Philadelphia. Its only advantage was its elevation, from which a small force might defend against a larger enemy. Otherwise, according to one of Washington's generals, it was "a desert."[27] In the absence of any winter engagements, Washington, of course, could have returned to the comfort of Mount Vernon, but he knew that if he deserted the army, the troops would have done the same, and he determined to set an example by wintering with his men.

"The General has wrote to me that he cannot come home this winter," Martha wrote to her brother-in-law Burwell Bassett, "but . . . he will send for me, if he does I must go." Tears streamed down Martha's face as she tried responding to Bassett's own letter that his wife, Anna Maria (Nancy), Martha's beloved younger sister, had died. The two Bassett sons, eleven and thirteen, had just spent several weeks with Martha at Mount Vernon to be inoculated against smallpox. "I doe most sincearly lement and condole with you, on the loss of our dear departed Friend," Martha wrote. "She has I hope made a happy exchange—and only gon a little before us the time draws near when I hope we shall meet never more to part. . . .

> I must one [own] to you that she was the greatest favorite I had in the world—it will always give me the greatest pleasure, if I could be useful to you or the children in anything. . . . nothing in this world do I wish for more sincerly than to be with [you], but alass . . . I cannot leve home. . . . Nelly Custis . . . is hear and Expect every day to be brought to bed—is the reason I cannot come down . . . my dear sister in her lifetime often mentioned my taking my dear Fanny [Anna Maria's ten-year-old daughter] if she should be taken

away before she grew up—If you will lett her come to live with me, I will with the greatest plasure take her and be a parent and mother to her as long as I live. . . . I sincearly . . . pray god to enable you to support yourself under your great affliction—and bless your children—I am with love to them. . . .

> My Dear Brother your ever
> affectionate
> Martha Washington.[28]

On New Year's Eve 1777, Nelly Custis delivered Martha's third grandchild—like the previous two, a girl.

Martha's letter to George announcing Nancy's death came with one from Lund Washington that torrential rains had ruined Mount Vernon crops—"all our Wheat destroyed, our Mill idle, and but a short Crop of Corn . . . We could not Plow it at all, for I coud not ride through the Field without mireg my Horse . . . we shall not have more than 400 Barrels for Sale if so much."[29]

Late in January, Washington found a private home in sight of the army encampment, and he sent for his wife. She arrived with an entourage of eighteen slaves, but had to send most of them back to Mount Vernon. Washington's house was only sixteen feet square.

Although a large fireplace kept their stone structure warm enough, Washington had barely enough room to conduct business, let alone get a comfortable night's sleep and entertain friends and guests. He solved the space problem in part by building a log cabin extension to the house as a dining area, where Martha organized a morning sewing circle for other wives at camp to sew and knit for the troops.

"I never in my life knew a woman so busy from early morning until late at night as was Lady Washington, providing comforts for the sick soldiers," one camp follower wrote. "Every day, excepting Sunday, the wives of the officers in camp, and sometimes other women, were invited . . . to assist her in knitting socks, patching garments and making shirts for the poor soldiers when material could be procured. Every fair day she might be seen, with basket in hand, and with a single attendant, going among the keenest and most needy sufferers, and giving all the comforts to them in her power."[30]

Mounting criticism of Washington's military leadership drew the immediate ire of Washington's young officers. His three surrogate sons—Hamilton, Laurens, and Lafayette—organized a letter-writing campaign by Valley Forge officers to their governors and congressmen. Lafayette tried consoling Washington in broken English: "I don't Need telling You How I am Sorry for all what Happens Since Some time it is a necessary dependence of my most tender and Respectful friendship for You, which affection is as true and Candid as the Sentiments of my Haert and much Stronger than a So newe acquaintance Seems to admit. . . . I wish You Could know as well as myself, what difference there is Betwen You and Any other man Upon the continent."[31] Lafayette promised Washington that "I am now fixed to your fate, and I shall follow it and sustain it as well by my sword as by all means in my power."[32]

Deeply moved by the evident affection and loyalty of his "three sons," Washington responded warmly. He thanked the marquis for "that friendship and attachment which I have happily experienced since the first of our acquaintance, and for which I entertain sentiments of the purest affection. It will ever constitute part of my happiness to know that I stand well in your opinion . . . but we must not in so great a contest, expect to meet with nothing but Sun shine. I have no doubt but that every thing happens so for the best; that we shall triumph over our misfortunes, and shall, in the end, be ultimately happy; when, My Dear Marquis, if you will give me your Company in Virginia, we will laugh at our past difficulties and the folly of others."[33]

The winter at Valley Forge worked several subtle changes in Washington, softening the hard shell that seldom allowed sentiment to interfere with business decisions. When Lund Washington suggested selling unproductive slaves to pay property taxes, George forbade their sale "without their consent."[34]

On February 6, 1778, the king of France recognized American independence and signed two treaties, one treaty of amity and commerce and a second establishing a military alliance if and when war broke out between France and Britain. Word of the French alliances reached Valley Forge at the end of April, and so moved Lafayette that he spontaneously grasped his commander in chief in his arms and kissed him on both cheeks—certainly a first for the usually staid Virginian. Officers and soldiers at Valley Forge burst into spontaneous celebration, and Washington joined in, playing games with children and displaying a grin few had ever seen. "It having pleased the Almighty Ruler of the Universe," he proclaimed, "to defend the Cause of the United American-States . . . by raising us up a powerful Friend among the Princes of the Earth to establish our liberty and Independence op[on] lasting foundations, it becomes us to set apart a day for gratefully acknowledging the divine Goodness and celebrating the important Event which we owe to his benign Interposition."[35]

The next morning, an official day of "public celebration" began with morning religious services, followed by military parades, marching, and the firings of cannon and musketry. When the ceremonies ended, the Washingtons "gave a grand banquet in the camp," General Johann Kalb recalled. "Fifteen hundred persons sat down to the tables, which were spread in the open air. All the officers with their ladies. . . . Wine, meats, and liquors abounded, and happiness and contentment were impressed on every countenance. Numberless hurrahs were given for the King of France. . . . It was a fine day for us, and a great one for General Washington. Let me say that no one could be more worthy of this good fortune. His integrity, humanity, and love for the just cause of his country, as well as his other virtues, receive and merit the veneration of all men."[36]

In Virginia, the privateer that Jacky Custis had purchased—the *George Washington*—set sail to prey on British vessels.

7

An Affectionate Friend

IN THE SPRING OF 1778, fears of a French invasion forced the British to evacuate Philadelphia and mass forces in New York. At Valley Forge, Washington sent Martha home to Mount Vernon, then led his little army to pursue and harass the rear guard of the long British column. After a week, the redcoats encamped at Monmouth Courthouse (now Freehold, New Jersey), with the Americans six miles behind. Washington ordered English-born General Charles Lee to attack the center of the British line at dawn with four thousand troops, while two smaller forces under "Mad" Anthony Wayne and Lafayette sliced into the British flanks. Washington would hold the main army in readiness three miles back. After the attack began, Washington sent Hamilton to reconnoiter troop movements. To Hamilton's astonishment, he saw Lee's force retreating in chaos, leaving Lafayette's column trapped behind enemy lines. Intuiting what was happening, Wayne, on the opposite flank, lived up to his sobriquet by ordering an insane charge that forced the British to retreat long enough to allow both Wayne's and Lafayette's men to escape capture.

Outraged at Hamilton's report, Washington galloped into Lee's camp and demanded, "What is the meaning of this, Sir?" Lee replied that the Americans were unequal to British bayonets, to which an enraged Washington shouted, "You damned poltroon [coward], you never tried them." Another general at the scene described Washington shouting "till the leaves shook on the trees."[1] Washington ordered Lee to the rear, took command, and spurred his horse into the midst of retreating American troops, shifting right, left, turning full circle, rearing up on his mount, and herding the men back into line as he called out, "Stand fast, my boys! The southern troops are advancing to support you!" He was back at Fort Necessity, charmed by the sounds of whistling bullets—this time in command as he had not been before—a vengeful titan risen from some nether world.[2]

"General Washington was never greater in battle than in this action," Lafayette recounted. "His presence stopped the retreat; his strategy secured the victory. His stately appearance on horseback, his calm, dignified courage, tinged only by the anger caused by the unfortunate incident in the morning, provoked a wave of enthusiasm among the troops."[3]

Hamilton agreed: "I never saw the general to so much advantage. His coolness and firmness were admirable. . . . By his own good sense and fortitude he turned the fate of the day."[4]

In Washington's heart, soul, and gut, Monmouth compensated for his personal humiliations in the French and Indian conflict and Revolutionary War and all the "secret, insidious attempts to wound my reputation." He had won the day, proved to the world—and to himself—that he was a great soldier and military leader worthy of the title "commander in chief." Adding to his joy were the courageous successes of his three military "sons": Lafayette had led his troops out of death's jaws; Laurens had fought valiantly on horseback—and on foot after his horse was shot out from under him. Hamilton, who had long bristled under confinement of office work, jumped into combat in "a frenzy of valor," thrusting himself before retreating troops and leading them back into battle with bayonets fixed. Like Laurens, he lost his horse to British bullets. Badly injured by the falling beast, his aides helped him from the field.

Before Washington could seal his victory and destroy the British force, darkness set in, and the exhausted forty-six-year-old commander in chief spread a mantle on the ground beneath a tree where, according to Lafayette, he and his adopted French son lay side by side for the night. As they slept, the British deprived Washington of final victory by quietly slipping away to Sandy Hook, a spit of land on the northern Jersey shore at the entrance to New York

Bay, where transports carried them to New York. Although Monmouth was not decisive, the Americans claimed victory, with Washington writing to Martha and then to his brother "Jack" (John Augustine), on July 4, that Monmouth had "turned out to be a glorious and happy day. . . .

"Without exaggerating," he wrote to Jack, "their trip through the Jerseys in killed, Wounded, Prisoners, and deserters, has cost them at least 2000 Men and of their best Troops. We have 60 Men killed, 132 Wounded, and abt. 130 Missing, some of whom I suppose may yet come in. . . . As the Post waits I shall only add my love to my Sister and the family, and Strong assurances of being with the Sincerest regard and Love, Yr. most Affectt. Brother."[5]

Washington had good reason for his enthusiastic assessment: not only did his ragtag army of farmers and hunters show itself equal in battle to British and Hessian professionals, Americans were now in nominal control of a huge swath of territory in the mid-Atlantic region, stretching from the Massachusetts coast to the shores of Lake Erie, down through New Jersey into Pennsylvania and Maryland. Only New York City, Long Island, and Newport, Rhode Island, remained in British hands in the North. Washington's heroic personal performance at Monmouth lifted the morale of American troops and civilians alike and raised Washington to legendary status. Congress rewarded him with almost dictatorial powers "to superintend and direct the military operations in all the departments in these States."[6]

Henry Laurens, the president of Congress—and John's proud father—sent Washington and his army the unanimous thanks of Congress: "Love and respect for your Excellency is impressed on the heart of every grateful American, and your name will be revered by posterity."[7] Laurens invited George and Martha to Philadelphia to receive the thanks of Congress and attend a magnificent formal ball in their honor. Martha glowed—and led the stately opening dance with her husband to the applause and cheers of the nation's notables.

To Martha's relief, Monmouth ended Washington's career as a battlefield soldier. At the same time, however, it elevated him to the pinnacle of his career as a military commander. For the first time, he now took charge of the entire war, moving military divisions and

Washington at the Victory Ball. A consummate dancer, Washington enjoyed attending "assemblies," as balls were called.

their various commanders from sector to sector like a chess master. He continued to lose more battles, but both he and the British knew he could forestall British victory indefinitely by ceding the coast, retreating into the interior, and stretching British supply lines too far to maintain. On the other hand, he knew he could not win the war without a powerful army to push English forces into the sea. Early in 1779, Lafayette agreed to return to France to coax King Louis XVI to send Washington the help he needed for victory. Emotion got the better of the young Frenchman before sailing: "To hear from you," he wrote to Washington, "will be the greatest happiness I can feel. . . . Farewell, my most beloved general; it is not without emotion that I bid you this last adieu, before so long a separation. Don't forget an absent friend."[8]

Washington set up winter headquarters for 1778–1779 at Middlebrook (now Bound Brook), New Jersey, just northwest of New Brunswick. When Martha joined him, she bore distressing news from Jacky Custis. Because of "an insufferable Quantity of Muskitoes," he was considering the sale of a magnificent plantation Washington had purchased with funds from Jacky's estate as both an investment and a potential home for him and Nelly.[9]

Although Washington could not prevent its sale, he was furious at his stepson's poor judgment, writing that

> a Moments reflection must convince you of two things. first that Lands are of permanent value . . . and secondly that our Paper Currency . . . has depreciated considerably . . . the advice I shall give in consequence of it, is this, that you do not convert the Lands you now hold into Cash . . . exchange Land for Land . . . if our currency, unfortunately, continue to depreciate in the manner it has done in the course of the last two years, a pound may not, in the space of two years more, be worth a Shilling.[10]

Jacky hated supervising overseers, workers, and slaves, however, and found it demeaning to bargain with merchants over the sale of crops; he preferred the races, cards, and evenings with Virginia's notables. In the end, he ignored his stepfather's advice and sold his plantation for cash.

With the breakup of winter quarters and Martha's return to Mount Vernon, Washington sorely missed the companionship, good humor, and twisted syntax of Lafayette. The young Frenchman embodied the kind of son he had always hoped Jacky Custis would—but couldn't—become.

"When my dear Marquis shall I embrace you again?" he wrote after an afternoon of toasting on July 4. "Shall I ever do it? or have the charms of the amiable and lovely Marchioness, or the smiles and favors of your Prince withdrawn you from us entirely?"[11]

Later that summer, Washington opened his heart as never before, except to Martha:

> Your . . . strict and uniform friendship for *me* [his italics], has ripened the first impressions of esteem and attachment which I imbibed for you into such perfect love and gratitude that neither time nor absence can impair. . . . after our Swords and Spears have given place to the plough share and pruning hook . . . I shall welcome you in all the warmth of friendship . . . to my rural Cottage, where

homely fare and a cordial reception shall be substituted for delica-
cies and costly living . . . and if the lovely partner of your happiness will consent to participate with *us* in such rural entertainment
and amusemts. I can undertake in behalf of Mrs. Washington that
she will do every thing in her power to make Virginia agreeable to
the Marchioness. My inclination and endeavours to do this cannot
be doubted when I assure you that I love everybody that is dear to
you, and, consequently participate in the pleasure you feel in the
prospt. of again becoming a parent and do most Sincerely congratulate you and your Lady on this fresh pledge she is about to give
you of her love.[12]

Washington went on to give Lafayette page after page of troop
movements of the previous year's campaign. Then he turned playful
to a degree seen only in the intimacy of closest friends and family:

You are pleased my dear Marquis to express an earnest desire of
seeing me in France . . . but remember my good friend, that I am
unacquainted with your language. that I am too far advanced in
years to acquire a knowledge of it. and that to converse through a
medium of an interpreter upon common occasions, especially with
the *Ladies* must appr. so extremely awkward, insipid, and uncouth,
that I can scarce bear it in idea. . . .

But to conclude, you requested from me a long letter, I have
given you one; but methinks my dear Marquis, I hear you say, there
is reason in all things; that this is too long. I am clearly in sentiment with you, and will have mercy on you in my next. But at
present must pray your patience a while longer, till I can make a
tender of my most respectful compliments to the Marchioness. Tell
her (if you have not made a mistake, and offered your *own* love
instead of *hers* to me) that I have a heart susceptible of the tender-
est passion, and that it is already so strongly impressed with the
most favourable ideas of her, that she must be cautious of putting
loves torch to it; as you must be in fanning the flame. But here
again methinks I hear you say, I am not apprehensive of danger.
My wife is young, you are growing old and the atlantic is between
you. All this is true, but know my good friend that no distance can
keep *anxious* lovers long asunder, and that the Wonders of former
ages be revived in this. But alas! will you not remark that amidst
all the wonders recorded in holy writ no instance can be produced
where a young Woman from *real inclination* has preferred an old

man. This is so much against me that I shall not be able *I fear* to contest the prize with you, yet, under the encouragement you have given me I shall enter the list for so inestimable a jewel.

I will now reverse the scene, and inform you, that Mrs. Washington . . . often has in, her letters to me, enquired if I had heard from you, and will be much pleased at hearing that you are well, and happy. In her name . . . I thank you for your polite attention to her; and shall speak her sense of the honor conferred on her by the Marchioness.

When I look back to the length of this letter I am so much astonished and frightened at it myself, that I have not the courage to give it a careful reading for the purpose of correction. You must therefore receive it with all its imperfections, accompanied with this assurance that though there may be many incorrections in the letter, there is not a single defect in the friendship of my dear Marquis Yr., etc.[13]

In contrast to the joy with which he filled his letters to Lafayette, he felt nothing but annoyance writing to his stepson, who had not only ignored his advice on land sales but seemed intent on destroying the value of his once huge inheritance by selling off his plantations for cash.

"I candidly acknowledge I am at a loss what advice to give you with precision respecting the Sale of your Estate upon the Eastern shore," Washington wrote to Custis. He again warned that

the rapid depreciation of currency . . . will continue. . . . You must be sensible that it is not £40,000, £400,000 nor any nominal sum whatever that would give you the value of the Land in Northampton; instance your unfortunate sail of the York estate . . . for £20,000 [$152,000 today] which I suppose would now fetch £100,000 [$760,000 today]. . . . The present profit of your Land on the Eastern shore . . . retains in itself an intrinsic and real value, which rises nominally in proportion to the depreciation . . . suppose that it should continue to depreciate as it has done for the last 10 Months, where are you then? why bereft of your Land and in possession of a large sum of money with which you can buy nothing.

Washington urged Custis to stop selling lands unless he immediately invested the funds "in the purchase of something else of equal value . . . in fact this is but another name for barter or exchange . .

this was my advice to you before; and I now repeat it." Instead of signing his letter with "love," he ended it "with great truth."[14]

As the year progressed, Jacky Custis turned to gambling and threatened to undermine his mother and stepfather's fortune as well as his own. Two years after taking the combined Custis-Washington cattle herds to market, he had yet to send a penny of Washington's share of the proceeds or pay rents on Martha's dower lands. George knew Custis was gambling, but was helpless to stop him and dared not tell Martha.

Washington and Martha wintered in Morristown again in 1780—in weather even more frigid than it had been at Valley Forge. Although the Washingtons lived in a comfortable house, a blizzard in early January left them and the army buried under the deepest snow drifts in memory. High winds and bitter cold paralyzed the nation, with the island of Manhattan surrounded by solid ice for the first time since white men had landed. Chesapeake Bay froze from its head to the mouth of the Potomac.[15] Washington's army came close to "dissolution or starving," he told one congressman. "Sometimes it has been 5 or Six days together without bread. at other times as many days without meat, and once or twice two or three days without either . . . at one time the Soldiers eat every kind of horse food but Hay."[16]

As spring finally arrived to thaw the American north, a messenger arrived at the Washingtons' door with a letter that sent them into each other's arms in joyful tears:

> At the entrance of Boston harbour, 27th April 1780.
>
> Here I am, my dear general, and, in the midst of the joy I feel in finding myself again one of your loving soldiers, I take but the time of telling you that I came from France on board a frigate which the king gave me for my passage. I have affairs of utmost importance which I should at first communicate to you alone. In case my letter finds you any where this side of Philadelphia, I beg you will wait for me, and do assure you a great public good may be derived from it. To-morrow we go up to the town, and the day after I'll set off in my usual way to join my beloved and respected friend and general.

Adieu, my dear general; you will easily know the hand of your young soldier.

My compliments to the family.[17]

With the first light of dawn the next day, Washington sent his "young soldier" a letter welcoming him "home":

My dr. Marqs: Your welcome favour of the 27th. of April came into my hands yesterday. I received it with all the joy that the sincerest friendship could dictate, and with that impatience which an ardent desire to see you could not fail to inspire. . . .

I most sincerely congratulate with you on your safe arrival in America and shall embrace you with all the warmth of an affectionate friend when you come to head Qrs. where a bed is prepared for you. adieu till we meet. Yrs.[18]

Martha and George Washington fluttered, flittered, and fussed about the house like nervous schoolgirls awaiting their first suitor's knock at the door. The anticipated return of "our Marquis" was the first good news the Washingtons—and other patriot leaders—had received in months. On May 10 the Frenchman reached Morristown with an escorting cavalcade of cheering officers and soldiers, among them his beaming friend Lieutenant Colonel Alexander Hamilton. Washington's "eyes filled with tears of joy . . . a certain proof of a truly paternal love," Lafayette recalled. "After the first pleasure of meeting was over, General Washington and I retired into a private room to talk over the state of affairs. . . . It was then that I told the commander-in-chief what had been arranged [in Versailles] and the help he could now expect."[19]

Washington was ecstatic: Lafayette had obtained French government pledges to send six thousand French troops, enough clothing and arms for fifteen thousand American troops, and a French battle fleet to provide offshore support for joint Franco-American land operations. Adding to Washington's joy was the news that Lafayette's wife had given birth to their first son the previous Christmas Eve and named him George-Washington Lafayette. Lafayette asked Washington to be the boy's godfather.

The Washingtons looked at each other, then exulted and embraced their young French friend. George-Washington Lafayette, they laughed, was their first foreign-born godchild! Between them, George and Martha at forty-eight had already become godparents to what seemed like an entire generation of Americans. They were godparents not only to a myriad of nieces named Martha and nephews named George, but to an army of newborn George Washingtons in the military. They were everywhere: Patrick Henry had one; Major General Nathanael Greene. . . . The thought of them all at Mount Vernon . . . !

Lafayette's return—and the subsequent arrival of the French army—did not, of course, end the war. Indeed, the following spring saw the British send an armed sloop up the Potomac to punish the area's plantation owners, many of them political leaders who had helped start the Revolution. Washington had long anticipated such raids and warned Lund Washington to remove the most valuable articles from his house. "I am prepared for the worst that can happen to them, to hear therefore of their being plundered, or burnt, will be no surprize to me."[20]

When the British assault ship arrived, many of Washington's slaves and those of Lund Washington fled. To prevent the British from looting and burning the Mansion, Lund Washington risked his life by going aboard with food for the officers and agreeing to provision the ship if the commander would return the slaves and sail on, leaving Mount Vernon untouched. Knowing that some of his neighbors had watched their houses burn in retribution for supporting the Revolution, Washington was embarrassed and furious. He tried his best to convey his thoughts to his cousin without alienating him. Lund, after all, had single-handedly saved the vast Mount Vernon enterprise from bankruptcy, and he had saved the Mansion from destruction: He began, referring to Lund's lost slaves,

> I am very sorry to hear of your loss. I am a little sorry to hear of my own; but that which gives me most concern, is, that you should go on board the enemys Vessels, and furnish them with refreshment. It would have been a less painful circumstance to me, to have heard, that in consequence of your non-compliance with their request, they had burnt my House, and laid the Plantation in ruins. You ought to have considered yourself as my representative, and should have reflected on the bad example of communicating with the enemy, and making a voluntary offer of refreshments to them with a view to prevent a conflagration. . . .

I am thoroughly perswaded, that your desire to preserve my property, and rescue the buildings from impending danger, were your governing motives. But to go on board with a parcel of plundering Scoundrels, and request a favor by asking the surrender of my Negroes, was exceedingly ill-judged, and 'tis to be feared, will be unhappy in its consequences. . . .

Mrs. Washington joins me in best and affectionate regard . . . and does most sincerely regret your loss. I do not know what Negroes they may have left you; and as I have observed before, I do not know what number they will have left me by the time they have done; but this I am sure of, that you shall never want assistance, while it is in my power to afford it.[21]

Washington, of course, had no conception of what was in his power to afford. Like other southern plantations, Mount Vernon had relied on the British to absorb its huge tobacco and grain crops. With local markets unable to absorb much, Lund let many fields lie fallow, and when the value of local currency plunged to one-fortieth of its previous value, he reduced production to only those amounts needed to feed the Washington household and plantation workers, slaves, and other residents. At the beginning of the war, Washington had guided Lund with long, detailed, weekly letters of instruction, but the demands of his public life made it impossible to continue the practice.

"My whole time is . . . so much engrossed by the public duties of my station," he wrote to William Crawford, the overseer of Washington's western Pennsylvania lands, "that I have totally neglected all my private concerns, which are declining every day, and may, possibly, end in capital losses, if not absolute ruin, before I am at liberty to look after them."[22]

A colonel in the Pennsylvania militia, Crawford had ridden over large sections of Washington's lands and warned that squatters were threatening to overrun the western wilderness. There was little Washington could do except yield to the inevitable in his reply:

If the Settlers on the Land, either through ignorance or disbelief of its being mine, have made improvements of value thereon and wish to live on and enjoy them, I would agree they should remain Seven years longer . . . on terms which should in their own eyes appear moderate and easy . . . subject nevertheless at the expiration of that term to such reasonable Rents as the Land and Improvements are worth. . . . Upon these terms I would give Leases for lives, or a great length of years; provided also . . . some mode can be adopted to let the value of the Rents every Seven or ten years, be so raised as to bear some proportion to the increased value of the Land.[23]

Washington was not feeling well. His teeth were deteriorating badly and causing considerable pain—and problems eating. Over the years, dentists had removed them one by one and implanted a variety of bone or ivory prosthetics—or actual teeth purchased from the poor. Set in the sockets of the original teeth and wired to neighboring natural teeth, they nonetheless shifted about uncomfortably and often painfully. "A day or two ago," he wrote to a dentist in Philadelphia, "I requested . . . a pair of Pincers to fasten the wire of my teeth.. . . . I now wish you would send me one of your scrapers, as my teeth stand in need of cleaning."[24]

On September 9, 1781, Washington's heart swelled with joy as he reached "my own Seat at Mount Vernon" for the first time since he had left for the Second Continental Congress in Philadelphia more than six years earlier. Martha and Jacky and Nelly Custis greeted him with the four Custis children, including four-month-old George Washington Parke Custis, who had already acquired such nicknames as "Mr. Tub," "Washy," and "Wash." As before the war, visitors filled the house—Washington's aides, French commanding general Jean-Baptiste-Donatien Rochambeau and his aides, and a number of other, high-ranking French officers.

"A numerous family now present. All accommodated," noted the young Colonel Jonathan Trumbull Jr., the Connecticut governor's son who had become a Washington aide and had never before visited a southern plantation. "An elegant seat and situation, great appearance of opulence and real exhibitions of hospitality and princely entertainment."[25]

After three days, Washington's entourage set off for Williamsburg, and, on September 28, the combined Franco-American armies and the French fleet laid siege to the British fortifications at Yorktown. On October 8, shells breached British inner fortifications, and in a gesture fraught with romance that belied his often rigid demeanor, Washington gave each of his three "sons" the honor of leading a brigade into the breach to seal the victory. From his vantage atop a huge white horse, Washington watched his three cherished protégés charge into history: Colonel Alexander Hamilton led the advanced corps in assaulting and capturing two British redoubts on the left; Colonel John Laurens led the capture of a third redoubt; and Major General Marquis de Lafayette led a bayonet charge into the breaches of the British fortifications, with him and his men flinging themselves at British defenders with "an ardor" that sent the redcoats fleeing in terror.

"The bravery exhibited by the attacking Troops," Washington wrote in his diary, "was emulous and praiseworthy—few cases have exhibited stronger proofs of Intrepidity coolness and firmness than were shown on this occasion."[26]

To Washington's consternation, Jacky Custis showed up in the midst of the assault on Yorktown to offer his services as a civilian aide. Jacky had never wanted any part of soldiering, but, having hunted with his stepfather, he savored the kill, and he wanted to witness the destruction of the British army.

On October 17, the twelfth day of the siege, Cornwallis sent Washington a message under a flag of truce:

> SIR, I propose a cessation of hostilities for twenty-four hours, and that two officers may be appointed by each side . . . to settle the terms for the surrender of the posts of York and Gloucester.
>
> I have the honour to be, &c
>
> Cornwallis

Washington replied politely but firmly:

> Camp before York, October 17, 1781
>
> My LORD: I have had the Honor of receiving Your Lordship's Letter of this Date.
>
> An Ardent Desire to spare the further Effusion of Blood, will readily incline me to listen to such Terms for the Surrender of your Posts and Garrisons of York and Gloucester, as are admissable.

Washington sent John Laurens, and Rochambeau sent Lafayette's brother-in-law, the viscomte de Noailles, to negotiate the surrender.

On October 19, eight thousand British troops laid down their arms. After the ceremony, Washington ordered an aide to send a masterfully understated dispatch to the president of Congress:

> Sir, I have the Honor to inform Congress, that a Reduction of the British Army under the Command of Lord Cornwallis, is most happily effected. The unremitting Ardor which actuated every Officer and Soldier in the combined Army in this Occasion, has principly led to this Important Event, at an earlier period than my most sanguine Hope had induced me to expect.[27]

Washington sent a copy, with a personal note to Martha, then began planning strategy to end the war by forcing the British from their remaining bases in New York; Wilmington, North Carolina; Charleston, South Carolina; and Savannah, Georgia.

As great a victory as Yorktown had been for Washington, the public leader, it proved tragic for the private man and his wife and family. The Yorktown battlefield teemed with rotting human and equine corpses and body parts that polluted the air and water and generated widespread disease. "Camp fever," or typhus, transmitted by body lice, was endemic, and Jacky Custis was not immune. After witnessing the surrender, he fainted and was carried back to his quarters burning with fever. George ordered a carriage to take him to the Bassett home, thirty miles away in Eltham. Washington sent word to Martha, who immediately left Mount Vernon for Eltham with Nelly. George arrived on November 5.

"I came here in time to see Mr. Custis breath his last," Washington wrote to an aide. "About Eight o'clock yesterday Evening he expired. The deep and solemn distress of the Mother, and the affliction of this amiable young Man, requires every comfort in my power to afford them; the last rights [sic] of the deceased I must also see performed; these will take me three or four days; when I shall proceed with Mrs. Washington and Mrs. Custis to Mount Vernon."[28]

8

The Long Journey Home

AFTER JACKY'S FUNERAL, George and Martha Washington returned to Mount Vernon, where he coaxed her to accompany him to Philadelphia rather than roam the Mansion alone with her dead children's ghosts. Not coincidentally, he needed her to chase his own ghosts. All three of his young soldier "sons" had fled his military nest after Yorktown: Lafayette to France; Hamilton to New York to run for Congress; and Laurens to fight with Greene's army encircling the British at Charleston. Together, then, George and Martha settled into a beautiful Philadelphia mansion, where she resumed her role as Lady Washington, entertaining the city's notables. Members of Congress, in turn, wined and dined them on French food—by then the great fashion, of course. Inevitably they drew crowds as they strolled the capital's lovely lanes.

By spring 1782 the British lost their collective will to pursue the war and agreed to negotiate peace. Washington nonetheless insisted on returning to his army, encamped in Newburgh, New York, fifty miles up the Hudson River from New York City. "There is no measure so likely to produce a favorable termination of the war," Washington growled, "as vigorous preparations for meeting the enemy."[1]

His officers found him an adequate, albeit rustic home, where Martha joined him for Christmas for a year of persistent boredom. Although the war had not ended, the Americans had fought their last battle and left Washington with no strategy to plan. The French army had left, and the British had ceded the South. The cession of

Charleston, South Carolina, though, came at a high personal price for Washington. A squad of redcoats foraging outside the city came upon John Laurens and his men, and in an absolutely useless exchange of gunfire, young Laurens fell.

"Poor Laurens is no more," a tearful Washington wrote in disbelief to Lafayette. "He fell in a trifling skirmish in South Carolina, attempting to prevent the Enemy from plundering the Country of rice."[2]

Christmas 1782 was melancholy for the Washingtons. They had aged seven years during the war; his close comrades—and their often delightful wives—had returned to civilian life, and the Washingtons had little in common with the new, younger officers, most of whom were too ill at ease to do anything but stare at the legendary general and His Lady. Christmas dinner proved particularly embarrassing. Washington could not chew properly and left the table to write to Lund Washington: "In a drawer in the Locker of the Desk which stands in my study, you will find two small (fore) teeth; which I beg of you to wrap up carefully, and send inclosed in your next letter to me. I am positive I left them there, or in the secret drawer in the locker of the small desk."[3]

In addition to his failing (and falling) teeth, his eyesight was deteriorating, and David Rittenhouse, the renowned Philadelphia astronomer, sent him two pairs of spectacles.

"The Spectacles suit my Eyes extremely well," Washington replied by way of thanks, "as I am perswaded the reading glasses also will when I get more accustomed to the use of them. At present I find some difficulty in coming at the proper Focus; but when I do obtain it, they magnify properly and shew those objects very distinctly which at first appear like a mist blended together."[4]

In addition to social isolation in Newburgh, pressing problems at home added to the Washingtons' discomforts. Martha's younger brother, Judge Bartholomew Dandridge, who lived near the Custises, had agreed to be executor for Jacky Custis's estate, but refused to assume responsibility for Jacky's four young children. "I perceive your unwillingness to undertake the Guardianship of Mr. Custis's Children," Washington pleaded with his brother-in-law, "and tho' your reasons have weight in them . . . I cannot help . . . expressing my wish to see you vested with it. Indeed I know no other in whom it can be placed . . . with more convenience and ease."[5]

Dandridge pleaded illness, however, and left the Washingtons no choice under English law but to assume responsibility for their daughter-in-law, Nelly Custis, and guardianship of her four children. In addition to the Custis family, Washington faced problems with his own kin. His brother Samuel had died at age forty-seven. Married five times, he left his fifth wife destitute with their baby and his three boys and little girl from his previous marriages.

"In God's name," Washington wrote to his brother Jack, "how did my Brothr. Saml. contrive to get himself so enormously in debt? Was it by purchases? By misfortunes? or shear indolence and inattention to business?"[6]

With Samuel's wife penniless, only George among the surviving brothers was in a position to keep his children from being scattered in separate foster homes or even sold into bondage. Jack was overburdened with the care of his own children, and Charles, the youngest of the Washington brothers, "spent his hours . . . in intoxication."[7] George felt he had no choice but to assume responsibility for Samuel's three youngest children: George Steptoe Washington, eight; Lawrence Augustine Washington, six; and four-year-old Harriot. The oldest child, fourteen-year-old Ferdinand, was old enough to work and remained with his stepmother, but, like his father and so many of the Washington men, he would die young of tuberculosis—only four years later.

In addition to Samuel's debts, Washington faced new money demands from his increasingly irrational mother, who had humiliated her son by appealing to the Virginia legislature for a bill of assistance, saying she was "in great want owing to the heavy taxes she was obliged to pay."[8]

"I learn from very good authority," Washington wrote to Jack, "that she is upon all occasions, and in all Companies complaining . . . of her wants and distresses . . . which not only makes *her* appear in an unfavourable point of view but *those* also who are connected with her. I wish you to represent to her in delicate terms the impropriety of her complaints and acceptance of favors even where they are voluntarily offered, from any but relations."[9]

Washington's letter to Jack had actually begun with a promise to help Jack's son Bushrod, who had graduated from William and Mary College in Williamsburg and gone to Philadelphia to study law. Jack worried that given his family name, an unsophisticated boy such as Bushrod might fall into "the wrong company" in so large a city. Jack had sought no money from his brother—only counsel and guidance, which Washington was always quick to provide the young, especially when they were as deserving as Bushrod. In December 1776 Bushrod had helped found the Phi Beta Kappa literary society at William and Mary to assert student rights of assembly and free speech—and had then enlisted in the Continental Army.

"Dear Bushrod," wrote his proud uncle. "You will be surprised perhaps at receiving a letter from me; but if the end is answered for which it is written, I shall not think my time misspent. Your Father . . . seems to entertain a very favorable opinion of your prudence, and I hope you merit it. . . . Therefore, as a friend, I give you the following advice.

> Let the object, which carried you to Philadelphia, be always before your Eyes; remember, that it is not the mere study of the Law, but to become eminent in the Profession of it which is to yield honor and profit; the first was your choice, let the second be your ambition and that dissipation is incompatible with both. I am not such a Stoic as to suppose you will, or to think it right that you ought, always to be in Company with Senators and Philosophers, but, of the young and juvenile kind let me advise you to be choice.

After warning his nephew against gambling, excessive drink, and overspending on pretentious clothes, he urged him to "let your *heart* feel for the affliction, and distresses of every one, and let your *hand* give in proportion to your purse. It will add not a little to my happiness, to find those, to whom I am so nearly connected, pursuing the right walk of life; it will be the sure road to my favor, and to those honors, and places of profit, which their Country can bestow, as merit rarely goes unrewarded."[10]

Washington's unexpected letter initiated a close friendship and relationship with his nephew that both would treasure for the rest of their lives.

Bushrod Washington. The son of Washington's younger brother
John Augustine ("Jack"), Bushrod was the only one of Washington's
many nephews who fulfilled his ambitions for them, by reaching the
highest level of government leadership as a United States Supreme
Court justice. Washington bequeathed the Mansion Farm at Mount
Vernon to him. He is buried in the new vault at Mount Vernon
with his uncle. Portrait by Henry Benbridge, 1783.

In the spring, the Washingtons received a letter from Lafayette
announcing the birth of his third child, whom he named Virginie, to
honor the regiment he had led at Yorktown as well as Washington's
home state. "Virginia I am perswaded," Washington answered, "will
be pleased with the Compliment of the name; and I pray as a member of it she may live to be a blessing to her parents. . . . It only
remains for me to add . . . how much we all love and wish to embrace
you. . . . I hope it is unnecessary to repeat to you, that . . . after the
olive branch shall have extended itself over this Land (for which I
most devoutly pray) I shall be happy to see you on Columbias shore.
The inhabitants of my humble Cottage will salute you with the richest marks of grateful friendship."[11]

As he wrote, Britain officially recognized American independence and signed peace accords. While Adrienne de Lafayette thanked God at Mass, her husband thanked Washington:

> You, my dear general, who truly can say you have done all this, what must your virtuous and good heart feel on the happy instant where the revolution you have made is now firmly established. I cannot but envy the happiness of my grand children when they will be about celebrating and worshipping your name—to have had one of their ancestors among your soldiers, to know he had the good fortune to be the friend of your heart will be the eternal honour in which they shall glory. . . . In the month of June, I will embark for America. Happy, ten times happy will I be in embracing my dear General, My father, My best friend.[12]

Lafayette went on to express his many political and social concerns for the new nation, proposing a new constitution and "a plan . . . which might become greatly beneficial to the black part of mankind. Let us unite," he urged Washington, "in purchasing a small estate where we may try the experiment to free the Negroes, and use them only as tenants.

> Such an example as yours might render it a general practice, and if we succeed in America, I will chearfully devote a part of my time to render the method fashionable in the West Indies. If it be a wild scheme, I had rather be mad that way than to be thought wise on the other tack.
>
> Adieu, adieu my dear General. . . . My best, most affectionate respects wait upon Mrs. Washington. . . . With every sentiment of love and respect, I am for ever your most devoted and affectionate friend.[13]

Several days later, Washington sent Lafayette a long, emotional reply expressing "the sensibility of my Heart at the communications in your letter. . . . We now stand an Independent People. . . . We are placed among the Nations of the Earth, and have a character to establish; but how we shall acquit ourselves time must discover."

Washington went on to praise Lafayette's role in the American victory and said he looked forward to his own retirement from service and return to Mount Vernon. "I will endeavor," he wrote morbidly, "to glide down the stream of life 'till I come to that abyss, from where no traveller is permitted to return." Finally he turned to Lafayette's thorny question on slavery—a question that had preyed on him. During his years in the North, he had learned that many Americans assumed that the struggle for individual liberty applied to "all men"—as stated in the Declaration of Independence. As a farmer and industrialist, he had not failed to notice the higher productivity of northern farms, where workers paid by the piece had far more incentive to work than slaves driven by only the whip.

Washington was, therefore, quite receptive to Lafayette's proposal. Indeed, he believed the isolated Dismal Swamp might be the perfect place to emancipate slaves without arousing the ire of planters opposed to emancipation. "The scheme, my dear Marquis, which you propose as a precedent, to encourage the emancipation of the black people of this Country from that state of Bondage in wch. they are held, is a striking evidence of the benevolence of your Heart. I shall be happy to join you in so laudable a work; but will defer going into a detail of the business, 'till I have the pleasure of seeing you."[14]

Although the Washingtons were eager to return to Mount Vernon, he could not abandon his military command until the last British troops evacuated New York, their last base in the original thirteen colonies. Thousands of loyalists had flocked to the city for British protection and delayed the departure of troops while the British found enough ships to evacuate them.

The Washingtons could do nothing but bide their time and do their best to prepare their return to Mount Vernon:

"I shall thank you, Gentlemen," he wrote to one merchant house "for forwarding . . . two Pipes [126 gallons each] of old Madeira Wine . . . to Mr. Lund Washington on Pomk. River; 10 Miles below Alexa. in Virginia; who will pay the freight of them. . . . I have only to entreat that they may be committed to safe hands, to prevent wasteage or adulteration." Washington ordered "a like quantity of wine [claret]"[15] before beginning another letter on a matter of great import: "Having some Teeth which are very troublesome to me at times," he wrote to a knowledgeable friend, "of wch I wish to be eased . . . I would thank you for making a private Investigation of this . . . Dentist of whose skill much has been said . . . if he really is skillful, I should be glad to see him. . . . I would not wish that this matter should be made a parade of."[16]

In contrast to his professed intention of retiring from public life, Washington ordered a curiously large number of books on techniques of national governance. In one order, he asked a book dealer for "Charles the 12th of Sweden"; "Lewis [sic] the 15th 2 Vols."; "History of the Life and Reign of the Czar Peter, the Great"; "Robertsons History of America 2 Vols"; "Voltaires Letters"; "Vertots Revolution of Rome 3 Vols.—If they are Esteemed"; and "D[itt]o of Portugal."

Throughout the long winter at Newburgh, he immersed himself in the world's great literary works, still trying to compensate for his academic inadequacies. His close contact with the superbly educated commanders of the French army had made him overly sensitive to his lack of a university education. In fact, the extent and depth of his readings gave him an education that surpassed that of the vast majority of the formally educated men he had encountered—French, British, or American. Like Franklin, he was a brilliant autodidact, who, whenever and wherever he could, snapped up—and fully enjoyed—every opportunity to learn. He quoted easily and extensively from a wide variety of works that he often reread, not the least of which were such classical Latin works as Caesar's *Gallic Wars* and Cicero's *Orations*. Along with these standard works, he ordered such ponderous studies as an eight-volume "Accot. of the New Northn Archipelago," a four-volume "Histy of the U[nite]d Provinces of the Netherlands," and a two-volume "review of the characters of the principal Nations in Europe."[17] He also read for pleasure and, when he could control his laughter, he enjoyed reciting passages from memory and describing "battles" in Laurence Sterne's *Tristram Shandy*. Washington went out of his way to form relationships with academics and intellectuals, including presidents of Yale, Harvard, Princeton, and William and Mary. Yale conferred an honorary degree on Washington that matched the similar award from Harvard—and made him the first American to hold degrees from both institutions.

Washington's thoughts were never far from his plantation, however, and he ordered many works on agriculture. His search for up-to-date techniques brought him stacks of articles on a variety of crops, including "several little essays . . . to cultivate the foreign grape, for Wine" from French notables such as French minister of state and royal councillor Chrétien Guillaume de Lamoignon de Malesherbes, who offered to send him cuttings of French vines.

"I hardly know how to express my gratitude," Washington replied. "The spontaneous growth of the [wild] Vine in all parts of this Country, led me to conclude that by a happy choice of the species I might succeed better than those who had attempted the foreign vine;

accordingly, a year or two before hostilities commenced I selected about two thousand cuttings of a kind which does not ripen with us (in Virginia) 'till repeated frosts in the Autumn meliorate the Grape and deprive the Vines of their leaves. It is then, and not before, the grape (which is never very pallitable) can be eaten.

Several little Essay's have been made . . . to cultivate the foreign grape, for Wine but none had well succeeded . . . which I ascribed to the ripening of their grape in our Summer or Autumnal heats. This consideration led me to try the wild grape of the Country. . . . Thus my good Sir, have I given you the history of my proposed cultivation of the Vine. . . .

If . . . Monsr. de Malesherbes will honr. me with a few sets, or cuttings of any *one* kind (and the choice is left altogether to himself) I will cultivate them with the utmost care. I will always think of him when I go into my little Vineyard; and the first fruits of it shall be dedicated to him as the Author of it. If to these he would add a few sets of the several kinds of Eating Grapes for my Gardens it would add much to the obligation he seems so well disposed to confer on me.[18]

Martha contracted "bilious fevers and cholic" during the summer, and with George eager to confer with Congress about the military establishment, the Washingtons transferred to Princeton, New Jersey, to await the British evacuation of New York. Congress had fled there to escape riots in Philadelphia by soldiers demanding back pay. The house in Princeton was not Mount Vernon, but it was decidedly not Newburgh, and for that, both Washingtons were grateful. Early in September, he and Martha invited members of Congress to an outdoor dinner that earned a place in congressional folklore for generating numerous public quips by the commander in chief, who consumed more than his usual amount of wine. Told that Superintendent of

Finance Robert Morris "had his hands full" dealing with unpaid soldiers, Washington snapped, "I wish he had his pockets full." And as they sat to dinner, someone noted that the maker of the odd-looking wine goblets had "turned Quaker preacher," to which Washington retorted, "I wish he had been a Quaker preacher before he made the cups."[19]

Despite his professed yearning to return to private life, Washington could not resist meddling in national affairs. He issued a four-thousand-word circular to Congress calling for payment of all state and national debts, establishment of a permanent military establishment, and establishment of "an indissoluble Union of the States under one Federal Head."[20] Martha, however, had wearied of her husband's posturing, and insisted that he either retire or stop talking about it and run for Congress. He did as she wanted and turned almost full-time to preparations for a return to private life. Together they made lists of their needs at Mount Vernon, and despite a lack of cash to pay for anything, he ordered six dozen each of wine, beer, and water glasses from a Philadelphia merchant, along with "a neat and compleat sett of blue and White Table China . . . and a proportionable number of Deep and other Plates, Butter Boats, Dishes and Tureens."

While Martha wasn't looking, he added a sheepish postscript that indicated some awareness of his cash position: "Will you be so good as to inform me what Goods, for family use, are very low in New York, and if they are to be had cheaper, than Goods of the same kind and quality, at Philadelphia."[21]

He then wrote to his nephew Bushrod Washington in Philadelphia to "make enquiry of some of the best Cabinet makers, at what price, and in what time, two dozen strong, neat and plain, but fashionable, Table chairs (I mean chairs for a dining room) could be had. . . .

> Since I have already chalked out so much business for you, I will go further, and ask you to enquire at what prices several kinds of French and other wines (Madeira excepted, of which I have enough) of good quality, can be bought; and whether the stock on hand, or the quantity expected, is said to be large. . . . I wish also that you would enquire, if there is any blue and white table china, to be had in settes and the price. Table china frequently comes in packed up in compleat setts, amounting to a gross, or gross and a half of pieces, all kinds included.

There is another thing likewise which I wish to know, without having it known for whom the enquiry is made; and that is, whether French plate is fashionable and much used in genteel houses in France and England; and whether, as we have heard, the quantity in Philadelphia is large, of what pieces it consists, and whether among them, there are Tea urns, Coffee pots, Tea pots, and other equipage for a tea table, with a tea board, Candlesticks and waiters large and small, with the prices. These enquiries you may make in behalf of a friend, without bringing my name forward, 'till occasion (if a purchase shou'd happen) may require it.[22]

Exactly how Washington expected Bushrod Washington to keep the family name out of his transactions was the subject of some discussion between George and Martha, who insisted that her husband also write to Lafayette in Paris, where French plate would certainly be less expensive than in Philadelphia. Washington was somewhat embarrassed, but he did as Martha directed and excused himself to Lafayette by saying that after warring with England for eight years, "I do not incline to send to England (from whence formerly I had all my goods) for anything I can get upon tolerable terms elsewhere. . . .

As I persuade myself it would rather give you pain than pleasure, were I to apologize for any liberty I might take with you, which does not exceed the rules of propriety and friendship; I shall proceed without further hesitation or ceremony to beg the favour of you to send me of the plated wares (or what formerly used to be called French plate) the articles contained in the enclosed memorandum to which, as I am not much of a connoisseur in, and trouble my head very little about these matters, you may add any thing else of the like kind which may be thought useful and ornamental ["no dishes, plates and spoons," Martha interrupted him], except Dishes, plates and Spoons, of the two first I am not inclined to possess any, and of the latter I have a sufficiency of every kind. . . .

"I have not My Dr. Marqs sent . . . money for . . . these articles . . . but a bill shall be remitted to you the moment I am informed of the cost; in the mean while I am sure you will have no hesitation in becoming responsible to the workman for the payment. . . .

A LIST OF PLATED WARE TO BE SENT

Everything proper for a tea-table, and these it is supposed may consist of the following Articles: A Large Tea salver, square or round

as shall be most fashionable; to stand on the Tea table for the purpose of holding the Urn, teapot, Coffee pot, Cream pot, China
Cups and saucers &ca. [Again, Martha was dictating. She was as
obsessive about her table as George was about his gardens.]

A large Tea-Urn, or receptacle for the water which is to supply
the tea pot, *at the table.* 2 large Tea pots, and stands for Ditto,
1 Coffee Pot and stand, 1 Cream Pot, 1 Boat or Tray, for the Tea
spoons, 1 Tea-chest, such as usually appertains to tea or breakfast
tables, the inner part of which, to have three departments, two for
tea's of different kinds, the other for Sugar. . . .

> Also, Two large Salvers, sufficient to hold twelve common
> wine glasses, each.
> Two smaller size Do for 6 wine glasses, each.
> Two Bread-baskets, middle siz.
> A Sett of Casters, for holding oil, Vinegar, Mustard, &ca.
> A Cross or Stand for the centre of the Dining table.
> 12 Salts, with glasses in them.
> Eight Bottle sliders.
> Six large Goblets, for Costers.
> Twelve Candlesticks. Three pair of snuffers, and stands for them.

And any thing else which may be deemed necessary, in this
way. If this kind of plated Ware will bear engraving, I should be
glad to have my arms thereon, the size of which will, it is to be pre-
sumed be large or small in proportion to the piece on which it is
engraved.[23]

As the Washingtons prepared to return to Mount Vernon, they tried
to restore the past by urging their old friends George William and
Sarah Fairfax to return to Virginia and "once more become our
Neighbours.

> Your House at Belvoir I am sorry to add is no more, but mine
> (which is enlarged since you saw it) is most sincerely and heartily at
> your Service till you could rebuild it . . . and till you forbid me . . . I
> shall not *despair* of seeing you and Mrs. Fairfax once more the
> Inhabitants of Belvoir, and greeting you both there, the intimate
> companions of our old Age, as you have been of our younger years.[24]

On the morning of November 25, General Washington rode a magnificent gray horse alongside New York governor Clinton down

Broadway to assume sovereignty of New York. A week of festivities and fireworks followed before the last British masts dropped over the horizon. In the midst of the festivities, Washington could not control his passion for shopping—especially at the bargain prices overstocked stores were offering goods they had anticipated selling to the British aristocracy. By the morning of December 4, he was able to write to Lafayette that "I have made a purchase of so many pieces of the plated ware, as to render it unnecessary for you to comply with the request of my [last] letter . . . and have to beg the favor of you to take no step in consequence thereof."[25]

Later that morning, Washington invited ranking officers in New York to meet at noon at Fraunces Tavern, at the southern tip of the island, to say farewell. During the war, tavern owner Samuel Fraunces had frequently sent Washington secret reports on British troop and naval strength in the city, and Washington showed his gratitude by staging his farewell reception at Fraunces' establishment and ensuring the tavern's fame.

Of the twenty-nine major generals with whom Washington had served, only three were present, and of these, only Henry Knox was a close personal friend. Seven others had resigned during the war, six had died, and one—Benedict Arnold—had betrayed the Revolution. Nonetheless, other officers filled the "Long Room" at Fraunces Tavern to get a glimpse of the man they had served. When each had filled his glass, Washington's voice cracked, "With a heart full of love and gratitude, I now take leave of you. I most devoutly wish that your later days may be as prosperous and happy as your former ones have been glorious and honorable."

After they raised their glasses and drank, his tears got the better of him.

"I cannot come to each of you, but shall feel obliged if each of you will come and take me by the hand." As senior officer, Knox stepped forward first, having served his commander with unswerving loyalty and devotion for eight years. Washington put his arms around his three-hundred-pound friend and, with tears streaming down both their faces, kissed his chief of artillery on the cheek.[26]

When he had shaken the last officer's hand at Fraunces Tavern, Washington walked to the wharf, where a decorated barge awaited to take him to New Jersey and the beginning of the road home to private life at Mount Vernon. It proved longer than he anticipated, but he reveled in the mad adulation that awaited him on every road and in every town. Crowds cheered and public officials hailed his heroics at celebrations in New Brunswick, Trenton, and Princeton. President of Congress John Dickinson and the magnificent City Troop of Light Horse escorted him into Philadelphia, where church bells clanged and cannons boomed as he rode through the crowds into the center of the city. Still professing his eagerness to retire, he spent a week in Philadelphia attending dinners and balls in his honor, then rode to Wilmington, Delaware, for another "elegant supper" and festivities, and on to Baltimore and another dinner and ball, which lasted until 2:00 A.M. on December 19. He had promised Martha he'd be home for Christmas dinner, but with all his carousing, he had yet to meet with Congress, which was in Annapolis, awaiting official surrender of his commission as commander in chief. He arrived on December 20 for a formal dinner sponsored by the president of Congress. Two days later, Congress staged a magnificent ceremonial dinner, which one congressman described as "the most extraordinary I ever attended. In the evening of the same day, the Governor gave a ball at the State House. To light the rooms, every window was illuminated. . . . The General danced every set, that all the ladies might have the pleasure of dancing with him, or as it since has been handsomely expressed, get a touch of him."[27]

Washington appeared before Congress at noon on December 23. Throngs filled the streets leading to the State House. "The ladies occupied the gallery as full as it would hold, the Gentn: crouded below stairs. Silence ordered, by the Secretary, the Genl. rose and bowed to congress, who uncovered [removed their hats], but did not bow. 'Sir,' President Mifflin addressed the general, 'the United States in Congress assembled are prepared to receive your communications.'" He then delivered his speech, ending with a prayer "commending the Interests of our dearest Country to the protection of Almighty God. . . . Having now finished the work assigned me, I retire from the great theatre of action; and bidding an Affectionate farewell to this August body . . . I here offer my commission, and take leave of all employments of public life."[28]

Washington then "drew his commission from his bosom and handed it to the president. He replied in a set speech, the General bowed again to Congress, they uncovered and the General retired. After a little pause . . . Congress adjourned. The General . . . bid every member farewell and rode off from the door, intent upon eating christmas dinner at home."[29]

He rode past dark that evening then rose at dawn on December 24 and set off at full pace to reach his wife's arms in time for dinner with her, Nelly Custis, and Nelly's four children. After dinner the Washingtons had coffee, which, like other Americans, they had learned to enjoy instead of English tea.

9
A Broken Promise

HEAVY SNOWS ALL BUT BURIED Washington's Mansion at Mount Vernon in early 1784. With few travelers about, the Washingtons had almost no visitors, and Washington had hoped to put his voluminous papers in order, review his financial affairs, and reply to hundreds of accumulated letters of adulation. A swarm of children all but shattered his hopes. They were everywhere, waddling and gadding about, with slave girls and boys frantically chasing after, desperately trying to follow Martha's admonitions to keep the children out of mischief.

The youngest were Martha's two grandchildren, five-year-old Nelly and three-year-old Mr. Tub, or "Washy," whom the Washingtons had "adopted" after the death of their father, Jacky Custis. He had left his wife, Nelly, with four children. Unable to cope, she settled into a house in Alexandria with her two oldest and gratefully surrendered the two youngest to the Washingtons to raise at nearby Mount Vernon. The Washingtons also were caring for the three children of George's late brother Samuel: eight-year-old Harriot, ten-year-old Lawrence Augustine Washington, and twelve-year-old George Steptoe Washington. Left destitute, they faced a difficult life—even bondage, perhaps—had the Washingtons not taken them in.

The two oldest "children" in the snowbound Mansion were Martha's sixteen-year-old niece Fanny Bassett, and George's twenty-six-year-old nephew and godson George Augustine Washington, who was suffering from tuberculosis. Martha had offered to raise Fanny in 1777, after the death of Fanny's mother, Nancy Bassett, and she moved into the Mansion when Martha returned for good at the end of the war in November 1783. At sixteen, Fanny was old enough to be a welcome companion for Martha and young enough to be an equally welcome playmate and part-time caretaker for Nelly and Washy. George Augustine Washington was the son of his godfather's youngest brother, Charles Washington, an inadequate provider and a drunk. George Augustine had emulated his uncle George by enlisting and serving gallantly in the war—and earning his uncle's trust and affection. The elder Washington rewarded him by appointing him personal aide to Lafayette.

"At length my Dear Marquis," Washington wrote to Lafayette amid the din of squealing children, "I am become a private citizen on the banks of the Potomac, & under the shadow of my own Vine & my own Fig tree, free from the bustle of camp & the busy scenes of public life, I am solacing myself with those tranquil enjoyments, of which the Soldier who is ever in pursuit of fame . . . can have very little conception. . . .

> Envious of none . . . I will move gently down the stream of life, until I sleep with my Fathers . . . come with Madame la Fayette & view me in my domestic walks—I have often told you, & I repeat it again, that no man could receive you in them with more friendship & affection than I should do; in which I am sure Mrs Washington would cordially join me. We unite in respectful compliments to your Lady & best wishes for your little flock. With every sentiment of esteem, Admiration & Love, I am, My Dr Marqs Your Most Affecte friend
>
> G: Washington[1]

For fifty-two-year-old Martha, Nelly and Washy were a cherished new beginning. She wanted more from retirement than running a household and planning dinners. George had his crops, his livestock, his flowers and fruit trees; she wanted children and reveled in their presence.

"My little family are all with me," she exulted. Without them, "I almost despair of ever enjoying happiness."[2]

Fanny Bassett, Martha's niece and
"adopted daughter," painted by Robert
Edge Pine in 1785, when she was
eighteen.

Though somewhat less sanguine, Washington adored children,
and having failed to inspire Washy's father to notable achievements,
he looked forward to raising Washy—George Washington Parke
Custis—in the Washington rather than the Custis mold. "His family,
fortune and talents," Washington was convinced, "give him just pretensions to become a useful member of Society, in the Councils of
his Country."[3]

"My little Nelly," as Martha called her, and "my pretty little boy"
were far easier to love than Samuel Washington's children. Older and
set in their ways, they were often unruly, unkempt, and distant, and
when the snows melted, the Washingtons sent the boys to board
and study with the Anglican priest at Christ Church in Alexandria.
Although Harriot remained at the Mansion, she drifted uneasily
on the fringes of family life, inadequate with words, ungainly, her
hair and frock in constant disarray—no matter how often Martha
combed her hair or straightened and smoothed her dress. Occasionally George's sister Betty Lewis relieved Martha by taking the girl to
her house for a few weeks.

In the early morning hours when the children slept, and at night
when they went to bed, Washington answered letters, and, despite
his pompous pledges to retire under his proverbial "vine and fig tree,"

he showed no intention of relinquishing his unique status as a national hero to influence, if not dictate, national affairs. Even as he eschewed the center stage of public life, he eagerly slipped into the prompter's box, sending letters to the governors of Virginia, Maryland, and Pennsylvania to revive the great waterways project he envisioned connecting midwestern lakes and rivers to Chesapeake Bay via the Potomac River. To Martha's consternation, he also meddled in national political affairs with a call for government reform.

"The disinclination of the individual states," he wrote to Virginia governor Benjamin Harrison, "to yield competent powers to Congress for the Federal Government—their unreasonable jealousy of that body & of one another . . . will, if there is not a change in the system, be our downfall as a Nation."[4] He invited Harrison to visit Mount Vernon with Mrs. Harrison, who was Martha's cousin by marriage. He then established a steady, two-way flow of correspondence with political leaders in other states. By early spring, the volume of Washington's correspondence was diverting his attention from his plantation at a time when the latter needed his full focus. Friends, relatives, political figures, and admirers inundated him with mail. Lafayette sent him four letters on a single day—all of them endearing, but too voluminous for any response. Even Lafayette sensed as much as he began his *fourth* letter of the day:

> My dear General   Paris, March the 9th 1784
>
> Had I Not So perfect a Confidence in Your friendship, I Would Very Much Fear to tire You with My Scribbling of this day—But Cannot leave My Penn Before I Have Again Mentionned My tender Respectfull Affections to My dear General—I want to tell you that Md. de lafayette and My three Children are Well, and that all of us in the family Heartly join to Present their dutiful Affectionate Compliments to Mrs Washington and Yourself—Tell Her that I Hope Soon to thank Her for a dish of Tea at Mount Vernon— Yes, My dear General, Before the Month of June is over You will see a Vessel Coming Up Potowmack, and out of that Vessel Will Your friend jump With a Panting Heart and all the feelings of Perfect Happiness.

Washington replied immediately that he "ardently" longed "for the moment in which I can embrace you in America. Nothing could add more to the pleasure . . . than the happiness of seeing Madame La Fayette with you . . . and assure her of the sincerity of my wishes, & those of Mrs Washington; that she wou'd make Mount Vernon her home, while she stays in America. . . . it is unnecessary to tell you how much I am Yours &ca &ca."[5]

Spring increased the flow of visitors to Mount Vernon. The Lewis and Bassett clans and the various Washington relatives arrived regularly, often for a week or more. Nelly remarried and arrived with her new husband, Dr. David Stuart, who practiced in Alexandria. They brought Nelly's two older daughters to visit their younger sister and brother—Martha's two "babes"—Nelly and Washy. In addition to relatives, as many as a dozen or more visitors appeared at the Mansion each day—many of them men of note, whom the hospitable Washington often invited to the dinner table and to stay the night. The Washingtons were grateful he had had the foresight to build a "back stairway" that allowed them to slip away from the crowd unseen to the quiet of their common bed and bedroom.

As the year progressed, George Augustine became too sick to work, and Washington sent him to the warm waters at Berkeley Springs, then to Barbados. To George and Martha's delight, George Augustine proposed marriage to Fanny Bassett before he left, and she accepted.

"Honord Uncle," young Washington wrote after his arrival in Barbados,

> I sensibly feel the inexp[r]essible obligations I am under to You for Your unbounded goodness, and how I shall ever be able to acknowledge it I know not, but should I be so happy as to [be] bless'd with a restoration of my health, nothing in the compass of my power shall ever be omitted—that parental affection I have ever experienced from Mrs Washington lays me under equal obligations and it will ever be my study to make her Amends . . . may you experience the most perfect happiness this world is capable of affording, is the sincere wish of Your truely affectionate Nephew.

Of all the visitors who trooped through Mount Vernon over the summer, none gave the Washingtons more pleasure than Lafayette. Before he arrived, Lafayette's wife, Adrienne, had written to tell them he was on his way, but she had not dared risk the voyage with three young children. She also enclosed a note in the carefully crafted hand-writing of a seven-year-old that sent both Washingtons into gales of laughter.

> Dear Washington   Paris the 18th June 1784
>
>   I hope that papa whill come back Son here, I am very sorry for the loss of him, but I am very glade for you self. I wich you a werry good health and I am whith great respect, dear sir, your most obedient servent,
>
>   anastasie le fayette[6]

On August 17, 1784, Washington embraced his Lafayette on the carriageway in front of the Mansion at Mount Vernon. Martha was equally effusive. George Augustine Washington had returned by then, and he, too, embraced his former commander, as the grandchildren danced around merrily, not quite knowing how to respond to the tall Frenchman. The Washingtons had changed visibly since he had seen them last, but in his joy he ignored Martha's added heft—and George's missing teeth.

"Washington in retirement," Lafayette wrote to Adrienne, "is even greater than he was during the Revolution. His simplicity is truly sublime, and he is deeply involved in the details of managing his lands and home as if he had always been here. . . .

> There are two of Mrs. Washington's grandchildren here. As you know she was married before. The general has adopted them and loves them deeply; it was quite funny when I arrived to see the curious looks on those two small faces who had heard nothing but talk of me the entire day and wanted to see if I looked like my portrait. The general loved reading your letter and that of Anastasie, and I've been charged with sending you the most loving regards of the entire family, and Mrs. Washington told me today that, with both of them so old, you must not deprive them of the joy of receiving you and our little family; I made a solemn vow, sweetheart, to bring you with me on the next trip; Mount Vernon stands on the most beautiful site; it is as if the Pottowmack was created for it. The house is most beautiful and the countryside is charming. . . . we often speak of you, our children and everything else that has to do with the family.[7]

The Home of Washington—an engraving by Thomas Oldham Barlow—shows Washington on the piazza of the Mount Vernon mansion talking with Lafayette in 1784. In the grouping on the right are Martha's niece Fanny Bassett, Martha, and Martha's granddaughter Eleanor ("Nelly") Parke Custis. On the left, George Washington ("Washy") Parke Custis plays with the dogs.

During his visit, Martha covered the table with hams, breads, and bottles of peach and other fruit brandies that captivated Lafayette's palate almost as much as little Nelly and Squire Tub captivated his heart. Washington awakened at four each morning and took Lafayette on predawn rides across his five farms. They were back at the house for breakfast at seven, after which Washington guided Lafayette through his gardens, orchards, and new greenhouse, pointing out rare species of plants and flowers that admirers from around the world had sent. Washington gave Lafayette a sampling of seeds the king of France had requested for his gardens in Versailles from American flowers, shrubs, and trees unknown in Europe.[8]

On September 1, Washington accompanied Lafayette to Alexandria, where Washington was to begin his anticipated trip west to inspect his properties, while Lafayette set out for Annapolis, Philadelphia, and other cities for parades and festivities in his honor. They said their farewells in a tavern, where Lafayette admittedly got "a little tipsy," but shed none of his usual tears, because they planned to spend more time together before he returned to France.

A week later, Washington reached Berkeley Springs, where he spent a few days luxuriating in the waters and ordered construction of a two-story vacation home for his family. The rest of his western adventure would not be as pleasant. At Washington Bottom, one of his properties near Fort Pitt, he found the mill abandoned, inoperative, and in disrepair. Squatters' hovels littered his other properties, and when he confronted them, many scoffed at his ultimatum to pay rent or vacate. Washington appointed local agents to take legal action or evict them and set off for the Ohio River Valley to inspect his "bounty" lands. When passersby reported widespread Indian unrest in the area, however, he turned back and returned home three weeks early, without having improved his personal financial affairs.

Although he put the more than thirty-two thousand acres of Ohio River Valley lands up for sale, he grew more determined than ever to pursue the national waterways project, which would add considerable value to the western properties he retained on the Youghiogheny River. He would need the backing of legislatures in states through which the waterways would operate—Virginia, Maryland, and possibly Pennsylvania. His efforts would take him back onto center stage of national public life.

Washington first went to Richmond. Lafayette met him there, and arm in arm they strode into a banquet in their honor, to the roars of the state's leading citizens. Patrick Henry announced he would name his next son Fayette. (He already had a "George" in a brood that would eventually number seventeen children and inspire remarks that Henry, not Washington, was the real father of his country.) After a week of festivities (and successful lobbying for the waterways project), Washington and Lafayette left Richmond and spent two days of intimate camaraderie on the road to Mount Vernon, talking of their families, homes, and gardens, but also discussing social issues such as slavery and political issues—especially the need for a strong federal union with Washington at its head. They reached Mount Vernon on November 24. Four days in the bosom of Washington's family ended in torrents of tearful farewells—from little Squire Tub and Nelly, George Augustine Washington and Fanny

Bassett, and Martha Washington herself. Washington could not bring himself to say good-bye and chose to accompany Lafayette to his boat in New York.

They arrived the next day at Annapolis to the usual clangs, booms, and clatter of church bells, cannons, fireworks, and cheering crowds—the governor's welcome, the General Assembly speeches, and the governor's ball. Washington's unexpected presence added to the tumult and so tired him that he decided to forgo visiting Philadelphia and New York, where more exhausting celebrations awaited and would most certainly deprive the two friends of any quiet moments together.

On December 1, Washington and Lafayette embraced each other and parted. Neither could speak; Washington pressed two notes into Lafayette's hand: one was for Adrienne:

> The pleasure I received in once more embracing my friend could only have been encreased by your presence. . . . The Marquis returns to you with all the warmth and ardour of a newly inspired lover. We restore him to you in good health with wreaths of love and respect from every part of the Union. That his meeting with you, his family and friends, may be propitious, and as happy as your wishes can make; that you may long live together revered and beloved, and that you may transmit to a numerous progeny the virtue which you both possess, is the . . . vow and fervent wish of your devoted and most respectful Humble Servant.
>
> G: Washington
>
> N.B. In every good wish for you Mrs Washington sincerely joins me[9]

The second note was for Anastasie:

> Permit me to thank my dear little correspondent for the favor of her letter . . . & to impress her with the idea of the pleasure I shall derive in a continuation of them. Her Papa is restored to her with all the good health, paternal affection & honors, her tender heart could wish.
>
> He will carry a kiss to her from me, (which might be more agreeable from a pretty boy) & give her assurances of the affectionate regard with which I have the pleasure of being her well wisher.[10]

On December 21, 1784, New York governor George Clinton and a large crowd of dignitaries escorted Lafayette on a lavishly decorated barge to the French frigate that was to carry him back to France. Nathanael Greene, Alexander Hamilton, and Henry Knox took turns embracing him, and, as Clinton bid him farewell, he slipped a letter into Lafayette's hand. It was from Washington, who had written it on his return to Mount Vernon.

> In the moment of our separation upon the road as I travelled, & every hour since—I felt all that love, respect & attachment for you, which length of years, close connexion & your merits have inspired me. I often asked myself, as our Carriages distended, whether that was the last sight, I ever should have of you? And tho' I wished to say no—my fears answered yes. I called to mind the days of my youth, & found they had long since fled to return no more; that I was now descending the hill, I had been 52 years climbing—& that tho' I was blessed with a good constitution, I was of a short lived family—and might soon expect to be entombed in the dreary mansions of my father's—These things darkened the shades & gave a gloom to the picture, consequently to my prospects of seeing you again: but I will not repine—I have had my day.
>
> It is unnecessary, I persuade myself to repeat to you my Dr Marqs the sincerity of my regards & friendship—nor have I words which could express my affection for you, were I to attempt it. My fervent prayers are offered for your safe & pleasant passage—happy meeting with Madame la Fayette & family, the completion of every wish of your heart—in all which Mrs Washington joins me.[11]

With almost all his teeth missing, Washington invited the French dentist Jean Pierre le Mayeur to come to Mount Vernon to perform tooth transplants. Le Mayeur had assured him that he had transplanted "four fronts and one Eye tooth and are at this day perfectly secure and two others . . . are in a promising state and will be perfectly ferm."[12] The Frenchman bought teeth from the poor, advertising "three guineas for good front teeth from anyone but slaves."[13]

Within a month, the Virginia and Maryland legislatures appropriated funds to develop Potomac and James river navigation and build portage roads to Ohio River tributaries. The states sent representatives to a meeting at Mount Vernon and named Washington president of the Potomac Company. Leaders in both states hailed his success. In just four months he had succeeded in organizing the greatest public works project in North American history and unified two states that had hitherto been ready to war with each other over rights to the waterways involved.

"The earnestness with which he espouses the undertaking is hardly to be described," James Madison wrote to Jefferson, "and shows that a mind like his, capable of grand views, and which has long been occupied with them, cannot bear a vacancy."[14]

In ratifying the waterway agreement, Virginia and Maryland agreed to review interstate commercial relations annually. Maryland invited neighboring Delaware and Pennsylvania to participate because of their proximity to the waterway. Virginia went a step farther and urged that all states participate to consider unifying interstate and foreign commerce regulations, eliminate interstate trade restrictions, and facilitate establishment of trade agreements with foreign nations.

In the months that followed, Washington's financial situation continued deteriorating. Although he received rents from his lands in the Shenandoah, his agents had failed to extract rents from squatters on his western lands, and his advertisements had yielded no offers for Ohio River Valley bounty lands. After a long, wet winter, a drought ruined his spring crops at Mount Vernon and left his mill there without water to operate. And, without knowing how it happened, he gradually became "the national host" to swarms of uninvited guests who devoured his food and drink.

"My house," he complained ingenuously, "may be compared to a well resorted tavern, as scarcely any strangers who are going from north to south, or from south to north, do not spend a day or two in it."[15]

Although many were unwelcome strangers and even boors, most were relatives with open invitations and equally welcome former comrades in arms or notables such as John Dickinson, Robert Morris, James Madison, or Benjamin Lincoln. Washington's personality was such that he could not—did not know how—to turn them away. "Before strangers," wrote a British visitor, "he is generally very reserved and seldom says a word. I was fortunate in being in his company with his particular acquaintances. The General with a few glasses of champagne got quite merry, and being with his intimate friends laughed and talked a good deal."[16]

The great banker and agriculturalist Elkanah Watson offered another portrait. "He soon put me at ease," Watson said of Washington, "by unbending, in a free and affable conversation. The cautious reserve, which wisdom and policy dictated, was evidently the result of consummate prudence, and not characteristic of his nature." Watson was not only a pioneer in sheep and cattle breeding, he had studied canal systems in the Low Countries and found an eager listener in Washington. "I observed a peculiarity in his smile," Watson continued, "which seemed to illuminate his eye; his whole countenance beamed with intelligence. . . . I found him kind and benignant in the domestic circle, revered and beloved by all around him; agreeably sociable, without ostentation; delighting in anecdote and adventures."

Watson arrived at Mount Vernon with a bad cold, and that night, as he lay awake coughing, he heard his door open. "On drawing my bed-curtains, to my utter astonishment, I beheld Washington himself, standing at my bedside table, with a bowl of hot tea in his hand. . . . This little incident, occurring in common life with an ordinary man, would not have been noticed; but as a trait of the benevolence and private virtue of Washington, deserves to be recorded."[17]

Not until June 30 did the stream of visitors to Mount Vernon suddenly stop and allow George and Martha Washington a quiet evening together in their dining room—an event that George noted with surprise in his diary that evening: "dined with only Mrs. Washington. I believe [it] is the first instance of it since my retirement from public life."[18]

The stream renewed its flow the following day, though, with the entire Bassett clan arriving for dinner—along with an uninvited congressman. In the days that followed, artists and sculptors appeared at Mount Vernon to produce likenesses of Washington and his family. The renowned English artist Robert Edge Pine stayed three weeks painting portraits of both Washingtons, the four Custis grandchildren, and Fanny Bassett. French sculptor Antoine Houdon showed up later in the year, commissioned by Thomas Jefferson to make duplicate busts for the Virginia Capitol and the Paris City Hall (see frontispiece). Like Houdon, sculptor Joseph Wright made a life mask of Washington with plaster. "I consented with some reluctance," Washington recalled. "He oiled my features over, and placing me flat on my back, upon a cot, proceeded to daub my face with the plaster. Whilst in this ludicrous attitude, Mrs. Washington entered the room, and seeing my face thus overspread with the plaster, involuntarily exclaimed. Her cry excited in me a disposition to smile, which gave my mouth a slight twist or compression of the lips, that is now observable in the busts Wright afterwards made."[19]

Washington grew to like having his portrait painted—or perhaps resigned to it. "I am so hackneyed to the touches of the Painters pencil," Washington wrote to Pennsylvania jurist Francis Hopkinson, "that I am *now* altogether at their beck, and sit like patience on a Monument whilst they are delineating the lines of my face.... At first I was as impatient ... and as restive under the operation, as a Colt is of the Saddle—The next time, I submitted very reluctantly, but with less flouncing. Now, no dray [wagon] moves more readily to the Thill [shaft], than I do to the Painters Chair."[20]

Between sittings, Washington spent time planting ornamental shrubs and shade trees—lilacs, dogwoods, poplar, holly, mulberry, willows, mountain laurel, peach and pear trees, various nut trees, pine trees, etc. He also applied many of Elkanah Watson's new principles of agriculture gleaned from England, where crop rotation had become essential to renewing and maintaining soil fertility on a limited landmass. In 1785, though, a severe drought decimated his crops and destroyed much of the new landscaping around the Mansion. Washington was devastated.

"Most of my transplanted trees," he lamented in his diary, "have a sickly look. The small Pines in the Wildernesses are entirely dead. ... Almost the whole of the Holly are dead Many of the Ivy ... seem to be declining. Few of the Crab Trees have put forth leaves. Not a single Ash tree has unfolded its buds.... The lime trees ... are now withering."[21] With his crops gone, Washington had to buy a thousand bushels of wheat for his mill to make bread for the household and an equal amount of corn to feed his animals and slaves.

The Washingtons nonetheless pressed forward with plans for the wedding of his nephew George Augustine Washington to Martha's niece, Fanny Bassett. Both Washingtons were thrilled with the union of their own kin. The flow of champagne convinced some guests that Washington was one of the most successful planters in America. "I fancy," said one, "he is worth £100,000 sterling [$6 million today], and lives at the rate of three or four thousand a year [$200,000 and $250,000]."[22]

The wedding so elated the Washingtons that they invited the newlyweds to make Mount Vernon their home until they could find a home of their own to raise a family.

After the wedding, Washington's cousin Lund Washington announced his decision to retire as manager of the plantations after twenty-one years. Although George Augustine eagerly offered to succeed Lund, Washington knew that his nephew was not strong enough physically for the work or knowledgeable enough. Washington had no choice but to take over the task himself, but by the end of 1785, he recognized he had assumed too many burdens. A few months later he received an application from a young Harvard graduate to serve as his secretary and personal aide and relieve Washington of some of his nonfarming burdens. Recommended by former major general Benjamin Lincoln, Tobias Lear was twenty-four years old, from a prominent New Hampshire family, had lived in Europe, and was fluent in French. Lincoln assured Washington that Lear's "abilities are surpassed by few and his integrity by none."[23] Washington took to the young man immediately: he was exactly the sophisticated, intellectually gifted, erudite young gentleman Washington had tried to become as a youngster, and he invited Lear to make the Mansion his home. Lear had strong reservations about slavery, but relented when Washington expressed his intentions to emancipate his slaves and explained how, in the meantime, they would be safer, better off economically, and, indeed, happier living with the Washingtons than anywhere else.

Like Lafayette, Laurens, and Hamilton, young Lear all but worshiped Washington, and within a few weeks Washington, Martha, and the rest of the Washington clan embraced him as one of their

Tobias Lear, Washington's secretary, who also tutored Martha's young grandchildren Washy and Nelly. Artist unknown.

own—especially little Nelly and "Washy," whose formal education became Lear's responsibility.

With Lear organizing his enormous correspondence, Washington sought professional help for his agricultural enterprise and hired James Bloxham, "a plain, honest farmer . . . hard working Servant, capable of Ploughing, Sowing, Hedging, Ditching, Shearing, Mulling and Brewing . . . particularly attentive to Stock, and not inferior to any Man . . . in Thatching of Houses and Barns."[24] Washington combined his own knowledge with Bloxham's skills to "go into an entire new course of cropping" that replaced what he called the "ruinous mode of farming" that had exhausted the land on so many Virginia plantations.

Washington experimented tirelessly, passionately, with sixty different crops to find the best combinations for each of his fields, which varied according to the depth of the topsoil. He wrote of his experiments to agriculturists across the nation and around the world, and they, in turn, sent him different varieties of seeds and cuttings. He tried mingling crops, planting rows of corn eight feet apart, "with Irish potatoes or carrots, or partly both, between." He found that "corn planted in this manner will yield as much to the acre as in any other. That the quantity of potatoes will at least quadruple that quantity of corn, and that the potatoes do not exhaust the soil."[25]

He eventually settled on a six-year rotation of corn plus potatoes; wheat; peas (or "a medley" of buckwheat, turnips, and pumpkins);

Depiction of Washington's gardens at Mount Vernon, with the vegetable and flower gardens flanking the mansion and outbuildings, and fruit trees just visible on the extreme right.

spring barley or oats; clover; a season for the ground to lay fallow, with heavy applications of manure, before returning to a planting of corn.

In addition to cash crops, Washington maintained extensive fruit and vegetable gardens for his own table. Two acres of walled gardens produced such Washington favorites as peas and artichokes—and a full range of herbs. A four-acre fruit garden and orchard held a variety of berry patches, some two dozen different species of apple, plum, peach, pear, and cherry trees, and, of course, Washington's beloved (and oft-cited) grape vines and fig trees. His apple orchards yielded 120 gallons a year of sweet cider, applejack, and apple brandy. In addition to experimenting with various species of vegetables and plants, he experimented with new types of tools, often modifying or redesigning them to improve their efficiency—or inventing new ones as needed. He perfected several types of plows, including a barrel plow that combined tilling, seeding, and harrowing in a single tool. He burned successive rows of holes through the side of a small barrel, varying the diameter of the holes in each row to permit only one type of seed to pass through. He corked all the rows of larger holes, thus permitting only one size and type of seed to escape with each revolution of the barrel. Attached to plowshares that opened the row ahead, the barrel plow deposited its seeds at precise intervals, while a brush harrow attached behind covered the seeds with soil.

As he noted to his gardener, "I am never sparing . . . in furnishing my Farms with any, and every kind of Tool and implement that is calculated to do good and neat work . . . [and] will contribute to the improvement . . . of my farms."[26]

A brilliant, self-taught architect as well as engineer, he designed new barns—one of them a one-hundred-foot-long behemoth for storing grains, potatoes, turnips, and other root crops. It needed thirty-six thousand shingles to cover its roof. To fertilize his more than seventy-five hundred acres, he combined the manure from his livestock with compost, using a "Plan of the Dung Pit" in Thomas Hale's *A Compleat Body of Husbandry* (1758–1759) as a guide for building a thirty-one-foot-by-twelve-foot "Repository for Dung" with a cobblestone floor near the stables. He had studied the benefits of compost in John Spurrier's text *The Practical Farmer* (1793), and he ordered workmen to "rake, and scrape up all the trash of every sort about the houses, and in the holes and corners, and throw it . . . into the Stercorary [L. stercus: excrement]."[27]

In addition to his passion for agriculture, Washington was one of the nation's foremost breeders of livestock—130 horses, 350 cattle, 350 sheep, several hundred hogs and countless poultry, and mules. Together they produced raw materials—wool and hides, food, manure, and—often forgotten—hundreds of jobs for slaves, indentured workers, and freemen. A breeder of horses for racing and pleasure riding, Washington was a pioneer in breeding workhorses and, for his work in improving and promoting the use of mules, the agricultural world dubbed him "Father of the American Mule." In addition to breeding Arabian riding horses, he acquired a myriad of mares—twenty-seven from the army alone after the Revolution—to breed the most productive horses for his fields. He also bought Conestogas—then considered the finest draft horse—from German farmers in Lancaster County, Pennsylvania, where the breed was developed.

His studies, however, soon convinced him that mules had more strength and stamina than workhorses and consumed less food. Never one to ignore the wishes of his "beloved general," Lafayette wrote to the king of Spain, whose herd of jackasses were renowned for their strength and stamina as work animals. The king, in turn, sent Washington two prize jackasses, one of which died at sea. The other, which Washington named Royal Gift, was, at first, unmoved by "female allurements," Washington wrote to Lafayette. "I have my hopes that when he becomes a little better acquainted with republican enjoyments, he will amend his manners & fall into our custom of doing business."[28] When Bushrod Washington expressed interest in a mule, his uncle responded that, for the moment, Royal Gift seemed "too full of royalty, to have anything to do with a plebean race."[29] It would take Royal Gift many months to lower his social (and sexual) standards, and in the meantime, Lafayette sent Washington a Maltese jack and two jennets (females) hoping they would be "less frigid than those of His Catholick Majesty."

Washington conducted a series of experiments to test the strength of his mules pulling plows, harrows, and carriages, and he began breeding them for a variety of tasks, ranging from saddle and light carriages to heavy, slow draft. "From these," he noted, "I hope, all together, to secure a race of extraordinary goodness that will stock the Country."[30] Planters quickly sought to breed their mares with his jacks, and breeding mules became a rich new source of income. Soon he was advertising across the state and beyond:

> ROYAL GIFT. A JACK ASS of the first race in the kingdom of Spain, will cover mares and jennies at Mount-Vernon. . . . The first for ten, the latter for fifteen pounds the season. Royal Gift is four years old, is between 14 1-2 and 15 hands high, and will grow, it is said till he is 20 or 25 years of age. He is very bony and stoute made, of a dark colour, with light belly and legs.[31]

Later he sent Royal Gift on a breeding tour of the South and so promoted the use of mules that a century later the mule and donkey population of the United States would reach almost 2 million. Before the arrival of Royal Gift, Washington stabled 130 horses and no mules. Fourteen years later, the plantation counted 25 horses and 58 mules.

Apart from mules, Washington had already been among the first Virginia planters to raise sheep, having increased his flock to more than 200 before the war, and restoring it to 350 by 1785. Eventually Mount Vernon counted more than 600 sheep, which, because of his

172 THE UNEXPECTED GEORGE WASHINGTON

constant experimental breeding, produced wool as fine as that in England—and succulent mutton. He proved equally skilled with cattle, increasing his herd to 166 head by the mid-1780s and developing a breed of oxen more powerful than the largest draft horses and more efficient for pulling heavy field equipment. Again, he studied the subject intensively and bred a herd of two dozen oxen that were able to work until they were eight years old, after which he put them out to pasture for a year to "tenderize" them before slaughter. He carefully controlled the makeup of his herd of cattle—largely red Devon—to provide Mount Vernon an adequate supply of beef, veal, and milk and milk products such as butter, cream, and cheese.

Washington also perfected pig and hog production. (Pigs are classified as hogs when they weigh more than 120 pounds at slaughter.) In summer he let all the swine run wild to feed off the land until fall, when he penned them up for fattening (to 140 pounds or more) and slaughter for ham, salted pork, bacon, sausage, and lard. The 128 hogs he slaughtered just before Christmas in 1785 yielded 17,000 pounds of pork.

Washington bred and raised a wide variety of chickens, turkeys, ducks, and geese for eggs and meat. Although most of his poultry were standard breeds, he enjoyed raising exotic birds he received as gifts, including two partridges and seven pheasants—four of them rare gold-colored Chinese pheasants and two silver French pheasants that Lafayette sent him from the royal aviary at Versailles. Washington's brother Jack gave him a swan and four wild geese, and Virginia's Episcopal bishop contributed "a Goose & Gander of the Chinese breed."

Washington's genius went beyond agricultural production and animal husbandry, however. He studied and mastered the intricacies of food processing and distribution, for example, and learned that a Delaware inventor, Oliver Evans, was developing milling technology to automate grain processing. Four years before Evans would publish details of his new technology, Washington convinced him to install it at the mill at Mount Vernon. (Few could resist the exhortations of a national idol, especially an insistent national idol as tall and powerfully built as Washington.)

Evans's ingenious process consisted of vertical, bucket conveyors that carried the wheat or grain from its entry into the mill to the grindstone, where, after processing, a mechanical rake spread the meal to cool. Another assembly of bucket conveyors carried the flour and poured it into casks and barrels that rolled down a ramp for loading onto wagons. Driven by water wheels, the process would send shock waves through the milling industry, with owners of small mills complaining that Evans's equipment would put them out of business. Washington's business acuity saw it as a means of reducing labor costs, speeding production, improving quality, and increasing profits—and he was right on all counts. The Evans equipment increased his sales of flour tenfold, to about 150,000 pounds, and helped make Washington's Mount Vernon an agricultural showplace.

Among the most successful of Washington's prewar enterprises had been his fishery. Although production had slowed during the war, it required almost no new investment to return it to prewar profitability—only new nets. Restoring his other enterprises to profitability, however, had required huge new investments and left him ever deeper in debt. He desperately needed to collect moneys owed by relatives, friends, tenants, and customers, but saw no way to do so "without suit and I hate to sue them. I have offered lands for sale at very moderate prices but have not, been able to sell them."[32]

Just as Washington was trying to restore his plantation's profitability, he received a letter from John Jay in mid-March 1786 that heralded the end of his idyll beneath his vine and fig tree: "[A]ltho' you have wisely retired from public Employments," Jay wrote, "I am persuaded you cannot view . . . your country . . . with the Eye of an unconcerned Spectator. . . .

> Experience has pointed out Errors in our national Government, which call for Correction. It is in Contemplation to take measures for forming a general convention . . . I am fervent in my Wishes, that it may comport with the Line of Life you have marked out for yourself, to favor your country with your counsels on such an important & single occasion. I suggest this merely as a Hint for your consideration.[33]

"I coincide perfectly in sentiment with you," Washington replied somewhat too eagerly, "that there are errors in our National Government which call for correction; loudly I will add. . . . That it is necessary to revise, and amend the Articles of Confederation, I entertain *no* doubt . . . something must be done."[34]

With the arrival of Tobias Lear, Washington stepped up the pace of his correspondence, exchanging views with every American of consequence on the shape of a new national government. Washington also corresponded with foreign emissaries to the United States and influential figures overseas. All provided him with a flow of commercial and political intelligence that made him one of the best-informed and most knowledgeable Americans in both domestic and foreign affairs—and belied his stated intentions to retire from public life. He knew all too well the failings of the Articles of Confederation, which had emasculated Congress and left foreign nations unable to obtain satisfactory trade agreements. To conclude a trade agreement with one state often meant negotiating agreements with all the surrounding states through which the imports and exports would travel to the first state. It was so complex that most foreign nations gave up trying, and foreign trade all but halted in many areas.

To avoid upsetting Martha, Washington pretended to remain aloof, but his correspondence carried his views across the nation. "I do not conceive we can exist long as a nation," he warned John Jay, "without having lodged somewhere a power which will pervade the whole Union. . . . Retired as I am from the world, I frankly acknowledge I cannot feel myself an unconcerned spectator. Yet having happily assisted in bringing the ship into port & having been fairly discharged: it is not my business to embark again on a sea of troubles."[35]

In October 1786, Washington learned that his trusted wartime comrade Nathanael Greene had died. As always, he acted to help his friend's orphaned boy. If Mrs. Greene thought it "proper to entrust my namesake G: Washington Greene to my care," he wrote the executors of Greene's estate, "I will give him as good an education as this country . . . will afford and will bring him up to either of the genteel professions that his friends* may choose, or his own inclination shall lead him to pursue at my own cost and expense."[36] With absolutely no money to spare, it was fortunate for Washington that

---

* The word "friend" in eighteenth-century America was often used to mean a kinsman or near relative, and it is in this sense that both Washingtons consistently apply the term.

Lafayette, who was far wealthier, made the same offer to Mrs. Greene, and she opted to send her son to Paris for a year of schooling under Lafayette's guardianship.

Early in January 1787, Washington received the devastating news that his brother Jack—John Augustine Washington—had died. As usual, he choked for adequate words to express the deep sorrow that lay behind the stoic face. His diary acknowledges only "the sudden death . . . of my beloved Brother Colo. Jno. Auge. Washington," followed by a simple notation: "At home all day."[37]

In the winter of 1787, when Washington turned fifty-five, the Virginia General Assembly approved the call for states to convene in Philadelphia in May and unanimously elected Washington to head the state delegation. Martha tried to hide her hurt. After promising to retire by her side at Mount Vernon after the war, he was breaking his vow and going to Philadelphia. He had never before broken a promise to her, and she shuddered that he would ride away as he had in 1775 and answer the siren call of national leadership.

As in '75, he tried to comfort her, said he wouldn't go; he'd stay home with her, but in her heart she knew her husband all too well.

IO

"God Bless Our Washington!"

"IT IS THE GENERAL WISH that you should attend," Henry Knox pleaded with Washington a month before the convention of American states. "It is conceived to be highly important to the success of the propositions of the convention."[1] Named to lead the Virginia delegation, Washington feigned reluctance—much as he had always feigned reluctance for power as an almost certain means of obtaining it. For once, however, his reluctance was not a total pretense. He had elevated the surrender of his Revolutionary War commission before Congress to high drama by publicly pledging to retire from public life. Not only was he reneging on his pledge to the American people, he also was breaking his promise to Martha that he would retire. Nor were these his only concerns. He knew his financial condition was so shaky that a return to public life might bankrupt him. And his physical condition was almost as bad: he had only one tooth left, and his arthritis had become so painful that he had partially immobilized one of his arms in a sling. He was in the mood for bed, not a long, bumpy ride to Philadelphia. Still another factor in his considerations was his personal happiness. He adored his life at Mount Vernon, surrounded, as he was, by his grandchildren. He did not want to leave what seemed an idyllic life.

But Henry Knox, whom Washington had plucked out of obscurity to command the Continental Army artillery in the war, knew how to manipulate his patron after eight years of service together.

Washington family portrait by Edward Savage shows the aging
Washingtons in 1796, with their "adopted" children—actually Martha's
fatherless grandchildren, George Washington ("Washy") Parke Custis,
fifteen, on the left, and Eleanor ("Nelly") Parke Custis, seventeen, on
her grandmother's right.

After assuring Washington of his election to the presidency of
the convention, he predicted that the role would be "highly honorable to your fame . . . and doubly entitle you to the glorious republican epithet—The Father of Your Country."[2]

Knox knew the magic words, and early on May 9, Washington
left Martha holding back her tears at Mount Vernon while he set out
for Philadelphia, where he lodged at the luxurious mansion of finan-
cier Robert Morris. As before, church bells and cheering crowds
greeted his entry into the city, and his tall, stately figure commanded
everyone's attention wherever he went—spending money he didn't
have, shopping in the mornings, dining at the finest homes in the
afternoon, and thrilling Philadelphia ladies at festive balls in the
evening. Enough wine helped him forget his arthritis. But he did not
forget Martha or the family, writing each day to remind them (and
mollify Martha's displeasure), "if you . . . should want any thing here,
it would give me pleasure to oblige you."[3]

He had given his nephew George Augustine Washington temporary command of the Mount Vernon agricultural enterprise, and

young Washington fulfilled his uncle's expectations by sending detailed weekly reports to Philadelphia—as Lund had done during the war. Then as now, in the midst of his frenetic activities at the Constitutional Convention, Washington could not dismiss Mount Vernon from his thoughts. Indeed, he found that writing detailed instructions to his nephew a pleasant way to escape the stress of convention activities:

> If you tried both fresh, and Salt fish as a manure. . . .
>
> I have no objection to putting the ground . . . in Buckwheat. . . .
>
> How does the grass Seeds which were Sown with the grain & flax, seem to come on?[4]

To no one's surprise, the convention unanimously elected George Washington president. Of the thirty-seven delegates, twenty-seven had served with him in the Continental Army. By rule, all proceedings were to be kept secret, and, as president, he could not voice opinions at the convention, but his carefully crafted letters in the years following independence—and his conversations with delegates outside the hall and in nearby taverns—made his the loudest voice. And whenever he needed to, he unsheathed the weapon that had proved so successful in retaining command during the war: the threat of resignation.

"I almost despair of seeing a favorable issue to the proceedings of our Convention," he growled after two months, "and do therefore repent having had any agency in the business."[5] In the two months that followed, delegates hammered out a constitution. In the end, it was Washington's Constitution. He had shaped the ideas, implanted them in the minds of delegates, and all but wrote the actual words for them.

True to convention rules, however, Washington's longest diary entries relate to only his visits to nearby farms. At one farm, he marveled at the fertilizing effect "of plaister of Paris [similar to lime] . . . on a piece of Wheat stubble, the ground bearing which, he [the farmer] says. had never recd. any manure. . . . The white clover on this grd. . . . was full high enough to mow, and stood very thick."[6]

Washington knew he would be the nation's president if the states ratified the new constitution—that only he had the prestige and experience to ensure success for the new government. He also recognized, however, that success would depend on unanimous support, and experience had taught him the surest way to obtain such support was to feign disinterest.

Although Martha also feigned disinterest, she was unhappy with the prospect of her husband returning to public service and did her best to ignore the chatter about the presidency by focusing on her grandchildren. In a letter to her niece Fanny, Martha wrote that "we have not a single article of news but pollitick, which I do not conscern myself about. . . . I wish you could see the papers that comes hear every week as you are fond of reading them." Then she turned to her primary concerns: "My Dear little children have all been very well, till today my pretty little Dear Boy complains of a pain in his stomach. . . . I cannot say but it makes me miserable if ever he complains let the cause be ever to[o] trifeling—I hope the almighty will spare him to me. . . . The General is very well—as to myself I am as usual—neither sick nor well."[7]

As the nation deliberated the form of its future government, the priest at Alexandria Academy refused to continue boarding Washington's two nephews in his home because "it neither suits them or me."[8] Samuel Hanson, a teacher, agreed to take them, but within a week he wrote to Washington, "I will not conceal from you that there have been many disagreements between your Nephews & myself & family. The principal Subjects of those are the following: An obstinate habit . . . of Keeping Company with Servants . . . Going out without my permission . . . staying out late of Evenings, and sometimes the whole Night. I pass over the disrespect and insults with which they have treated Mrs. H. and myself." Hanson asked that, as a condition for keeping the boys, Washington consider "investing me not only with nominal, but an actual, authority over them."[9]

Washington agreed and warned the older nephew, fifteen-year-old George Steptoe Washington, "I hope this is the last complaint I shall ever hear while you remain in your present situation . . . as it will prevent me from using means to regulate your behavior which will be disagreeable to us both."[10]

No sooner had he dealt with his nephews than his sister Betty Lewis in Fredericksburg wrote him that their eighty-year-old mother had developed breast cancer and was dying. Knowing he might be called to the presidency, he rode to Fredericksburg "to discharge the last Act of *personal* duty, I may . . . ever have it in my power to pay my Mother."[11] As in the past, he fails to describe his mother as "beloved" in his diary entry—nor had he ever expressed the "love" for her that he routinely offered his sister, brothers, and in-laws in letters to them. His diary fails to describe his last visit to her or even note her death.

On August 5, Washington returned from the fields to find his thirteen-year-old nephew Lawrence, the younger of the boys at Alexandria Academy, sobbing in Martha's ever-protective arms, saying he was afraid to remain at Samuel Hanson's house. "He . . . offered to shew me some bruises he had received," Washington wrote to Hanson the next day. "Being prepared for it, I was going to correct him, but he begged so earnestly, and promised so faithfully that there should be no cause of complaint against him for the future that I have suspended the Punishment. . . . The letter which I have written to his Brother on the subject, is under this cover and open for your perusal."[12]

Washington, of course, had given Hanson permission to use corporal punishment, and Hanson had been doing just that when George Steptoe heard his younger brother's cries, rushed into the house, and leaped on Hanson's back to prevent the man from inflicting further punishment.

"Dear George," Washington wrote to his incorrigible nephew, "It was with equal pain and surprize I was informed by Colo. Hanson on Monday last, of your unjustifiable behaviour in rescuing your brother from that chastisement which was due to his improper conduct; and which you know, because you have been told it in explicit language, he was authorized to administer whensoever he should deserve it.

> Such refractory behaviour on your part, I consider as an insult equally offered to myself . . . and I shall continue to view it in that light, till you have made satisfactory acknowledgments to Colo. Hanson for the offence given him. . . . If the admonitions of friendship are lost other methods must be tried which cannot be more disagreeable to you than it would be to one who wishes to avoid it who is solicitous to see you and your Brother (the only

remaining Sons of your father) turn out well, and who is very desirous of continuing your Affecte Uncle

Go. Washington[13]

In his reply, the boy defended his actions, insisting that "what I did . . . was not to deny Col. Hansons authority, it was not to call in question the justice of his punishment, but I was driven to it by brotherly affection; if it has meet with your disapprobation, I am sorry for it . . . what is done cannot be undone, I shall persue that only method of atonement for folly, to be sorry for it, and do so no more.

"It only remains," the boy went on, "that I should express my thanks for your kind advise and assuring you that I will never deviate from any instructions which I shall be favoured with from you; these are the unaltered intentions. Of Dear Uncle Your most Obedient Nephew George S. Washington [P.S.] Both of us are in want of coats and a pair of breeche's."

A few days later, Washington made an entry in his account book: "By Messrs Geo. & Lawce Washington pd to Messr Porter & Ingraham on their Acct . . . 27.0.0 By ditto pd Rd Weightman for making their Cloaths . . . 5.2.7. By ditto pd for trimgs for making Cloaths for them . . . 0.4.5." He was as incorrigible in spoiling the boys as they were in misbehaving.

As ratification of the Constitution became a certainty, some of Washington's political friends decided to humor him rather than badger him. John Jay wrote from New York, "Some Gentlemen here and in Jersey have it in Contemplation to form a Society to promote the Breeding of good Horses and mules—in that Case we will endeavour to introduce some Jennies, of which we have none at present, and send them to your Jack."[14] And physician Benjamin Rush wrote from Philadelphia, "I received a small quantity of the mangel wurzel [a large, coarse beetroot grown as cattle feed] or Scarcity root Seeds a few days ago from Dr Lettsom of London. In distributing these Seeds among the friends of Agriculture in this country, I should have been deficient in duty, and patriotism, to have neglected a small portion of them to your Excellency."[15] Washington immediately planted it in his little "Botanical Garden," just behind the Mansion, where he experimented with rare plants and unusual species. He loved nothing more than dropping to his knees and plunging his fingers into the soil to stabilize fragile seedlings by cradling them in his huge hands. Working the soil was a spiritual experience. For a rare, brief moment he was a part of the earth but apart from the world, with his intellect and emotions at one with nature.

"No pursuit is more congenial with my nature and gratification, than that of agriculture," he would confess, "nor none I so pant after as again to become a tiller of the earth."[16]

New York's Gouverneur Morris—himself an avid farmer—acknowledged having promised Washington some

> Chinese Piggs—A promise which I can perform only by Halves for my Boar being much addicted to Gallantry hung himself in Pursuit of meer common Sows And his Consort to asswage her Melancholy (for what alas can helpless Widows do) took up with a Paramour of Vulgar Race and thus let her grunting Progeny have jowls and Bellies less big by Half than her Dam. Such however as I have such send I unto you And to piece and patch the Matter as well as I may In Company with the Piggs shall be sent a Pair of Chinese Geese Which are really the foolishest Geese I ever beheld for they chuse all Times for Sitting but Spring And one of them is now actually engaged in that Business.
>
> It would be too degrading to the Noble Race of Man should I introduce Politics after Hogs and Geese. This is a tolerable Excuse for saying . . . I am the Breed of Optimists and believe that . . . you will certainly be seated in the Presidents Chair.[17]

Alexander Hamilton knew his old commander too well to participate in the charade. Like Knox, he knew all the magic words that fired Washington's ambitions: "glory," "fame," "honor."

"I should be deeply pained my Dear Sir," Hamilton concluded, "if your scruples in regard to a certain station should be matured into a resolution to decline it." He agreed that "caution in deferring an ultimate determination is prudent," but insisted that "every public and personal consideration will demand from you an acquiescence in what will *certainly* be the unanimous wish of your country."[18]

Despite his expressed disinterest in the presidency, Washington was already preparing for the job—much as he had done before accepting leadership of the Continental Army. He pored over a vast array of books, knowing that the first president would have to invent a form of governing never before envisioned, let alone practiced in world history. His library of nine hundred books eventually included volumes on every form of government in every civilized nation, including Edward Gibbon's massive *History of the Decline and Fall of the Roman Empire*, which was just then being published piecemeal.

As he tried preparing himself for the presidency, however, the problems of his two nephews continued intruding. "Except beating Mrs. H., and striking myself," Samuel Hanson complained, "there is no outrage or indecorum they have not commited. Neither my servants nor my children have escaped their fury and violence."[19] Hanson insisted that Washington find another place to board the boys, and Washington turned in desperation to his old friend and physician sixty-year-old James Craik, a hardened Scotsman who had served at Fort Necessity and Braddock's Field and had cared for both the Washingtons and their children at Mount Vernon.

"As it is probable I shall soon be under the necessity of quitting this place," Washington wrote to his older nephew George Steptoe Washington, "I think it incumbent on me as your Uncle & friend, to give you some advisory hints . . . in regulating your conduct and giving you respectability. . . . You have now arrived to that age when you must quit the trifling amusements of a boy, and assume the more dignified manner of a man." In six pages of admonitions, Washington urged the boy to pay "attention to the moral values . . . to your studies, and employ your time of relaxation in proper company. . . . Decency & cleanliness will always be the first objects in the dress of a judicious & sensible man . . . you should always keep some clothes to wear to Church, or on particular occasions, which should not be worn every day."

Washington warned his nephew that

if you are determined to neglect your books, and plunge into extravagance and dissipation nothing I could say now would prevent it . . . should you or Lawrence, therefore, behave in such a manner as to occasion any complaints being made to me—you may depend upon losing that place which you now have in my affections—and any future hopes you may have from me. But if, on the contrary, your conduct is such as to merit my regard you may always depend upon the warmest attachment & sincere regard of Your affectionate friend & Uncle

Go: Washington[20]

At the end of March, Washington turned over management of his vast agricultural enterprise to his nephew George Augustine Washington, along with ten pages of detailed instructions on virtually every aspect of the enterprise—fish, timothy seed, rents, use of the jacks, brickwork, harvesting, cowpens, sheep folds, stables, gullies, tobacco, rum, flour, barley. The list ran on and on before concluding in typical Washington understatement:

> The general superintendence of my Affairs is all I require of you, for it is neither my desire nor wish that you should become a drudge to it—or, that you should refrain from any amusements, or visitings which may be agreeable either to Fanny or yourself to make or receive. Sincerely wishing you health & happiness—I am ever your warm friend and Affectionate Uncle
>
> Go: Washington[21]

At noon, April 14, 1789, a carriage pulled up to the Mansion door. Martha and George Washington stepped out to greet the aging Pennsylvania revolutionary Charles Thomson, who had been secretary of the Continental Congresses and sole witness to John Hancock's signature on the Declaration of Independence. He had been secretary to Congress under the Confederation, and had entertained the Washingtons—singly and together—at his home in Philadelphia. The Washingtons greeted Thomson warmly and exchanged pleasantries with him until a sudden pause allowed their smiles to dissolve into grim seriousness. Thomson announced he had come with a message from Congress. The Washingtons were prepared. Martha gathered the rest of the family around her as Thomson pulled a paper from his pocket, stepped back from his former commander in chief, and straightened his arthritic body to attention to read:

> Sir, I have the honor to transmit to your Excellency the information of your unanimous election to Office of President of the United States of America. Suffer me, Sir, to indulge the hope, that so auspicious a mark of public confidence will meet your approbation,

and be considered as a sure pledge of the affection and support you are to expect from a free and an enlightened people.[22]

Washington pulled a response from his own pocket:

Sir, I have been long accustomed to entertain so great a respect for the opinion of my fellow citizens, that the knowledge of their unanimous suffrages having been given in my favour scarcely leaves me the alternative for an Option. Whatever may have been my private feelings and sentiments, I believe I cannot give a greater evidence of my sensibility for the honor they have done me than by accepting the appointment. . . . I shall therefore be in readiness to set out the day after to morrow, and shall be happy in the pleasure of your company. For you will permit me to say that it was a peculiar gratification to have received the communication from you.[23]

Two days later, on the morning of April 16, 1789, George Washington, Charles Thomson and Washington's secretary Tobias Lear climbed into Washington's ornate carriage and began the ride to glory in New York, the temporary capital of the new republic. He left a list of instructions for the overseers of his various farms, and he reminded the English gardener to plant Indian corn, flax, and buckwheat before the end of the month, and to plant peas and pumpkins in May, potatoes in June, turnips in June and July, and so forth until the deep frost set in. Martha stood in the doorway, forcing herself to smile as she watched the carriage pull away from the Mansion, then stepped back inside and, to the dismay of Nelly and Washy, hurried up to her room with tears streaming down her face.

"I am truly sorry to tell that the General is gone to New York," she wrote to her nephew a few days later.

Mr Charles Thompson [sic] came express to him, on the 14th— when, or wheather he will ever come home again god only knows,— I think it was much too late for him to go in to publick life again, but it was not to be avoided, our family will be deranged as I must soon follow him

I am greved at parting, and sorry to part with your sister [Martha's niece "Patty" was visiting Mount Vernon] as well as the rest of the family,—I expect to set out the middle of may . . . the same Horses that carred the General is to return for me to carry me to New York—

My love and good wishes to your mother grandmother Brothers and sisters and believe me Dear

> John your most
> affectionate
> Aunt
> M Washington[24]

Martha's sorrow weighed on Washington throughout the day. He had tried unsuccessfully to comfort her before he left their bedchamber that morning, and he almost believed he had succeeded when she smiled like a good soldier at the door as his carriage pulled away. But he knew better, and, indeed, he had mixed feelings about leaving. "About ten o'clock I bade adieu," he wrote in his diary that evening, "I bade adieu to Mount Vernon, to private life, and to domestic felicity; and with a mind oppressed with more anxious and painful sensations than I have words to express, set out for New York . . . to render service to my country in obedience to its call, but with less hope of answering its expectations."[25]

His ride to New York fulfilled any and every ambition for glory he—or any other leader, for that matter—might ever have harbored.

Over the next eight days, every city and village greeted Washington and his party with elaborate—often interminable—festivities, complete with church bells, fireworks, bands, marches, floral arches, balls, and, of course, speeches—endless speeches, often late into the night. Washington was hard put to rise before daybreak, but he had no choice if he was to cover enough ground to get to New York in time for his own inauguration. The extravagance disquieted Washington, as he wrote in his diary. How would those same mobs react if he failed?

"I greatly apprehend," Washington wrote, "that my Countrymen will expect too much from me. I fear, if the issue of public measures should not corrispond with their sanguine expectations, they will turn extravagent . . . praises which they are heaping upon me at this moment, into equally extravagant . . . censures."[26] Washington wanted to write to Martha, but decided against adding his own fears to those he knew she already harbored.

On April 30, 1789, the morning of the inauguration of the first president of the United States, cannons saluted Washington. His body servant powdered his hair, then helped him dress. At nine, church bells across the city called the public to worship and pray to "the Great Ruler of the universe for the preservation of the President," according to Tobias Lear.

> At twelve the troops of the city paraded before our door, and soon after, the committees of Congress and heads of departments came in their carriages to wait upon the President to the Federal Hall. At half past twelve the procession moved forward, the troops marching in front with all the ensigns of military parade. Next came the committees and heads of departments in their carriages. Next the President in the state coach . . . foreign ministers and a long train of citizens.
>
> About two hundred yards before we reached the hall, we descended from our carriages, and passed through the troops, who were drawn up on each side, into the Hall and Senate-chamber, where we found the Vice-President, the Senate, and House of Representatives assembled. They received the President in the most respectful manner, and the Vice-President conducted him to a spacious and elevated seat at the head of the room. A solemn silence prevailed.[27]

Adams welcomed Washington before announcing, "Sir, the Senate and House of Representatives are ready to attend you to take the oath required by the Constitution."

"I am ready to proceed," Washington replied. Grim-faced, he stood and followed Adams through a door onto a small portico overlooking Wall and Broad streets. New York governor Clinton waited with Henry Knox. Samuel Otis, the secretary of the senate, lifted a red cushion that held a Bible on which Washington placed his huge right hand. New York chancellor (chief justice) Robert R. Livingston administered the oath as thousands looked up from the streets below. It was one in the afternoon:

"Do you solemnly swear that you will faithfully execute the office of President of the United States and will, to the best of your ability, preserve, protect, and defend the Constitution of the United States?"

"I solemnly swear that I will faithfully execute . . ." he repeated the oath, then added, "So help me God" and bent over to kiss the Bible.

"It is done," declared Livingston, who turned to the crowd, raised his arms, and shouted, "Long Live George Washington, President of the United States."[28]

According to Lear, "the air was rent by repeated shouts and huzzas,—'God bless our Washington! Long live our beloved President!'" Washington acknowledged the cheers, but his thoughts darted back to his beloved older brother Lawrence . . . Braddock's Field . . . Martha at Mount Vernon. Then a hand slipped under his arm to lead him back into the hall to address Congress.[29]

"It was a touching scene," said one congressman. Another described it as "elegant." But a third noted that Washington "trembled. This great man was agitated and embarrassed more than ever he was by the leveled cannon or pointed musket."[30] Never known for his great oratory, he had but one tooth left and pursed his lips to contain his ill-fitting false teeth. After a twelve-minute struggle, he ended his—and the nation's—first inaugural address with a solemn prayer "to the benign Parent of the human race, in humble supplication . . . to favour the American people, with . . . the security of their Union, and the advancement of their happiness."[31]

Still uncertain what he was to do in his new job, he rode back to the President's House, which filled with so many well-wishers, job seekers, hangers-on, and mere gawkers that he had to work out a policy for receiving guests and responding to invitations to visit others. Washington hired his old friend Samuel Fraunces, of Fraunces Tavern, as cook, and awaited the arrival of Martha to organize the rest of his household and social life. Two weeks after the inauguration, Martha set off for New York in the family coach with her two grandchildren, ten-year-old Nelly Custis and eight-year-old Washy. Her niece Fanny agreed to watch over George's niece Harriot at Mount Vernon. Martha stopped for a tearful farewell in Alexandria with her daughter-in-law, the elder Nelly Custis, and the two older Custis granddaughters, Elizabeth and Martha. The same clanging church bells, massive parades, cheering crowds, and thirteen-gun salutes that had greeted her husband welcomed her along the route north. Baltimore staged a display of fireworks followed by an endless "serenade" that lasted until 2:00 A.M. Two days later, two cavalry units met her carriage in Chester, Pennsylvania, to escort her into Philadelphia. Once the bells, cheers, and gunfire faded, Martha reverted to her old self and dashed to the most fashionable stores to buy shoes for Nelly, Betty, and Patty Custis in Alexandria—along with a panoply of clothes for little Nelly and Washy. And silks for herself.

> My dear Fanny
>
> I have the pleasure to tell you, that we had a very agreable journey,—I arrive in philadelphia on fryday after I left you without the least accident to distress us, were met by the President of the state with the city troop of Horse . . . a number of Ladies and Gentlemen came to meet me,—and after a cold colation we proceed to town,—I went to Mr. Morrises—the children was very well and chearfull all the way, Nelly complained a very little of being sick— as soon as I could I sent for the stay maker and gave him your measure . . . also two pair of shoes of a new fashioned kind those with Low Heels are for you, those with the high heels is for Mrs. [Martha's daughter-in-law Nelly] Stuart, with a pr apiece for the two dear little girls.[32]

After leaving Philadelphia, Martha and the children rode to Elizabeth Town, New Jersey, where the same decorated barge that had taken her husband to New York for his inauguration awaited— with the president on board to surprise his wife. "I set out on Monday," she continued her letter to Fanny, "and was met by the President . . . with the fine Barge you have seen so much said about of in the papers with the same oars men that carried the P. to New York—

> dear little Washington ["Washy"] seemed to be lost in a mase at the great parade that was made for us all the way we come—The Governor of the state met me as soon as we landed, and led me up to the House, the paper will tell you how I was complimented on my landing—I thank god the Prdt is very well, and the Gentlemen with him are all very well,—the House he is in is a very good one and is handsomely furnished all new for the General. . . . I have not had one half hour to myself since the day of my arrival—my first care was to get the children to a good school, which they are boath very much pleased at. . . . My Hair is set and dressed every day—and I have put on white muslin Habits for the summer—you would think me a good deal in the fashion if you could but see

me—My dear Fanny send me by some safe convance my Black lace apron and handkerchief they are in one of my drawers in the chest of drawers in my chamber and some thread lace or joining nett is in one of the Baskets on the shelf in my closet they were fine net Handkerchiefs which I intended to make cap boarders off— I think I shewed it to you. . . . I should think there could not be any impropriety in Hariot's going to see her cousin whenever she desires it.[33]

Instead of political problems, Martha found her husband forced to deal with congressional concerns over social etiquette—the number of "levees," or receptions the president should hold each week, at what time of day, and for how many people. There was also the question of the correct address: "Your Excellency"? "Your Highness"? "Your Exalted"? In the end, Congress decided on the simplest title of all—the President—and to address him with republican simplicity as a fellow citizen: "Mr. President." With Martha's staunch support, Washington decided on a "line of conduct which combined public advantage with private convenience." He would limit visitors to one hour, two days a week—Tuesdays and Fridays, between two and three in the afternoon—after which he would abandon his guests and join his family in the private quarters for dinner. Initially, Washington decided against all entertaining, but relented in favor of a weekly dinner with members of Congress. On other days, however, dinner was to be a private affair for his own family and members of his "presidential family," such as Tobias Lear or other close advisers. To limit demands on his time, he decided against accepting any invitations, although he reserved the right to attend theater and drive into the country to visit farms—and he could not resist attending a ball that the French minister hosted in his honor.

Too accustomed to entertaining at Mount Vernon, however, the Washingtons did not wait long to invite friends to dinner. Although the first guests apprized the offerings as "the least showy dinner that I ever saw," by summer's end both Washingtons had tired of republican simplicity, and Martha ordered foods and wines that she had served at Mount Vernon—and drew comments such as: "It was a great dinner . . . the best of the kind I ever was at."[34]

As word of Martha's lavish dinners reached the public, one newspaper complained that "in a few years, we shall have all the paraphernalia yet wanting to give the superb finish to the grandeur of our AMERICAN COURT! the purity of republican principle seems to be daily losing ground . . . we are on the eve of another revolution."[35]

Although the press reports infuriated the Washingtons, Martha imposed her personality on capital social affairs to dispel suspicions that she and her husband had monarchical ambitions. "She received me with great ease and politeness," wrote Abigail Adams of the First Lady after their first encounter. "She is plain in her dress, but that plainness is the best of every article. . . . Her hair is white, her teeth beautiful, her person rather short than otherwise. . . . Her manners are modest and unassuming, dignified and feminine, not the tincture of hauteur about her."[36] Evidently pleased by each other's unpretentiousness, the First and Second Ladies took to each other immediately. "Mrs. Washington," Abigail wrote in her second report on Martha, "is one of those unassuming characters which create love and esteem. A most becoming pleasantness sits upon her countenance and an unaffected deportment which renders her the object of veneration and respect. With all these feelings and sensations I found myself much more deeply impressed than I ever did before their Majesties of Britain."[37]

Washington spent much of the summer making appointments— 110 in all—and studying the detailed farm reports from George Augustine Washington at Mount Vernon. Martha, meanwhile, fussed over household arrangements and the grandchildren's education— and fretted continually over how Fanny and the rest of the young ones in Virginia would survive without her.

"I wish you to take a prayer book yourself," she wrote to Fanny in July, "and give one to Harriot the other two to be given to Betty & Patty Custis . . . give sweet little Maria [Fanny and George Augustine Washington's daughter] a thousand kisses for me—I often think of the dear little engaging child—I wish her with me to hear her little prattle."

The next day, she wrote again: "Nelly shall begin Musick next week—she has made two or three attempts to write you; but has never finished a letter—she is a little wild creature and spends her time at the window looking at carriages &c passing by which is new to her and very common for children to do." Martha longed desperately to be in Mount Vernon.[38]

Martha enrolled Nelly in a fashionable girls' school, where she was to study English, reading, spelling, grammar, plainwork (plain, as opposed to ornamental or "fancy," needlework and sewing), embroidery, cloathwork, painting, japanning, filagree, music, dancing, and French. She also asked George to trade in the spinet for a pianoforte, which had become the rage among music lovers. George did as Martha told him and went a step farther by arranging for the renowned concert pianist and impresario Alexander Reinagle to give ten-year-old Nelly her piano lessons. Reinagle was a composer of sorts, having conceived the then-memorable choral hallelujah to Washington's victory at Trenton: *Welcome, mighty Chief!*[39]

Toward the end of summer, two letters arrived from the South— one with startling news from Dr. Craik about his incorrigible nephews. "Since they come to live with me," the crusty old Scotsmen related, "they have behaved well I frequently admonish them and they seem to take it well."[40]

The second letter was from his sister Betty: their mother, Mary Ball Washington, was dead. Although he was named executor of the estate, Washington told his sister it was "impossible for me at this distance and circumstanced as I am, to give the smallest attention to the execution of her will." He suggested that Betty use the proceeds of the estate to pay all his mother's debts and divide whatever remained among the grandsons. He consoled his sister with a simple hope that their mother had been "translated to a happier place."[41] After a week of limited mourning, he ordered "twenty-six dozen bottles of claret and the same quantity of champagne," and Martha resumed the lavish dinners she knew pleased her husband.[42]

The first session of the First Congress adjourned on September 29, 1789, and Washington decided to make a grand tour of northeastern states "to acquire knowledge of the face of the Country the growth and Agriculture there of and the temper and disposition of the Inhabitants towards the new government."[43] In effect, he would introduce himself to the people and get to know them, their region, and their problems, examine their farms, and study their crops and methods of breeding livestock.

Before leaving, Washington dashed off a letter to Lafayette, apologizing for "a long interval of silence between two persons whose habits of correspondence have been so uninterruptedly kept up as ours; but the new and arduous scenes in which we have both been lately engaged will afford a mutual excuse."[44] Washington knew that Paris mobs had stormed the Bastille prison, that Lafayette had taken command of the Paris National Guard, and that King Louis XVI had agreed to establish a constitutional monarchy.

As president, however, Washington had to measure his words carefully. "The revolution, which has taken place with you," he wrote, "is of such magnitude and of so momentous a nature that we hardly yet dare to form a conjecture about it. We however trust, and fervently pray that its consequences may prove happy. . . . Mrs Washington joins me in best wishes to you and your amiable Partner. I am, my dear Marquis, with very great affection, Yours . . ."[45]

The president spent the next month traveling through Connecticut, Massachusetts, Maine, and New Hampshire, visiting industrial facilities—sawmills, gristmills, textile and silk-making facilities, glassworks, ship-building, sail-cloth manufacturing, card manufacturing: "Manufactury . . . seems to be going on with Spirit," he exulted in his diary. "They have manufactured 32 pieces of Duck of 39 or 40 yds. each in a week; and expect in a short time to increase it. . . . They have 28 looms at work & 14 Girls spinning with Both hands (the flax being fastened to their waste). Children (girls) turn the wheels for them, and with this assistance each spinner can turn out 14 lbs. of thread pr. day." Later he visited a card factory: "They have made 63,000 pr. of Cards in a year and can under sell the Imported Cards—nay Cards of this Manufactury have been smuggled into England."[46]

Social customs also pleased him: "There is a great equality in the People of this State," he noted after crossing from Connecticut into Massachusetts on the road from Hartford to Springfield. "Few or no oppulent Men. . . . The farms . . . are small not averaging more than 100 acres. These are worked chiefly by Oxen."[47] As president, Washington adopted a strict rule never to lodge in private homes, even refusing the invitation of Governor John Hancock to sleep at magnificent Hancock House on Beacon Hill in Boston. The use of public accommodations, Washington insisted, "leaves me unembarrassed by engagements, and by a uniform adherence to it I shall avoid giving umbrage to any by declining all such invitations of residence."[48] (So much for the claims that "George Washington slept here." He never did!)

On Sundays he searched out the Episcopal church in the morning, and, as often as not, attended Congregational services or the rites of other churches in the afternoon. Though dispassionate about religious rituals, he enjoyed attending church—any church—and believed that God, while unknowable, was omnipresent—a belief that spawned his conviction of God's presence in the houses of worship of all denominations.

In a festive and triumphant journey reminiscent of his preinaugural trip to New York, Washington spent seventeen days visiting towns, cities, and Revolutionary War sites, snubbing only Rhode Island, which had yet to ratify the Constitution. He so enjoyed his visits that he resolved to visit every state in the Union over the next year. As president, he had little else to do. While visiting Boston, Washington made a pilgrimage to Lexington and burst into laughter as he repeated the story of a British M.P. who accused American Minutemen of cowardice for firing from behind stone walls—to which Benjamin Franklin replied that there were two sides to every wall.[49]

While Washington guffawed in Lexington, Martha was miserable in New York. New York was a small, crowded, dirty little town, devoid of the charm and elegance of Philadelphia. Martha wanted desperately to return to Mount Vernon, but was unwilling to disrupt the children's education or upset her husband.

"I live a very dull life hear," she complained to Fanny, "and know nothing that passes in the town—I never goe to the publick place—indeed I think I am more like a state prisoner than anything else, there is certain bounds set for me which I must not depart—and as I can not doe as I like I am obstinate and stay at home a great deal." As always, Martha responded to boredom by shopping. "I have . . . sent you a watch," she wrote Fanny, "it is of the newest fashon, if that has any influence on your tast—The chain is of Mr [Tobias] Lears choosing and such as Mrs Adams the vice Presidents Lady and those in the polite circles wares. It will last as long as the fashon— and by that time you can get another of a fashonable kind—I send to dear Maria a piece of Chino to make her a frock—the piece of muslin I hope is long enough for an apron for you, and in exchange for it, I beg you will give me the worked muslin apron you have like my gown that I made just before I left home of worked muslin as I wish to make a petticoat of the two aprons—for my gown." Martha's ideas—and spelling—were sometimes convoluted, but always sincere and heartfelt.[50]

Washington returned to New York in mid-November bearing all the vestiges of a fortnight's banquets in a badly protruding belly. After declaring November 26 a national day of Thanksgiving, he began a program of regular exercise, riding his horse from nine to eleven each morning and walking for an hour in the afternoon after dinner.

Christmas only intensified Martha's dislike for New York and longing to rejoin her family in Virginia. "I little thought when the war was finished, that any circumstances could possible have happened which would call the General into public life again," she fretted to her old friend from Cambridge days, Mercy Otis Warren:

I had anticipated, that from this moment we should have been left to grow old in solitude and tranquility together . . . the first and dearest wish of my heart;—but in *that* I have been disappointed . . . yet I cannot blame him for having acted according to his ideas of duty in obaying the voice of his country . . . with respect to myself, I sometimes think the arrangement is not quite as it ought to have been, that I, who had much rather be at home should occupy a place with which a great many younger and gayer women would be prodigiously pleased.—As my grand children and domestic connections made a great portion of the felicity which I looked for in this world.—I shall hardly be able to find any substitute that would indemnify me for the Loss of a part of such endearing society. I do not say this because I feel dissastisfied with my present situation— no, God forbid . . . I am still determined to be cheerful and to be happy in whatever situation I may be, for I have also learnt from experiance that the greater part of our happiness or misary depends upon our dispositions, and not upon our circumstances; we carry the seeds of the one, or the other about with us, in our minds, wherever we go.

I have two of my grand children with me who enjoy advantages in point of education, and who, I trust by the goodness of providence, will continue to be a great blessing to me, my other two grand children are with thair mother in virginia.

The Presidents health is quite reestablished by his late journey—mine is much better than it used to be—we should rejoice to see you both, I wish the best of Heavens blessings, and am my dear madam with esteem and

regard your friend and Hble Sert
M Washington[51]

II

"Tranquillity Reigns"

GEORGE AND MARTHA WASHINGTON gasped as they peered between the drapes to the street: hysteria stretched as far as they could
see. It was New Year's Day, and all the world, it seemed, had come to
pay homage to the Father of His Country and His Lady. "The Vice-
President, the Governor—the Senators, Members of the House of
Representatives in Town—Foreign public characters and all the
respectable Citizens came between the hours of 12 & 3 to pay the
complimts. of the Season to me," Washington scribbled in his diary
that night, "and in the Afternoon a great number of Gentlemen &
Ladies visited Mrs. Washington on the same occasion."[1]

In contrast to New Year's Day, however, the rest of January and
the months that followed settled into a slow, dull routine that left
both Washingtons with less to do than in retirement at Mount Vernon. Congress had passed no laws to enforce as yet, and Alexander
Hamilton and Thomas Jefferson were perfectly capable of handling
the routine correspondence of the Treasury and State departments.
Washington spent more time posing for portraits than at the presidential desk. John Trumbull painted him into epic historical paintings,
and Edward Savage preserved his image for Harvard University and for
John Adams, who wanted a portrait for his home in Massachusetts.

After his first annual address to Congress, the president's routine was less than taxing: "Exercised with Mrs. Washington and the
Children in the Coach the 14 Miles round," reads his diary. "In the

Afternoon, walked around the Battery."* The following day's entry is no more revealing: "Exercised on Horse-back between 10 and 12, the riding bad." And again on succeeding days: "Exercised in the Coach with Mrs. Washington & the two Children abt. 12 Oclock." On one occasion he visited a farm to see a new threshing machine in operation; on another, a paper mill. One morning, he and Martha went to an exhibition of John Trumbull paintings and, on the next, to a picnic in northern Manhattan.[2]

Vice President John Adams had even less to do. "My country," he would later complain to his wife, Abigail, "has in its wisdom contrived for me the most insignificant office that ever the invention of man contrived or his imagination conceived."[3]

Dinners were always pleasant at the president's house—usually with his favorite personalities from Congress and the judiciary. Foreign envoys were always welcome, as were state governors and their wives. Adams, Jay, Jefferson, Knox, Hamilton, Madison, Randolph, and the rest of his old friends were regulars; some brought their older children. Martha's table was as elaborate as at Mount Vernon. In the course of one week in March, the Washingtons and their guests consumed fifty-four quarts of "cyder," thirty bottles of Madeira wine, thirty bottles of porter, four bottles of champagne, three bottles each of "spirits and brandy," and two bottles each of claret and rum— along with fourteen bottles of "common wine" for preparing sauces and other hot dishes. They did no entertaining on the Sabbath. They attended either St. Paul's Chapel or nearby Trinity Church[†] before returning home for a quiet family dinner, and an equally quiet afternoon and evening by themselves.

Congress dealt with only two issues of consequence in its first session: federal "assumption" of state debts from the Revolutionary

---

* The "14 Miles round" was a popular ride northward about six miles along the Hudson River, then northeastward through lovely forests across Manhattan Island to the Old Boston Post Road and south back to the city. The Battery was a fortress at the southern tip of Manhattan Island.

† By then, the formerly Anglican congregations in America had severed ties to the Church of England and adopted the name Protestant Episcopal.

War and situating the nation's capital city. Aimed at spreading the burden of war debts equitably among the thirteen states, "assumption" infuriated Virginia and other southern states that had spent little on the war and believed many of the huge debts accumulated by Massachusetts and other northern states had resulted from profligacy and waste. They acquiesced, however, after northerners agreed to situate the new federal capital in the South—in Virginia, near Georgetown. Washington signed both measures, pleased by the selection of a site so close to Mount Vernon and even more so by the role Congress granted to him to guide its planning and development. At last he'd have something to do!

In mid-March, Washington heard from Lafayette, whose letters were diminishing in length and frequency as his involvement with the French Revolution grew in complexity. "Give me leave, My dear General," wrote Lafayette, "to present you With a picture of the Bastille just as it looked a few days after I Had ordered its demolition, with the Main Key of that fortress of despotism—it is a tribute Which I owe as A Son to My Adoptive father, as an aid de Camp to My General, as a Missionary of liberty to its patriarch. . . . Adieu, My Beloved General, My Most Affectionate Respects Wait on Mrs Washington. . . . Most tenderly and respectfully Your Most Affectionate and filial friend . . . Lafayette."[4]

Washington searched for words to reply to Lafayette. Both he and his French protégé were actual or effective heads of state—precluded by their oaths of office from committing to paper any thoughts, let alone information, that might compromise their own governments or the relations of the two governments with each other and other nations.

"Happy am I, my good friend," Washington replied to the friend he loved like a son, "that, amidst all the tremendous benefits which have assailed your political Ship, you have had address and fortitude to steer her hitherto safely through the quick-sands and rocks, which threatened instant destruction on every side . . . you know full well my best wishes have never left you for a moment." Washington thanked Lafayette for the key, which he called "the token of victory gained by Liberty over Despotism by another."[5] Washington treasured the key and hung it in a small glass-enclosed frame on the wall in the central passage of the Mansion at Mount Vernon, where it remains today.

Washington received a bit of comic relief in a letter from Mount Vernon bearing a child's scrawl:

> I now set down to write to my dear Uncle as I have not wrote to him since he left this place I should have done it but I thought you had so much business that I had better write to Aunt Washington yet I am sure you would be very glad to see me improveing myself by writeing letters to my friend's.

Washington broke into laughter as he read. Fourteen-year-old Harriot was not bright, but she was sweet in her own way, and the Washingtons knew they were all she had:

> I am a going to ask you My Dear Uncle to do something for me which I hope you will not be against but I am sure if you are it will be for my good, as all the young Ladyes are a learning musick, I will be very much obleiged to you if you will send me a gettar, there is a man here by the name of Tracy that teaches to play on the harpsicord & gettar, a gettar is so simple an instrument that five or six lessons would be sufficient for any body to learns, If you think proper to send me a gettar I will thank you if you will send it by the first opportunity I was informed that you and Aunt Washington were certainly a comeing home this Summer which gave me a great deal of pleasure for I want to see you very much.
>
> If you please to give my love to Aunt Washington Nelly & Washington ["Washy"]. I am My Dear Uncle your Sincere Niece
>
> Harriot Washington[6]

Unfortunately for Harriot, Tobias Lear, Washington's aide who would have handled her request, had left for New Hampshire to be married, and the "gettar" would slip quickly from her uncle's thoughts.

Unable and unwilling to draft his own official correspondence, Washington broke his dull, daily routine with a five-day visit to Long Island, where he developed a bad cold that deteriorated into pneumonia by the time he returned home. Four doctors came to treat him. Six days into the illness, his breathing grew labored, and, according to Thomas Jefferson, "he was thought by the physicians to be dying."[7] As word spread to the public, "a universal gloom" spread "throughout the country."[8] Infuriated by the pessimism of the doctors, Martha took charge of the sickroom and applied home remedies that had always cured her grandchildren. She had lost one husband and two children; she was not going to lose this man, whom she adored more than any other living person. Whatever she did, it worked. "A copious sweat came on," Jefferson reported, "his articulation became distinct, and in the course of two hours it was evident he had gone thro' a favorable crisis."[9] As Washington's color improved, his fever diminished, and the next day Martha pronounced her husband out of danger.

"The sevear illness which the President was attacked . . . absorbed every other consideration, in my care and anxiety for him," Martha wrote to her friend Mercy Warren. "During the President sickness . . . He seemed less concerned himself as to t[h]e event, than peraps almost any other person in ye united states. Happily he is now perfectly recovered and I am restored to my ordinary state of tranquility, and usually good flow of spirits."[10]

As the novelty of the presidency lost its luster, the number of people attending his and Martha's "levees" diminished.

"Though I may not have a great deal of business of consequence to do," Martha rationalized, "yet I have a great many avocations of one kind or another which imperceptibly consume my time . . .

> In truth I should be very ungratefull if I did not acknowledge that everything has been done, which politeness, hospitality or friendship could suggest, to make my situation as satisfactory and agreeable as possible. My grandchildren have likewise good opportunities for acquiring a useful and accomplished education. In their happiness, my own is, in a great measure, involved. But for the ties of affection which attract me so strongly to my near connection and worthy friends, I should feel myself indeed much weaned from all enjoyments of this transitory life.
>
> If Congress should have a recess this summer . . . I hope to go home to Mount Vernon for a few months: and from that expectation I already derive much comfort. Especially as, I believe, the exercise, relaxation and amusement to be expected from such a journey, will tend very much to confirm the President's health. This is also the opinion of all his Physicians.[11]

As the summer progressed, Washington resumed his normal activities, riding and walking again, as vigorously as his strength permitted. In June he went on a three-day fishing trip with Jefferson and other friends and caught sea bass. Washington also went to Rhode Island, which he had bypassed during his earlier trip north because of its failure to ratify the Constitution. It finally voted to ratify in June 1790, and he, Jefferson, and other friends of note boarded the comfortable "packet"—a pleasant passenger, mail, and cargo vessel—for a two-day cruise on the calm waters of Long Island Sound to Newport. During his two days there, he made a point to visit America's oldest Jewish congregation, which had been founded in 1658 with the arrival of fifteen Jewish families. Moses Seixas, the leader of the congregation and a leading town merchant, welcomed Washington:

> Permit the children of the Stock of Abraham to approach you with most cordial affection and esteem . . . in welcoming you to New Port. . . . For all the Blessings of civil and religious liberty which we enjoy . . . we desire to send up our thanks . . . beseeching . . . the Angel who conducted our forefathers through the wilderness into the promised land, may graciously conduct you through all the difficulties and dangers of this mortal life: and, when like Joshua full of days and full of honour, you are gathered to your Fathers, may you be admitted into the Heavenly Paradise to partake of the water of life and the tree of immortality.[12]

Seixas could not have selected more pleasing biblical allusions and metaphors for the president, who responded emotionally, albeit unthinkingly: "It is now no more that toleration is spoken of," Washington replied, "as if it was by the indulgence of one class of people, that another enjoyed the exercise of their inherent natural rights. . . . I am pleased with your favorable opinion of my Administration, and fervent wishes for my felicity. May the Children of the Stock of Abraham, who dwell in this land, continue to . . . sit in safety under his own vine and figtree, and there shall be none to make him afraid."[13]

After two days at Newport, the president and his friends sailed to Providence for two days before sailing back to New York to move all his papers and his family's personal effects to the new temporary capital, in Philadelphia. Once the move was completed, the Washingtons set off for Mount Vernon for the long congressional autumn recess.

On September 11 the Washingtons and their huge entourage arrived home for the first time in seventeen months. His nephew had done such an efficient job managing his plantations that the Washingtons were able to spend their time enjoying favorite pastimes. Washington resumed his exhilarating morning rides, returning to the Mansion for dinner, where Martha gathered all her and George's dearest relatives at the dinner table. They did not return to Philadelphia until the end of November, and early in December Washington wrote to his seventeen-year-old nephew George Steptoe Washington, who, with his younger brother, fifteen-year-old Lawrence, was about to finish his education at Alexandria Academy. Both boys had abandoned their recalcitrant behavior and achieved good academic results. Washington knew he could ill afford the costs of continuing their support and education—and that of his two grandchildren—but as their legal guardian, he believed he owed them the opportunity of attending college in Philadelphia if they pledged to seize the opportunity to full advantage:

> After you and Lawrence have carefully perused and well considered . . . the enclosed account of studies and expences . . . I wish you to determine whether you will come or not—If your determination should be in favor of coming on, I must impress this upon you both in the strongest manner viz.—That you come with good dispositions and full resolutions to pursue your studies closely, conform to the established rules and customs of the College—and to conduct yourselves, on all occasions, with decency and propriety.
>
> Should you enter upon the course of studies marked out you must consider it as the finishing of your education, and, therefore, as the time is limited, that every hour mispent is lost forever—and that future *years* cannot compensate for lost *days* at this period of your life. This reflection must shew the necessity of an unremitting application to your studies. . . . Much more might be added to shew the necessity of application and regularity, but, when you must know that without them, you can never be of service to your country, assistance to your friends, or consolation to your retired moments, nothing further need be said to prove their utility.
>
> As to your clothing . . . I shall always wish to see you clothed decently and becoming your stations; but I shall ever discountenance extravagance or foppishness in your dress. At all times and

upon all occasions I shall be happy to give you both such marks of my approbation, as your progress and good conduct merit. . . .

Your Aunt joins me in love to you both . . . I am dear George, your sincere friend and affectionate Uncle.[14]

His stern though generous letter obviously sparked the boys' ambitions. They took the stage from Alexandria to Philadelphia, enrolled at the College of Philadelphia (later, the University of Pennsylvania), and boarded in a home nearby. The Washingtons had no room for them at the presidential mansion, which housed the two Custis grandchildren, Tobias Lear and his expectant wife, and more than a dozen servants and slaves. Washington paid for the boys' room and board as well as tuition and provided them with money for books, paper, pens, and other school supplies, along with firewood to heat their rooms. He stinted on nothing, paying for all their clothes, laundry, and sewing—even for "dressing" their hair, tickets to the theater, and $1 each for pocket money. Within weeks of their arrival, Washington gave George Steptoe £9.15 (about $700 today) to buy a violin and music sheets, then paid $4 a month ($85.50 today) to a music teacher for the boy's lessons. To their credit, they would graduate in 1792.

In February 1791 "a French gentleman" offered Washington 6,000 French crowns (about $45,000 today) for all his bounty lands in the Ohio River Valley. Washington exulted over the prospects of wiping out his debts. Tobias Lear's wife then added to Washington's joy by giving birth to a baby boy in the president's house. Lear named the boy Benjamin Lincoln and asked Washington to be his godfather. Lincoln had been Lear's patron and had recommended him to Washington for his current post. Washington was ecstatic and left on his long-awaited trip south to fulfill his promise to visit all the nation's states.

"I performed a journey of 1887 miles," he wrote when he returned. "It has enabled me to see with my own eyes the situation of the country. . . . The country appears to be in a very improving state. . . . Tranquillity reigns among the people."[15]

In contrast to the South's tranquillity, turmoil had engulfed much of the rest of the world while the president was traveling. The British were inciting Indian raids against American settlers in the West;

slaves had rebelled in French-owned Santo Domingo (now Haiti) and disrupted American trade in the West Indies; the Revolution had spread across France—the king was prisoner in his own palace; and France and Britain were poised for war, with potentially devastating consequences for American trade.

"I assure you, my dear Sir, I have not been a little anxious for your personal safety," Washington wrote to Lafayette, trying carefully to express his feelings without violating diplomatic protocol.

> Your friends in this Country are interested in your welfare & frequently enquire about you with an anxiety that bespeaks a warm affection. . . . Hamilton, Knox, Jay & Jefferson are well & remember you with affection—Mrs. Washington desires to be presented to you in terms of friendship & warm regard, to which I add my most affectionate wishes & sincere prayers for your health & happiness—and request you to make the same acceptable to Madm. Lafayette & your children.[16]

Washington also faced problems at home—in both his presidential family and in the presidential mansion. Alexander Hamilton and Thomas Jefferson—two trusted department heads who were both warm, personal friends—were feuding like schoolboys, no longer talking to each other and writing bitter, libelous articles about each other in the press. Hamilton favored a strong powerful executive to direct national economic growth—regardless of popular sentiment, which he distrusted. Jefferson and his sycophants supported the people's right to govern themselves and distrusted government.

Washington's problems in the presidential mansion resulted from a Pennsylvania law that automatically freed any slave who lived in the state for six consecutive, uninterrupted months. Washington told Lear to send his slaves home to Mount Vernon if there was any risk they might seek emancipation—especially Martha's "dower" slaves from the Custis estate.

> It behves me to prevent the emancipation of them, otherwise I *shall* not only loose the use of them, but may have them to pay for. If upon taking good advice it is found expedient to send them back to Virginia, I wish to have it accomplished under pretext that may deceive both them and the Public;—and none I think would so effectually do this, as Mrs. Washington coming to Virginia next

month. . . . This would naturally bring her maid and Austin—and Hercules under the idea of coming home to *Cook*. . . . I request that these Sentiments and this advise be known to none but *yourself & Mrs. Washington*.[17]

As it turned out, one slave returned to Mount Vernon at his own request to see his wife, and Lear complied with Washington's instructions and sent four others back before they could claim residency in Pennsylvania.

"You will permit me now, Sir, to declare," Lear reminded Washington, "that no consideration should induce me to take these steps to prolong the slavery of a human being, had I not the fullest confidence that they will at some future period be liberated, and the strongest conviction that their situation with you is far preferable to what they would probably obtain in a state of freedom."[18]

Late in November, Washington reached the end of his patience with Hamilton and Jefferson. He called his department heads together for what was the first "cabinet" meeting in American history and stripped them of powers to formulate policy independently. Henceforth they would meet as a body, determine administration policy as a group, and govern by consensus, with the president breaking any tie votes. Every cabinet member would either support group decisions or resign. There would be no more public feuding among cabinet members.

On February 22, 1792, Washington turned sixty and decided not to seek reelection the following year. Unlike his previous professions of disdain for public office, he sincerely intended stepping off the public stage. He viewed the presidency as largely ceremonial and was bored. Although he recognized the contribution he had made in bringing divergent regions and interests together, his travels across the nation convinced him that the national fabric was strong enough to survive without him. From the personal standpoint he had culled every honor, glory, and triumph known to man as a military, political, and social leader; he had masterminded the creation and establishment of a new nation with liberties that ordinary men had never before enjoyed anywhere in the history of the world.

He had done his job—more than his job. He was old, had lost all his teeth, was losing his eyesight and memory, and suffering painful rheumatism in his back, ankles, knees, and fingers. His old friends and all but one of his brothers were dead. His generation had passed. At sixty, Washington had already lived far longer than all the endemically tubercular men in his family, and he wanted to spend whatever years were left to him doing what he loved most—planting, farming, and riding at the place he loved most—Mount Vernon—with the people he loved most—Martha, a brood of children and grandchildren, and groups of friends and relatives to share his table and his wines. It was time for a younger man to lead; Washington was going home.

12

The Voice of
Your Country

MARTHA WAS ECSTATIC about her husband's plans to retire, but she was alone in her enthusiasm.

When Washington asked James Madison to help prepare a farewell address, Madison used Washington's own fears of factionalism to argue against his retirement, saying he was the only one who could quell it. The cabinet supported Madison, with Jefferson insisting that "the confidence of the whole union is centered in you. You being at the helm will be more than an answer to every argument which can be used to alarm & lead the people in any quarter into violence or secession. . . . North and South will hang together if they have you to hang on."[1]

Washington stood determined, however, and left for Mount Vernon with Lear to shape his farewell address away from political influences. His nephew George Augustine Washington had gone to Berkeley Springs to treat his tuberculosis, but Fanny was there to greet him with her children—and his niece Harriot. Harriot fully expected her "dear uncle" to arrive with a "gettar"—and left him blushing and sputtering trying to explain how he had forgotten her simple request.

To his pleasant surprise, Washington found his fields planted, new crops sprouting strongly, and the rest of his Mount Vernon enterprise—the fishery, mill, even the stercorary—functioning perfectly.

Satisfied that all was well, he worked out a farewell address with Lear and returned to Philadelphia convinced that even without his nephew, he had organized his Mount Vernon enterprise so efficiently that he would be able to manage it himself when he retired.

"I now take up my pen to write to my dear Uncle," his niece Harriot wrote after his departure. She was obsessed:

> I hope you arrived safe in Philadelphia, and at the time you expected, I should not trouble you for a guttar, if I was not certain I could learn myself, every person that I have asked say's that It is the easiest instrument to learn on that is, and any body that can turn a tune, can play on a Guittar, but Mrs Bushrod Washington, has been so kind as to offer to teach me if I could not learn myself.
>
> If you please to give my love to Aunt Washington Nelly and Washington. I am My dear Uncle Your affectionate Niece
>
> Harriot Washington[2]

Washington handed the letter to Lear and sent him to find a "guttar" to end Harriot's incessant pleas. He found one for $17, and Martha took care of the rest. "The President has given miss Harriot a guittar," Martha wrote to Fanny. "I have inclosed the key it is sent in the vessel with several other things. . . . The President has fixed on the 12th [July] to leave this place if nothing happens to prevent us."[3]

After thirty-three years of marriage, Martha knew exactly how she wanted every nook and cranny of her home to look. "[I] wish my dear Fanny," she continued, "that you would make Frank clanse the House from the garret to the sellers—have all the Beds aird and mended and the Bed cloths of every kind made very clean and the Bed stead also well scalded—and the low bedd steds put up to be ready to carry out of one room into another as you know they are often wanted.

> I have not a doubt but we shall have company all the time we are at home—I wish you to have all the china looked over, the closet clened and the glasses all washed and every thing in the closet as clean as can be than they will be ready when wanted with much less troable than to have them to look for when ever in hurry they may be wanted.
>
> I do not wish to have the clouded cotten made into chear covers—nor the chares stuffed, or done anything to, till I come home

as it is probable that the old covers will last as long as I shall stay home by a vessel that will live [deliver] this in a day or two. . . . I am glad that Fayette* is recovered and hope I shall find you and the children quite well—impress it on the gardener to have every thing in his garden that will be nessary in the House keeping way as vegetable is the best part of our living in the country—I dare say you have made the table cloths as well as they can be done—as to the window curtain and bed curtain they may as well be put up—I shall send a carpit for our parlor so that it will be ready by the time I get there if the vessel lives this on Tuesday as we expect.[4]

In mid-July the Washingtons arrived home for what would be their longest stay at Mount Vernon since the beginning of his presidency. Children romped and squealed about the house again—Nelly and "Washy" and so many others: Martha's two other grandchildren, Nelly's and Washy's older sisters Elizabeth (variously called Eliza or Betty) and Martha (called Patty); Fanny Bassett and George Augustine Washington's three children, Anna Maria, Charles, and baby Fayette. The president had difficulty remembering their names, but Martha had gifts for them all. Although the flow of mail did not cease, Washington's answers did. The Lears had gone to visit his parents in New Hampshire, and Washington left letters from all but his intimates unopened to focus on preparing his farm for his retirement. "The President is buried in solitude in Mount Vernon," Secretary of War Knox reported to his wife.[5]

Alexander Hamilton, however, succeeded in disturbing the solitude with a letter warning the president that a refusal to serve a second term would be "deplored as the greatest evil, that could befall the country . . . and as critically hazardous to your own reputation." Hamilton knew Washington's weaknesses, insisting that "the clear path to be pursued by you will be again to obey the voice of your country . . . to . . . sacrifice of your tranquility and happiness to the public good."[6]

Hamilton's letter infuriated Washington. He responded by assailing both Hamilton and Jefferson for creating the very political divi-

---

*Fanny and her husband, George Augustine Washington, had named the older of their two sons after Washington's wartime commander the marquis de Lafayette.

sions they now said required his presence to heal. "I believe it will be difficult, if not impracticable," he railed at Jefferson, "to manage the Reins of Government or to keep the parts of it together . . . if . . . after measures are decided on, one pulls this way & another that, before the utility of the thing is fairly tried, it must, inevitably, be torn asunder—And, in my opinion, the fairest prospect of happiness & prosperity that ever was presented to man, will be lost—perhaps for ever!

"My earnest wish, and my fondest hope, therefore is, that instead of wounding suspicions, & irritable charges, there may be liberal allowances—mutual forbearances—and temporizing yieldings on *all sides*."[7]

He used sterner language for Hamilton:

> Differences in political opinions are . . . unavoidable . . . but it is to be regretted, exceedingly, that subjects cannot be discussed with temper on the one hand, or decisions submitted to without having the motives which led to them, improperly implicated on the other: and this regret borders on chagrin when we find that Men of abilities—zealous patriots—having the same *general* objects in view, and same upright intentions to prosecute them, will not exercise more charity in deciding on the opinions, & actions of one another.[8]

On the eve of their departure for Philadelphia, the Washingtons received heartrending news from Tobias Lear that "the Marquis de la Fayette was taken . . . with eight other officers . . . and delivered to the Austrians."[9]

When the Washingtons returned to Philadelphia, they did so with every intent of winding up their affairs in the capital and moving back to Mount Vernon permanently, in time for Washington's sixty-first birthday. The Lears were there to greet them with their baby—a happy little fellow whose smiles so seduced the Washingtons they all but smothered him, what with Martha cuddling him in her arms, pressing his cheek to hers, while George's huge hand caressed him. He cooed through it all—which only provoked more kisses, hugs, tickles, and laughter.

Growing ever more enthusiastic about his forthcoming retirement, Washington drew extensive plans for new outbuildings and landscaping at Mount Vernon. He designed a radically new threshing barn that remains "a milestone in American farm architecture," according to modern authorities.[10] The two-story barn was radically different—a sixteen-sided, virtually round structure with second-story floor boards spaced one and a half inches apart. Threshing to separate grain from the stalks was an ancient process done outdoors, either by hand—with slaves beating loose the grain with flails—or by treading, with horses stamping loose the grain with their hooves as they trampled it. Washington's barn eliminated two costly drawbacks of outdoor threshing: exposure to wet weather and theft. He built it near an embankment to allow horses to enter the second-floor threshing room by an earthen ramp. As they walked in circles, stomping the stalks, the grain dropped through the cracks between the floorboards to the ground floor, where workers shoveled it to the center for cleaning and packing into barrels and bags for shipment to Washington's gristmill. At the end of the day, iron bars on the window and "a good lock . . . upon the lower door" prevented theft at night.[11]

In designing the barn, Washington calculated he would need 30,820 bricks—so costly a number that he decided to build a kiln and make the bricks himself. Not only would he cut his own costs, he would create a new brickmaking enterprise to profit from sales to area planters and builders. It was another of the profitable nonfarming enterprises he created from his need for costly materials. After sending the plan and a list of all materials (with quantities and dimensions) to his farm manager, he drew up an order for more than ninety ornamental deciduous and nondeciduous trees and flowering shrubs for landscaping the Mansion grounds: yews, junipers, boxwood, andromeda, hydrangeas, philadelphus (mock orange). He sent a copy to his farm manager, coding the name of each plant with a letter—"a" through "f"—indicating the type of soil and amount of sunlight it needed:

a rich, moist, loose or loamy soil, in shade of other trees.
b rich deep soil.
c wet moorish soil.
d Dry indifferent soil.
e A good loamy moist soil in any situation
f Any soil and situation[12]

On December 5, 1792, the Electoral College cast all but 3 of 135 votes for Washington as president, with 3 electors abstaining. There was no opposition. Although the official tally would not be announced until the opening of Congress in mid-February, the results had been a foregone conclusion, despite Washington's refusal to announce whether he would serve a second term. His increasing involvement with Mount Vernon seemed a strong signal to the contrary. He sent his farm manager long, detailed sets of instructions for rotating potato, buckwheat, and corn crops; for breeding pigs; and for packing shad from the next run. "Mrs Washington expected two barrels of *good* Shad," he noted carefully.[13]

In early December, Washington received a desperate plea from Adrienne de Lafayette:

"Without doubt you have learnt our misfortunes," she wrote, "you know that your disciple—your friend has not ceased to act in a manner worthy of you—

> You know that his unalterable attachment to the Constitution . . . drew upon him the unalterable hatred of a powerful faction which wished to destroy it. . . . His wish was that I should go with all our family and join him in England, that we might go & establish ourselves together in America. but . . . even before he reached a neutral Country . . . he was met and taken . . . to the Citadel of Spandau between Berlin & Potsdam. . . . They have not permitted him to write a line. . . .
>
> In the abyss of grief the idea of owing to the U.S. and to M. Washington—the life & liberty of M. Lafayette re-animates my heart. . . . I hope . . . through you, an Envoy . . . shall go to reclaim him in the name of the Republic of the U.S. . . . emancipate him from his captivity. . . . If his wife & his Children could be comprised [included] in this happy mission, it is easy to judge how sweet it would be to her and to them.[14]

Washington could do little. The United States had no diplomatic relations with Austria, which had not recognized American independence. Unable to state that his office precluded him from intervening directly, he sent Adrienne a brief, vaguely worded note and hoped she would understand:

> Madame,
>
> If I had words that could convey to you an adequate idea on the present Situation of Mr de la Fayette, this letter would appear

to you in a different garb. The sole object in writing to you now, is to inform you that I have deposited in . . . Amsterdam, Two thousand three hundred and ten guilders holland currency, equal to two hundred guineas [nearly $13,000 today] . . . to your orders.

The sum is, I am certain, the least I am indebted for services rendered to me by Mr de la Fayette, of which I never yet have received the account. I could add much, but it is best perhaps that I should say little on this subject. Your goodness will supply my deficiency. . . .

At all times, and under all circumstances, you, and yours, will possess the regard of him who has the honor to be Your most obedient & Most Hble Servant.[15]

In the rough draft of his letter, he had added these lines: "This letter must be considered as coming from me in my private character—as a public man I cannot at this moment address myself to you." He decided the words were too compromising and crossed them out, along with "affectionate regards." Washington also ordered Jefferson to instruct America's ministers in London, Amsterdam, and Paris to do whatever they could for Lafayette. What neither Washington nor Jefferson knew was that revolutionaries had already arrested Adrienne, carted her to prison in Paris, and sentenced her to death on the guillotine.

Washington turned most official correspondence over to Lear, while he spent his time writing to his manager at Mount Vernon. Indeed, his obsession with agriculture grew tiresome for even his closest friends. What had once been the liveliest dinner table in the capital had become "the most dull and unentertaining," according to George Hammond, the British minister to the United States.[16]

If the Washington home was "unentertaining" in 1792, it plunged into gloom in 1793. On January 4, Washington's close friend Burwell Bassett—Fanny's father and Martha's brother-in-law—died of a stroke. Adding to the family's melancholy was the deterioration of Fanny's husband, Washington's nephew George Augustine, who lay in the last, agonizing stages of tuberculosis. Then, in mid-January, Washington's farm manager, Anthony Whitting, added to their fiscal troubles by warning that all five Mount Vernon plantations needed major capital infusions: "a new barn at Dogue Run, Stable & Granary is wanting . . . a new Barn Stable & Granary at River plantn.

A thorough repair at Muddy hole . . . An Overseers House and Qu[arte]r at Ferry By the time these are compleated you will Sir find some thing necessary to be done at Mansion house these must be done before the places will look any way neat."[17]

Whitting also broached a difficult question—whether to proceed with the costly construction of a home that Washington's nephew had planned for himself and his family on land Washington had given him near the Mansion. "Poor Major Washington I believe has never contemplated his disorder is fatal," Whitting explained,

> but according to every account I hear of him it seems almost impossible he can recover When I mentiond a desire of carrying on his building it was from a wish not to be thought neglectfull in putting into execution what he had requested me to do, for in gratitude I know it is my Duty his treatment to me more like a Brother than a Stranger which I can never forget, And any thing I could do for him would be with the Greatest Chearfulness.[18]

Unnerved by Whitting's letter, Washington wrote immediately to his dying nephew but found it difficult to express his grief:

> My dear George,
>
> I do not write to you often, because I have no business to write upon; because all the News I could communicate is contained in the Papers which I forward every week; because I conceive it unnecessary to repeat the assurances of sincere regard & friendship I have always professed for you—or the disposition I feel to render every Service in my power to you and yours—and lastly because I conceive the more undisturbed you are, the better for you.
>
> It has given your friends much pain to find that change of Air has not been productive of that favorable change in your health, which was the wishes of them all—But the Will of Heaven is not to be controverted or scrutinized by the children of this world. It therefore becomes the Creatures of it to submit with patience & resignation to the will of the Creator whether it be to prolong, or to shorten the number of our days. To bless them with health, or afflict them with pain.
>
> My fervent wishes attend you, in which I am heartily joined by your Aunt & these are extended with equal sincerity to Fanny & the Children. I am always Your Affecte Uncle.[19]

George Augustine Washington died three weeks later.

Martha responded through her tears to the niece she adored as a daughter:

My dear Fanny,

Tho we were prepared to expect the event by every letter from you—yet we were much shocked to hear that our dear Friend was no more. I hope you will now look forward and consider how necessary it is for you to attend to your own health for the sake of your dear little Babes—you have, my dear Fanny, received a very heavy affliction; but while it pleases god to spare the President he will be a friend to you and to the children: he would have written to you by this post but is so pressed at this moment with public business that it is not in his power to do it, but will try by the next—we are all tolerable well; the President joins me in love and sincere condolence to you and your children.

My love to you your brothers and sisters . . . Nelly and Washington [Washy] send their love to you and children and Friends

> I am my Dear Fanny your
> truly affectionate
> M Washington[20]

In truth, the president was not too "pressed with public business" to write to Fanny, but each time he tried, his sadness so overwhelmed him he could not continue. Age was eroding his stoicism. Adding to Washington's sorrow was a letter from his farm manager Whitting, who said that he, too, had contracted tuberculosis.

A few days later, the Electoral College sent Congress the results of the presidential election. Because Washington had not withdrawn his name, the college had reelected him president. He knew he could not in all good conscience retire as planned.

"My dear Fanny," he finally summoned the resolve to write:

To you who know so well the affectionate regard I had for our departed friend, it is unnecessary to describe the sorrow with which I was afflicted at the news of his death; although it was an event I had expected many weeks before it happened. To express sorrow with the force I feel it, would answer no other purpose than to revive, in your breast, that poignancy of anguish, which, by this time, I hope is abated. Reason, and resignation to the Divine Will (which is wise & Just in its dispensations) cannot in such a mind as yours fail to produce this effect.

The object of the present letter is to convey to your mind the warmest assurances of my love, friendship, and disposition to serve you. These also I profess to have, in an eminent degree, for your Children.

What plans you have contemplated, or whether in so short a time you have thought of any, is unknown to me; and therefore I add that, the one which strikes me most favorably (by being best calculated to promote the interest of yourself & Children) is to return to your habitation at Mount Vernon. You can go to no place where you will be more welcome—nor to any where you can live at less expence, or trouble . . . which would ease you of that anxiety which the care of so large a family would, otherwise, naturally involve you in. It is unnecessary to observe to you, that House keeping under any circumstances and with the greatest economy, is expensive; and where provision for it is to be made, will be found, I fear, beyond your means.

You might bring my Niece, Harriot Washington with you for a Companion, whose conduct, I learn with pleasure, has given much satisfaction to my Sister.

Under the present view I have of the Subject, I shall be at Mount Vernon about the first of April for (perhaps) a fortnight; But your Aunt & family will not, I expect, be there before the middle of July. My love to the children—and with Affectionate Sentiments I am—always Yours

Go: Washington[21]

The national celebration of Washington's sixty-first birthnight* evoked the first attack on his character since the end of the Revolutionary War, with the *National Gazette* calling the festivities a "monarchical farce" and accusing the President of "every species of *royal pomp and parade*."[22]

Stung by the comments, Washington insisted on keeping the second inauguration simple. On Monday, March 4, 1793, Supreme Court justice William Cushing administered the oath of office in the Senate chamber, after which Washington delivered a 133-word inaugural speech, nearly half of which angrily challenged his critics: "The

---

*With most of the nation engaged in farming, it could ill afford to leave fields and livestock unattended during the day to celebrate Washington's birthday. Instead, Americans celebrated his birth*night*.

Constitution," he growled, "requires an oath of office . . . if it shall be found, during my administration of the Government, I have in any instance, violated, willingly or knowingly, the injunction thereof, I may (besides incurring Constitutional punishment) be subject to the upbraidings of all who are now witnesses of the present solemn ceremony."[23]

Congress immediately adjourned until December 2 and left town.

With Washington embedded in Philadelphia for four more years, he grew concerned for Fanny and her children. "The offer of a Residence at Mount Vernon," he reiterated, "was made you with my whole heart; but it is with you to consider nevertheless whether any other plan will comport better with the views which my nephew had, or with such as you may have entertained for your own ease, for the education of your Children . . . and your decision thereon will be perfectly agreeable to me; for I can assure you with much truth that I have no wish in the case beyond that of seeing you settled to your intire satisfaction. The Carriage which I sent to Mount Vernon for your use, I never intended to reclaim; and . . . may be . . . considered as your own—and I shall, when I see you, request that Fayette may be given up to me; either at that time, or as soon after as he is old enough to go to school; This will relieve you of that portion of attention which his education would otherwise call for."[24]

Fanny accepted Washington's offer to live at Mount Vernon and called "yours & my good Aunts guidance . . . a blessing to me. . . . My dear little Fayette shall be given up to your patronage, whenever you think proper; & I trust & hope Providence will reward your generous care of him."[25] The Washingtons would now have another small child to raise when they returned to Mount Vernon.

Martha was deeply disappointed about having to spend four more years away from home, and, recognizing the futility of complaining to her aging husband, she apparently took out some of her frustration on the children, forcing Nelly to practice at the keyboard as many as four or five hours a day. "The poor girl would play and cry, and cry and play, for long hours, under the immediate eye of her grandmother, a rigid disciplinarian in all things," Nelly's brother Washy recalled years later.[26]

In the spring, news arrived that the revolutionary government in France had executed King Louis XVI and declared war on England,

Holland, Spain, Austria, and Prussia. On April 8, a new French ambassador arrived demanding that the United States live up to the terms of the treaty from the Revolutionary War and support France militarily. Facing attack by British forces on the northern and western frontiers if the United States joined France, Washington responded by proclaiming the United States neutral—at peace with both Britain and France.

The neutrality proclamation, however, had the unintended consequences of polarizing the American people. "Citizen" Edmond Genet, the new French envoy, spurred those who had fought in the American Revolution to clamor for war against their former colonial oppressor. The conservative merchant class, which had rebuilt profitable trade relations with Britain, argued for stronger ties to England. The press joined the conflict, with a pro-French newspaper accusing Washington of "monarchical ambitions" and illustrating it with a cartoon showing Washington's crowned head beneath a guillotine blade. When Jefferson brought a copy to a cabinet meeting, Washington erupted in anger to a level few had ever witnessed in public. Jefferson reported the president shouting that if anyone wanted to change the United States into a monarchy "no man would set his face against it more." Jefferson then noted "that this was not what [Washington] was afraid of . . . that there was more danger of anarchy being introduced. . . . [the president] was evidently sore & warm."[27]

As pro-French mobs formed on street corners demanding Washington's head, the president feared for his wife's and grandchildren's safety. "Ten thousand people in the streets threatened to drag Washington out of his house and effect a revolution," John Adams recalled. Adams ordered arms from the War Department to protect his own house. "The town is one continuous scene of riot," the British consul wrote home. "French seamen range the streets night and day with cutlasses and commit the most daring outrages. Genet seems ready to raise the tricolor and proclaim himself proconsul."[28]

Washington raged at Jefferson to order Genet to remove his privateers from American waters. Genet refused and threatened to appeal the president's orders to the American people.

"Is the Minister of the French Republic to set the Acts of the Government at defiance, *with impunity*," Washington stormed at

Jefferson, "and then threaten the Executive with an appeal to the People? What must the World think of such conduct, and of the Governmt. of the U. States in submitting to it?"[29]

On July 31 Jefferson drew up a demand for Genet's recall, but Genet boarded a French warship and sailed to New York with the French fleet for refitting. On August 15 he issued drafts totaling $100,000 to local shipbuilders, then boarded his flagship, expecting pro-French crowds to serenade him. The waterfront was deserted, however, as thousands—regardless of political leanings—suddenly fled the city.

Yellow fever had broken out in New York!

"The coolest and the firmest minds," John Adams recalled later, "have given their opinions to me, that nothing but the yellow fever . . . could have saved the United States from a fatal revolution of government."[30] The pro-French Jefferson resigned as secretary of state at the end of the year.

As the epidemic spread southward, Philadelphians fled—some not soon enough. "We have had a melloncholy time hear for about a fortnight," Martha Washington wrote to Fanny. "Mrs. Lear was taken with a fever—the doctor was called in but to no purpose her illness increased till the eight day she was taken from us.—she never lost her senses till just before she expired—Mr. Lear bears his loss like a philosipher—she is generally lamented by all that knew her she was a pretty spritely woman—and always in good health. . . . I am truly sorry to hear of so many deaths—the wet raney season has made it sickly everywhere—I shall be glad when the frost comes to clear the air."[31]

After he buried his wife, Tobias Lear took his baby boy, Lincoln, and fled to his parents' home in the cool woods of New Hampshire, beyond the reach of the epidemic. The Washingtons left for Mount Vernon a month later, on September 10.

"It was my wish to have continued longer," Washington wrote to Lear. "But as Mrs Washington was unwilling to leave me surrounded by the malignant fever wch. prevailed, I could not think of hazarding her and the Children any longer by my continuance in the City the house in which we lived being, in a manner blocaded, by the disorder and was becoming every day more and more fatal. . . .

It gave Mrs Washington, myself and all who knew him, sincere pleasure to hear that our little favourite [Lear's boy] had arrived safe, and was in good health at Portsmouth. We sincerely wish him a long continuance of the latter, that he may always be as charming and promising as he now is, and that he may live to be a comfort and blessing to you and an ornament to his Country; as a testimony of my affection for him, I send him a Ticket in the lottery [for property rights in Federal City] . . . and if it should be his fortune to draw the Hotel it will add to the pleasure I have in giving it. . . . Mrs Washington . . . desires me to assure you of her sincere love for him in which I join and of her friendship and regard for you. In whatever place you may be or in whatever walk of life you may move my best wishes will attend you, for I am, and always shall be Your sincere friend &c.[32]

With the loss of his wife, Tobias Lear resigned from Washington's staff to establish his own business in the new Federal City that was rising on the Potomac near Georgetown. Washington adored the young man (and his baby boy) and gave him glowing references, despite his sadness at losing so vital an aide. Washington asked two nephews—Bartholomew Dandridge (Martha's nephew) and Howell Lewis (Betty Washington Lewis's son]—to handle Lear's job. He no sooner filled the void in his staff in Philadelphia, however, when Anthony Whitting, his farm manager, died. Toward the end of summer, Washington found another experienced manager, William Pearce, whom he spent the autumn teaching the elaborate Washington method of running Mount Vernon.

On September 18, the Alexandria Horse Troops arrived to escort Washington to Federal City, where a throng of Masons in their colorful regalia waited to greet him. With flags flying and bands playing, Washington dismounted, donned his Masonic apron, and, to the cheers of thousands, expertly troweled some cement onto the cornerstone of the new Capitol building of Federal City, which was officially renamed "Washington City." After cannons fired their acknowledgment, the president attended a public sale of lots, bought four, then sat down to a huge barbecue dinner.

As winter approached, cold weather ended the yellow fever epidemic, and government resumed operations in Philadelphia. Life

George Washington's plan for a "Rotation for a Farm of Six Fields" over a six-year period. In his own handwriting, the scheme is typical of the meticulous planning and careful research Washington performed for his farmlands.

remained glum, however—even at Christmas season. "Black seems to be the general dress in the city," Martha wrote to Fanny, "almost every family has lost some of thair friends. . . .

> Thank god we are all well . . . and not the least fear of the yellow fever while the weather is cold some people seemes to anticipate its return again in the summer. . . . they have suffered so much that it can not be got over soon by those that was in the city—the players are not allowed to come hear nor has there been any assembly [dances]. Yet the young people wish it and talk of having them soon. . . . there has been so many . . . people taken away by the fever—that it is with much difficulty any kind of work can be done the work men all complain of the want of hands to carry on every branch of business—The President joins me in love to you . . . kiss your dear little children for me—I have sent maria a fashenable sash.[33]

With little entertainment available, the Washingtons remained home almost every evening well into the new year. Washington responded to the ravages of the epidemic with a substantial donation for the education of orphans and children of indigent families. His emotional ties to orphans still ran deep: "I had pleasure in appropriating this money to such uses," he affirmed, "as I always shall in that of paying it."[34]

Neutrality proved a two-edged sword for the United States. Washington had hoped Americans would be able to trade nonmilitary goods with both Britain and France. But a British blockade cut all trade into French ports, and the British fleet seized or sank American ships on the high seas, regardless of cargo or destination, because of America's treaties with France. Facing national humiliation or war, Washington appointed Chief Justice John Jay to go to England to negotiate a rapprochement.

In the meantime, Secretary of the Treasury Hamilton sought to stave off government bankruptcy by enforcing collections of a two-year-old excise tax on distilled liquors— a tax western farmers considered legalized government theft and refused to pay. Almost every western farmer had a still to convert grain into whiskey, which was easier than bulk grain to transport over the mountains to eastern markets. After brutalizing Hamilton's tax collectors, they declared "a state of revolution,"[35] and on August 1 gathered by the thousands outside Pittsburgh on Braddock Field, a macabre landscape still littered with bones of British soldiers slaughtered by French and Indians nineteen years earlier. Armed and ready to march, they threatened to burn Pittsburgh and the properties of the monied class.

On August 7 Washington issued a proclamation ordering rebels to return to their homes or face arrest. His words were eerily similar to those of British governors to stamp tax protesters thirty-five years earlier. Washington dismissed comparisons and ordered Pennsylvania, Maryland, Virginia, and New Jersey to draft thirteen thousand troops for him to lead against the rebels.

In mid-September the Whiskey Rebels rejected Washington's ultimatum, and he issued a second proclamation "that the laws be faithfully executed." After vowing to lead the army himself, the aging president dismissed the meeting. Despite considerable pain from an accident on his horse the previous week, Washington all but ignored Martha's protests and called for a tailor to replicate the uniform he had worn as commander in chief in the Revolutionary War. Five days after signing the proclamation, he slipped his aged paunch into his new uniform, fully intending to ride his horse to war the next morning.

Later in the day, when she had stopped pouting, Martha called to him excitedly to read him a letter she'd received from Fanny. After embracing each other over its contents, they worked out a reply to disguise their excitement beneath a panoply of sage counsel:

"My dear Fanny," Martha wrote, with Washington commenting to correct her syntax. "I wish I could give you unerring advise in regard to the request contained in your last letter . . . you must be governed by your own judgement, and I trust providence will derect you for the best. . . .

> The person contemplated is a worthy man, and esteemed by every one that is aquainted with him; he has, it is concieved, fair prospects before him;—is, I belive, very industri[ous] and will, I have not a doubt, make sumthing handsome for himself.—as to the President, he never has, nor never will, as you have often heard him say, inter meddle in matrimonial concerns, he joins me however, in wishing you every happyness this world can give.—you have had a long acquaintance with Mr Lear, and must know him as well as I do.—he always appeared very attentive to his wife and child . . . he is I believe, a man of strict honor and probity; and one with whom you would have as good a prospect of happyness as with any one I know; but beg you will not let anything I say influence you either way. The President has a very high opinion of and friendship for Mr. Lear; and has not the least objection to your forming the connection but, no more than myself, would wish to influence your judgement, either way—yours and the childrens good being among the first wishes of my heart. . . .
>
> The President desired me to tell you he is not unmindful of his promise to take Fayette—he only waits till he is old enough to be put to a good school in this city. . . . The President . . . is to go

himself tomorrow to meet the troops: god knows when he will return again—I shall be left quite alone with the children.[36]

To the utter delight of the Washingtons, Fanny accepted Lear's proposal, and two of their favorite young people set August 1795 for their marriage. Lear planned building a home in Federal City, where he was establishing a business.

No longer the imposing warrior of 1775, Washington awoke the next day with his joints too stiff and achy to mount a horse. So he rode off to war like a docile old man, in a comfortable carriage with his aide, Martha's nephew Bartholomew Dandridge, and Alexander Hamilton, whom Washington had named field commander for the expedition. To assuage Martha's anxiety, he promised he would not engage in battle.

On October 16, Washington reached Fort Cumberland, where he had led 386 survivors of the Braddock massacre to safety in 1755. Old friends from the Revolutionary War awaited, among them Henry ("Light-Horse Harry") Lee, now Virginia governor, and Major General Daniel Morgan, whose "raiders" had played a vital role at Saratoga and, later, in the South Carolina campaign. Henry Lee out-ranked them all except Washington, and he took command. Among the horse troops Washington saw his nephew, Major George Lewis — his sister Betty's oldest son. "George," he called to him, "you are the oldest of five nephews that I have in this Army; let your conduct be an example to them, and do not turn your back until you are ordered."[37] Not only did he see Betty's three sons, he found his brother Charles's son, Samuel Washington, and, of all people, his late brother Samuel's once-incorrigible son, Lawrence Washington, who had successfully completed his studies at the College of Philadelphia at George Washington's expense.

Recognizing that he was too old to fight—and too essential to the government to risk his life in battle—Washington ordered the army to march to Pittsburgh without him, and on October 20, he watched his troops set off on the trail he had traveled as a young colonel nearly forty years earlier. A day later, he climbed into his coach and began the slow voyage eastward back to Philadelphia.

"The President returned from the westward very well," Martha wrote, expressing her deep relief to Fanny. "I thank god that we are all very well."[38]

On November 15 the army approached Braddock's Field, but the rebels had vanished. Although the troops captured twenty laggard Whiskey Boys, all the others had either returned to their homes or fled into the wilderness. Without firing a single shot—indeed, without even showing his face on the field of battle—Washington had crushed a revolution against constitutional rule.

Washington did not emerge unscathed, however. Many Americans—in and out of Congress—angrily criticized him for suppressing the very type of protest he had led during the Revolutionary War against taxation without representation. Most Whiskey Boys were either tenant farmers or frontiersmen who owned no property and therefore had no vote. Washington shrugged off the criticism, but his aura of infallibility evanesced after returning troops humiliated the twenty captured farmers by parading them through the streets of Philadelphia. Only two were ever convicted, and Washington pardoned both. Although most Americans continued to love and cherish Washington—and celebrate his birthnight—many ceased to idolize him or regard him, or any subsequent president, as other than a fallible human. Some of the press, too, changed their perception of the president and began a ceaseless crusade of criticism that would leave the old warrior bitter about having remained in office as long as he had. At a public dinner in Virginia, one critic proposed a toast that would have been unthinkable a decade earlier: "A speedy death to General Washington."[39]

The change in public perception wounded the president deeply. He grew more distant, appeared at fewer receptions; his solemn mood discouraged others from visiting the presidential mansion, and attendance at his levees thinned. "I can religiously aver," he complained, "that no man was ever more tired of public life, or more devoutly wished for retirement, than I do.[40]

13
Vine and Fig Tree
Revisited

WITH THE NEW YEAR of 1795, Henry Knox and Alexander Hamilton resigned from Washington's cabinet, leaving the aging president to run the nation without the men he trusted most—comrades who had advised him throughout the Revolutionary War as well as the presidency. Surrounded by young strangers, he grew reticent, almost morose at times—a mood that discouraged visitors and all but converted the presidential mansion into a private residence.

As Washington had anticipated, the Jay Treaty unleashed a chorus of acrimonious debate across the nation—in Congress, the press, and in the streets. Hailed by some for averting another brutal war with England, Washington found himself pilloried in many newspapers for pro-British bias. Opponents of the treaty warned that the president "insidiously aims to dissolve all connections between the United States and France, and to substitute a monarchic for a republican ally."[1] Although the Senate ratified the treaty in June, town after town passed resolutions demanding that Washington refuse to sign it. By midsummer the issue remained unresolved, and, feeling ever more isolated from his cabinet, Washington turned for counsel and comfort to an old friend. He invited John Adams, a man of his own time and generation, to a private dinner. Adams responded with "kindness and confidence." Until then, Adams had felt ignored—and with good reason. He was not a cabinet member, and Washington, a strict constitutionalist, had studiously avoided inviting Adams to participate in policymaking decisions. To Martha's delight, the two men restored their old friendship and set the stage for Martha to renew her friendship with Abigail. Washington gave the vice president "my best, and most cordial thanks," along with praise for Adams's twenty-eight-year-old son, John Quincy Adams, then serving as ambassador to Holland: "I shall be much mistaken," Washington told Adams, "if in as short a time as can well be expected, he is not found at the head of the Diplomatique Corps." (Twenty-two years later, Washington's prediction would prove correct, when President James Monroe named the younger Adams his secretary of state.)

Washington followed Adams's advice—went home to Mount Vernon, then returned to the capital in the heat of August while Congress was in recess and signed the treaty without public ceremony—or controversy.

On September 7 he was preparing to return to Mount Vernon when a courier arrived with a letter from Massachusetts senator George Cabot: sixteen-year-old George-Washington Lafayette—Washington's godson—was in Boston with his tutor, at Cabot's home and asking help in reaching the Washingtons. American ambassador James Monroe had arranged for Adrienne de Lafayette's release from prison and helped her and her two daughters flee to neutral Denmark, but—at her insistence—he had secreted her son and his tutor onto a ship bound for America and the safety of his godfather's home at Mount Vernon. With the boy waiting at Cabot's home for instructions, Washington strayed inexplicably from his core values of personal friendship as he weighed his obligations as the boy's godfather and as Lafayette's closest friend, against his political obligations and the diplomatic storm that would result if he granted asylum to a French fugitive in the *presidential residence*.

"Let me in a few words, declare that I *will be his friend*," Washington replied disingenuously, "but the manner of becoming so, considering the obnoxious light in which his father is viewed by the French government, and my own situation, as the Executive of the U. States, requires more time to consider in all its relations, than I can bestow on it at present; the letters not having been in my hands more than an hour, and I myself on the point of setting out for Virginia. . . .

The mode which, at the first view strikes me as the most eliga-
ble to answer his purposes and to save appears. is, 1. to administer
all consolation to the young Gentleman that he can derive from
the most unequivocal assurances of my standing in the place of and
becoming to him, a *Father, friend, protector,* and *supporter*, but 2dly,
for prudential motives, as they may relate to . . . my *official* character it would be best not to make these sentiments public; of course,
that it would be ineligable, that he should come to the Seat of the
genl. government where all the foreign characters (particularly of
his own nation) are residents, until it is seen what opinions will be
excited. . . . 3. considering how important it is to avoid idleness
and dissipation; to improve his mind; and to give him all the
advantages which education can bestow . . . he should enter as a
student at the University in Cambridge [Harvard] altho' it should
be for a short time *only*. The expence of which, as also every mean
for his support, I will pay.[2]

Fearing the boy's presence would further inflame passions over
the Jay Treaty, he asked that Lafayette use his patronymic family
name "Motier," rather than Lafayette. It was the first time in his life
Washington felt shamed by his uncharacteristic behavior toward
a godchild and son—perhaps an orphaned son at that—of a close
friend.

Washington stayed in Mount Vernon for only two weeks before
returning to the capital, and Martha cut short her stay and went with
him. It was fortunate she did; he needed comforting. Apart from
dealing with his guilt over the Lafayette boy, his administration was
in disarray. He had no secretary of state; his attorney general had
died; and, with few federal laws for anyone to challenge in the
Supreme Court, Chief Justice John Jay grew bored and left to become
governor of New York. One man, whom he barely knew—Secretary
of War Timothy Pickering—was running the entire government,
exercising authority that was not his. But there was no one else in
government to do the job and no one outside government willing to
abandon private interests to serve. Although Martha favored sending for young Lafayette and his tutor, she had no solution for her
husband's political problems. Washington turned to Alexander Hamilton for help with both: "What am I to do for a Secretary of State?"
Washington pleaded. "Aid me I pray you, with your sentiments."

Then: "The young gentleman [George-Washington Lafayette] must have experienced some unpleasant feelings from being kept at a distance from me," he anguished. "I am resolved to be in the place of a father and friend to him . . . under any circumstances. If therefore . . . you should think that good would come from it . . . I pray you to send them hither . . . without delay." He said he and Martha had "resolved . . . to take them at once into my family."[3]

Hamilton argued against Washington's bringing the boy to Philadelphia, however. "It seems to me . . . the factious might use it as a weapon to represent you as a favourer of the anti Revolutionists of France . . . perhaps it will be then best for you to write Young La Fayette a Letter, affectionate as your feelings will lead you to make it, announcing your resolution to be to him a parent and friend; but mentioning the very peculiar circumstances of the moment impose on you the necessity of deferring the gratification . . . desiring him at the same [time] to concert with me a plan for disposing of himself satisfactorily, and advantageously, in the mean time."[4]

Against his own—and Martha's—instincts, Washington did as Hamilton advised and sent the boy assurances of his "warmest affection and support; of my determination to stand in the place of a father and friend to you undr. all cir[cumstance]s." But in the next sentence he told Lafayette, "It is my desire, that you . . . would repair to Colo Hamilton, in the city of New York. . . . This gentleman was always in habits of great intimacy with, and is warmly attached to, Mr. de la Fayette; you may rely therefore on his friendship."[5]

His letter only added to his shame. "As there can be no doubt," he argued with Hamilton, "that the feelings of both are alive to every thing which may have the semblance of neglect or slight; and indeed, expectant as they must have been . . . of an invitation to fly to me without delay . . . it is necessary that every assurance and consolation should be administered. . . . I am distrustful of my own judgment in deciding on this business."[6]

This "business" continued tormenting him. He felt he had turned his back on the helpless child of one of his dearest friends. A month later, with Christmas but three days off, he grew frantic that he had not heard from young Lafayette. He berated himself for having abandoned the boy alone in a strange, foreign land. Washington wrote in panic to Hamilton: "Have you seen or heard more of young Fayette since you last wrote to me on that subject? Where did he go to? Did you deliver him the letter I sent under cover to you for him? His case gives me pain, and I do not know how to get relieved from it. His sensibility I fear is hurt, by his not acknowledging the receipt of my letter to him. . . . If he wants money, I am ready to furnish it. . . . With much sincerity and truth I am always Affectly Yours."[7]

Hamilton answered by return: "Young Fayette is now with me."[8] He and his tutor had been with the Hamiltons through the fall and would remain through winter and early spring.

The French government responded to the Jay Treaty by seizing American cargo ships in French ports and threatening war. French warships captured more than three hundred American ships on the high seas and either executed the seamen on board or tossed them into prison chains at Bordeaux.

Beset by events he could no longer control, the president looked for ways to reduce his responsibilities—in Philadelphia and Mount Vernon. To reduce his proprietary responsibilities, he put the remainder of his western lands up for sale and advertised in English, Scottish, and Welsh newspapers to lease four of his five farms at Mount Vernon—a total of eight thousand acres—for fourteen years "to *real* farmers of *good* reputation, and none others need apply."

With the approach of spring, Washington could no longer live with his shame for failing to see, let alone harbor, his godson, and he acted decisively to bring the boy and his tutor to Philadelphia.

"My dear young friend," he wrote to Lafayette. "My desire to see you, is such, that I request you and Mr. Festel [Lafayette's tutor] will make me a visit about the first of April at this city; by that time the weather will be settled, the roads good, and the travelling pleasant. . . . Anything of which you stand in need, will be furnished by Colo. Hamilton on my behalf. With best wishes and the most Affecte. regard I remain etc."[9]

When Lafayette responded somewhat tentatively, Washington wrote again—this time more forcefully and affectionately: "I again repeat my former request; and wish that without delay, you and Mr. Frestel, with your baggage &ca. would proceed immediately to this

City, and to my house; where a room is prepared for you and him."
Washington pledged "to render every service in my power to the Son
of my friend, for whom I have always entertained the purest Affections. These are too strong not to extend themselves to you. Therefore
believe me to be, as I really am, Sincerely and Affectionately Yours."[10]

On March 25, 1796, Martha's beloved niece Fanny died. She
had been ill since early winter, and, in an age of few medicines and
little medical knowledge, persistent illness often ended in death.
(Apparently she contracted tuberculosis from her late husband.) Lear
had written to the Washingtons twice in the week before her death.

"Your former letters prepared us for the stroke," Washington replied, as Martha sobbed, "but it has fallen heavily notwithstanding.

> It is the nature of humanity to mourn for the loss of our friends;
> and the more we loved them, the more poignant is our grief. . . . To
> say how much we loved, and esteemed our departed friend, is
> unnecessary. She is now no more! but she must be happy, because
> her virtue has a claim to it.
>
> As you talked of coming to this place on business, let us press
> you to do so. . . . At all times, and under all circumstances, we are,
> and ever shall remain, your sincere and affectionate friends.
>
> Go: Washington
> M Washington

Lafayette and his tutor arrived a few days later, and Lear a day
after that, with four toddlers in tow—Fanny's three children by
George Augustine Washington and Lear's little boy Lincoln, from
his previous marriage. The house was so crowded that Lear and Lincoln had to share a bedroom with young Lafayette and his tutor,
while the other children were stuffed into corners helter-skelter,
leaving the presidential mansion an unmansionly mess—and the
president and his wife to help care for four more infants. It was fortunate for Washington's precarious financial condition that as he
added children to the household, older ones were leaving—either
going to work or getting married. The two sons of Samuel Washington whom he had supported since childhood had finished college
and gone to work, and a young businessman in Fredericksburg now
asked for the hand of Samuel's nineteen-year-old daughter Harriot.

She married in July, and the president sent her $100 (about $2,000 today) for her trousseau.

Congress adjourned on June 1, and a few days later the Washingtons left for Mount Vernon with all their relatives, guests, and servants. Before leaving, Martha and George obsessed over instructions for the plantation caretaker:

"In a few days after *we* get there, we shall be visited, I expect, by characters of distinction," he wrote. "I could wish therefore that the Gardens, Lawns, and every thing else, in, and about the Houses may be got in clean and nice order." Then, with Martha commenting, he added,

> Let the Rooms in the Servants Hall, above and below, be well cleaned, and have the Beds and bedsteads therein put in order; after which have a good lock put on the door of the west room, above, and . . . suffer no person to sleep, or even go into it, without express orders. . . . Let exactly the same things be done with the Rooms over the Kitchen; as there will be a white Cook with us that will require one of them. . . . Tell the gardener, I shall expect everything that a Garden ought to produce, in the most ample manner. There may be many other things to be done.[11]

Indeed, there were eight more pages of things to be done—and Martha added a memo with her instructions!

After they resettled under their own "vine and fig tree," the Washingtons resumed the patterns of their lives before he had assumed the presidency. He still rose "with the Sun" and "if my hirelings are not in their places at that time, I send them messages expressive of my sorrow for their indisposition . . . by the time I have accomplished these matters, breakfast (a little after seven Oclock.) is ready. This over, I mount my horse and ride around my farms, which employs me until it is time to dress for dinner."[12]

Always home for dinner at three, he never knew whom to expect at the table. As before, guests ranged from "characters of distinction" to boorish intruders and curious travelers with the gall to barge in. Some insisted they had served under the general—sometimes in battles he never fought, such as Saratoga. "I rarely miss seeing strange faces," Washington complained, "come, as they say out of respect to me. Pray, would not the word curious answer as well . . . how differ-ent this, from having a few social friends at a cheerful board?"[13]

Washington usually appeared in a plain blue coat for dinner, his hair dressed and powdered, according to Benjamin Latrobe, a young English artist and friend of Bushrod Washington. "There was a reserve but no hauteur in his manner. . . . he placed me at the left hand of Mrs. Washington, Miss Custis seated at her right, and him-self next to her about the middle of the table." Latrobe said that Martha displayed "a good humoured free manner that was extremely pleasing and flattering. . . . A few jokes passed between the President and young Lafayette whom he treats more like a child than a guest. . . . As I drank no wine and the President drank only three glasses, the party soon returned to the Portico." Washington disappeared into his study after dinner, but returned at six for coffee on the piazza, the columned porch facing the Potomac. He often bemoaned his failing eyesight: "I have not looked into a book since I came home, nor shall I be able to do it until . . . the nights grown longer; when possibly I may be looking in doomsday book."[14]

Breakfast the next morning, Latrobe noted, was served "Virginia style, tea coffee and cold boiled meat; and for an hour afterwards he stood on the steps of the west door talking to the Company who were collected around him. Washington has something uncommonly majestic and commanding. . . . He is about 64 but appears some years younger. . . . He was sometimes entirely silent for many minutes . . . laughed heartily several times. . . . On the morning of my departure he treated me as if I had lived years in his house with ease and atten-tion. But in general I thought there was a slight air of moroseness as if something had vexed him."[15]

Latrobe's assessment was accurate. The president was both mo-rose and vexed—by the strangers who continued to penetrate his private world each day. He longed to end it. As Latrobe left, twelve Catawba Indians appeared. Washington sent an angry letter to Sec-retary of War James McHenry that he had been "incommoded . . . by a visit of several days . . . and should wish while I am in this retreat, to avoid a repetition of such guests."[16]

Despite the intrusion, Nelly would forever remember that sum-mer as idyllic. "I am as happy as a mortal can wish to be when they

View of the Mansion at Mount Vernon and its piazza, with the Potomac River in the left background. Engraving by L. Seymour of the drawing by William Birch.

are all here," she wrote to a friend. "I ride sometimes on Horse-back—walk, read, write french—work play & sing & always think the weeks go off too fast."[17]

In mid-August, Washington sent his Farewell Address to the *American Daily Advertiser* for publication on September 19. In his adieu to his countrymen, he offered a prayer "that Heaven may continue to you the choicest tokens of its beneficence; that your Union and brotherly affection may be perpetual."[18]

Washington returned to Philadelphia with Martha, Nelly, and Washy on October 31 for what George and Martha, at least, hoped would be their last sojourn in the nation's capital. While Nelly remained with her grandparents, fifteen-year-old Washy rode off to enroll at Princeton College.

"I rejoice to hear you went through your [placement] examination with propriety," the proud grandfather wrote Washy a few weeks later, "and have no doubt but that the president has placed you in the class which he conceived best adapted to the present state of your improvement." Washington's expectations for his grandson were so high that he was seldom able to end his letters without admonishing the boy for behavior the youngster had not even considered: "The more there are above you, the greater your exertions should be to ascend; but let your promotion result from your own application, and from intrinsic merit, not from the labors of others. The last would prove fallacious, and expose you to the reproach of the daw in borrowed feathers. This would be inexcusable in you, because there is no occasion for it." Washington signed his letters to his grandson, "your sincere friend."[19]

On December 7, Washington delivered the eighth and last of his annual addresses to Congress—indeed, his last public address to the nation. He ended it as he had the first—with a prayer:

> The situation in which I now stand, for the last time, in the midst of the Representatives of the People of the United States, naturally recalls the period when the Administration of the present form of Government commenced; and I cannot omit the occasion, to congratulate you and my Country, on the success of the experiment; nor to repeat my fervent supplications to the Supreme Ruler of the Universe, and Sovereign Arbiter of Nations, that his Providential care may still be extended to the United States; that the virtue and happiness of the People, may be preserved; and that the Government, which they have instituted, for the protection of their liberties, may be perpetual.[20]

As he stepped from the dais to the cheers of the House, Senate, and guests, Washington prayed silently that the rest of his days in office would be enjoyably ceremonial—but the pro-French republican press would not allow it.

"If ever a nation was debauched by a man," wrote the hate-filled *Aurora*, "the American Nation has been debauched by Washington. If ever a nation has suffered from the improper influence of a man, the American Nation has suffered from the influence of Washington. If ever a nation was deceived by a man, the American Nation has been deceived by Washington."[21]

Enough Americans—even his political opponents—ignored the barbs hurled at their hero to celebrate his last birthday in office as never before. A national holiday by then, February 22 began with church bells ringing, cannons firing, and militiamen marching to the music of parading bands. Flags flew from every perch in every city, town, and village in the nation. The President and First Lady attended an "elegant entertainment that evening," according to one guest, "with supper and dancing for 1,200 lasting well past midnight. Mrs. Washington was moved even to tears with the mingled emotions of gratitude for such strong proofs of public regard and the new prospect of uninterrupted enjoyment of domestic life. . . . I never saw the President look better, or in finer spirits, but his emotions were too powerful to be concealed. He could sometimes scarcely speak."[22]

In the days that preceded and followed his birthday, Washington received testimonies of appreciation for his service to the nation from each of the state legislatures, as well as thousands of citizens — including his grandson "Washy," who, at sixteen, was now addressed by his full name, Washington.

"Dear Washington," the president responded to the boy he had raised as his own son. "The affectionate sentiments . . . are highly pleasing to me. But that which affords a still higher gratification, is to hear that you are not only attentive to your studies, but pleased with them also. . . . Hence, I draw the most agreeable presages, that you will reward my care and anxieties to see you a polished Scholar, and a useful* member of Society."[23]

Washington hoped—prayed—that his grandson would emulate him. He believed strongly, and all too often repeated to others, that his grandson's "family, fortune and talents give him just pretensions to become a useful member of Society, in the Councils of his Country."[24]

Perhaps with Washy in mind, Washington thanked President-elect John Adams for his warm wishes with an equally warm father-to-father note expressing "a *strong hope* [his italics] . . . you will not withhold merited promotion for Mr. John [Quincy] Adams because he is your Son. For without intending to compliment the father or

---

*By "useful," Washington meant nothing less than a position of national leadership—the presidency, for example.

the mother . . . I give it as my decided opinion that Mr. Adams is the most valuable public character we have abroad and that he will prove himself to be the ablest of all our Diplomatic Corps. . . . and his country would sustain a loss if . . . checked by over delicacy on your part. With sincere esteem and affectionate regards."[25]

Washington and Martha spent their last nights in Philadelphia at theater, concerts, and other festivities, and on March 2, two days before he was to leave office, he wrote his last letters as president. One went to Henry Knox in Boston, the retired secretary of war who had served Washington faithfully since their first days with the Continental Army at Cambridge more than twenty years earlier. "Although the prospect of retirement is most grateful to my soul," Washington told his old friend, "yet, I am not without my regrets at parting with (perhaps never more to meet) the few intimates whom I love, among these, be assured you are one."[26]

On the eve of his departure from office, the Washingtons entertained for the last time in the presidential residence. "Ladies and gentlemen," the president raised his glass to the political notables there, "this is the last time I shall drink your health as a public man. I do so with sincerity, and wishing you all possible happiness." According to one witness, tears ran down the cheeks of those present as they tried to sip from their glasses.[27]

Just before noon the next day—Saturday, March 4—President Washington walked to Congress Hall, dressed in a black suit, a military hat, his hair powdered as usual. Greeted by thunderous applause, he climbed the speakers' platform and took his seat. The new vice president, Thomas Jefferson, followed and sat between Washington and the Speaker's chair. President-elect Adams followed, sat momentarily in the Speaker's chair, then rose to take the oath of office.

"A solemn scene it was indeed," President Adams wrote to his wife the next day, "and it was made affecting to me by the presence of the General, whose countenance was as serene and unclouded as the day. He seemed to me to enjoy a triumph over me. Methought I heard him say, 'Ay! I am fairly out and you fairly in! See which of us will be happiest!'"[28]

After the ceremonies, Washington—a private citizen for the first time in eight years—called on the new president before attending a lavish farewell dinner. The vicious newspaper *Aurora*, however, would not let Washington retire in peace: "If ever there was a period for rejoicing this is the moment. Every heart, in unison . . . ought to beat high with exultation that the name of Washington ceases from this day to give currency to political iniquity and to legalize corruption."[29]

While President Adams lodged at a hotel, the huge Washington family—including young Lafayette and his tutor—tried assembling their effects for the move to Mount Vernon, separating government from family property, then deciding which family property to keep and which to sell. Washington offered to sell the entire Green Drawing Room to Adams "at reduced prices," but the new president refused. Washington needed nearly one hundred boxes, fourteen trunks, forty-three casks, and thousands of yards of cord and baling wire to pack his things—and a sloop to carry them to Virginia. He ended up giving away many furnishings, including a chandelier, a mirror, and his private desk.

On March 9, the Washingtons, their granddaughter Nelly Custis, Lafayette, and his tutor climbed into the family coach with a dog and Nelly's parrot and began what the Washingtons hoped would be their last ride home to Mount Vernon. Six days later, they pulled into the Mount Vernon drive in time for dinner, after which Washington opened a letter marked "personal" in unfamiliar handwriting.

"Like a true woman," it began, "I take up my pen to address you, as you . . . have without design put into my possession the love letters of a lady addressed to you under the most solemn sanction; and a large packet too." Washington blanched. The letter continued,

> What will the goddess of prudence say to her favorite son and votary for his dereliction of principles to which he has hitherto made such serious sacrifices? Was the taste of your sex predominant in your breast;—and did the love of variety so preponderate that, because you had never blundered as President, was you determined to try its delights as a private gentleman? But to keep you no longer in suspense . . . I will with the generosity of my sex relieve you, by telling you that upon opening of the drawers of your writing desk I found a large bundle of letters from Mrs. Washington, bound up and labeled with your usual accuracy . . . from motives of

Delicacy I sealed them up And I trust it is unnecessary for me to add that they will be kept Inviolably until I deliver them.[30]

Washington had hidden Martha's letters to him in a secret compartment of his writing desk and had forgotten to open it when he gave the desk to Eliza Powel, the widow of the mayor of Philadelphia. She and the mayor had become close friends of the Washingtons during the presidential years, and Washington sighed with relief as he thanked her "for the delicacy with which they have been treated."[31] Her letter left it to Washington whether to tell Martha, and he had no hesitation. The letters, he said, were "more fraught with expressions of friendship, than of *enamoured* love. . . . if the ideas . . . should have been of the *Romantic order* . . . they might have been committed to the flames."[32] Eventually Martha did just that.

A sweet letter from their grandson Washington Custis also welcomed them home: "I congratulate you on a *thing* so ardently wished for by all those interested in your welfare," wrote the sixteen-year-old, trying his best to emulate Washington's writing style. He went on to describe his studies at Princeton and, to please his demanding grandfather, he pointed out that "the evident good effects resulting from an attention to [studies] . . . are now conspicuous. . . . The Roman History I have finished and am perfect, translating French has become pretty familiar, and the great deal of writing attending which has probably improved my hand."[33]

The former president replied, "It gives me singular pleasure to hear that your time has been so well employed . . . and that you are so sensible of the good affects of it yourself. If your improvement in other matters is equal to that which is visible in your writing, it will . . . redound much to your own benefit & reputation—& will make you a welcome guest at all times at Mount Vernon. . . . We are all on litter & dirt, occasioned by Joiners, Masons & Painters, working in the house; all parts of which as well as the out buildings, I find, upon examination, to be exceedingly out of repair. I am always and Affectionately yours . . . Go: Washington."[34]

Martha was as ecstatic as George to be home for good. "I cannot tell you, My dear friend," she wrote to Henry Knox's wife, Lucy, "how much I enjoy home after having been deprived of one so long, for our dwelling in New York and Philadelphia was not home, only a sojourning.

> The General and I feel like children just released from school or from a hard taskmaster, and we believe that nothing can tempt us to leave the sacred roof-tree again, except on private business or pleasure. We are so penurious with our enjoyment that we are loath to share it with any one but dear friends, yet almost every day some stranger claims a portion of it, and we cannot refuse.
>
> Nelly and I are companions. Washington is yet at Princeton and doing well. Mrs. Law and Mrs. Peter [Martha's two older granddaughters Eliza and Martha] are often with us. . . . Our furniture and other things sent to us from Philadelphia arrived safely; our plate we brought with us in the carriage. How many friends I have left behind. They fill my memory with sweet thoughts. Shall I ever see them again? Not likely, unless they shall come to me here, for the twilight is gathering around our lives.[35]

Early in April, Washington's sister Betty Lewis died, leaving him and his younger brother Charles, six years his junior, as the last surviving members of his generation of Washingtons. Like Martha, he sensed his own time approaching. Adding to the shock of Betty's death was a letter from Princeton warning that his grandson "Washy" was failing. The letter staggered Washington. He had failed to inspire the boy's father, Jacky Custis, to great achievements and was now failing with his grandson—despite having lavished him with every imaginable financial, cultural, and educational benefit.

In fact, Washington had raised a wonderful grandson—a sweet, normal, playful sixteen-year-old, eager to please both his grandparents. But his name was an enormous burden, and the prospect of emulating so colossal a figure as George Washington overwhelmed him. The boy could barely cope with day-to-day studies, let alone the intellectual, social, and political challenges of matching his grandfather's achievements. Like his father, Jacky Custis, Washy knew he could not follow his grandfather up Mount Olympus. No one could, and he didn't want to.

Just as Washington had not understood the boy's father, so he could not understand the son. Washington had willed himself to achieve, without benefit of formal education. He was convinced that the boy, like his father, was simply willful in refusing to achieve.

"From his infancy," Washington wrote to the Princeton president, "I have discovered an almost unconquerable disposition to indolence in every thing that did not tend to his amusements: and have exhorted him in the most parental and friendly manner, often, to devote his time to more useful pursuits.

> His pride has been stimulated, and his family expectation & wishes have been urged as inducements thereto. In short, I could say nothing to him now, by way of admonition—encouragement—or advice, that has not been repeated over & over again; and therefore I have judged it expedient . . . to let him understand what will be the consequences . . . as you will perceive by the enclosed letter open for your perusal.
>
> What effect this will have, I know not; but as the other mode has failed, it is necessary, I conceive, to try it.[36]

Although Washington's letter to his grandson has been lost, it apparently had its desired effect—temporarily.

"Dearest Sir," the boy wrote back immediately, knowing well the words to sooth his grandfather's anger and ambitions:

> Did you but know the effect your letter has produced it would give you as consummate pleasure, as my former one did pain—My very soul tortured with the sting of conscience at length called reason to its aid and happy for me triumphed, the conflict was long doubt-full till at length I obtained the victory over myself and now return like the *prodigal Son* a sincere penitent. . . . I will now shew all is not lost and that your Grandson shall once more deserve your favour, & Could you but see how happy I now am you would soon forget all that is past and let my future conduct prove the truth of my assertions.[37]

Washington responded warmly—as Washy knew he would: "Your letter eased my mind of unpleasant Sensations, and reflections on your account. It has indeed done more, it has filled it with pleasure, more easy to be conceived than expressed; and if your sorrow, and repentance for the disquietudes occasioned by the preceding letter . . . are sincere, I shall not only heartily forgive, but will forget also, and bury in oblivion, all that has passed." Washington could not, however, end there. He believed he could will the boy's success by insisting that he "think seriously of the advantages which are to be derived . . . from the steady pursuit of a course of study. . . .

> I am desirous of keeping you to your Studies. . . . These sentiments are dictated by the purest regard for your welfare, and from an earnest desire to promote your *true* happiness. . . . Your endeavours to fulfill these reasonable wishes . . . cannot fail of restoring you to all the attentions, protections and affection of one, who ever has been, and will continue to be Your sincere friend
>
> Go: Washington[38]

By the end of July, the Washingtons were aging visibly—tiring under the burdens of managing so vast an enterprise and entertaining almost daily. George asked his nephew Lawrence Lewis, the son of his sister Betty, whether "it is convenient to you to make this place your home. . . . As your Aunt and I are in the decline of life, and regular in our habits, especially in our hour of rising & going to bed, I require some person . . . to ease me of the trouble of entertaining company; particularly of Nights, as it is my inclination to retire . . . either to bed, or to my study, soon after candle light. In taking these duties . . . off my hands, it would render me a very acceptable Service." Lewis agreed, but postponed his arrival to find his runaway slave or, short of that, to buy a new one. Washington consoled the young man for "the loss of your servant" and predicted a sharp increase in the frequency of runaway slaves. "I wish from my Soul that the Legislature of this State could see the policy of a gradual abolition of Slavery; It might prevt much future mischief."[39]

Martha Washington was feeling her age as much as her husband. She had returned to Mount Vernon with a heavy, persistent cold that left her somewhat debilitated throughout the spring and summer. Making matters worse was the loss of both her cook and steward—and her teeth. A Maryland dentist came to fit her for new teeth, and her friend Mrs. Powel in Philadelphia promised to find a new cook and steward.

At the end of August, Washington sent his grandson $40 for his trip home to Mount Vernon for vacation. He was elated by the

George Washington, sixty-four, in
retirement at Mount Vernon. Painting
by Edward Savage, 1796.

prospects of riding out with Washy each morning across the farms,
but being who he was, Washington simply could not abandon the
ambitions he harbored for his grandson. "Although I persuade myself
that there is no occasion for admonition," he wrote, "yet, I exhort
you to come with a mind stedfastly resolved to return precisely at the
time allotted; that it may be guarded against those ideas and allurements, wch unbend it from study, & cause reluctance to return to it
again—better remain where you are . . . devoting your youthful days
in the acquirement of that knowledge which will be . . . the founda-
tion of your usefulness here & happiness hereafter."[40]

Washington was too late, however. Before the boy reached Mount
Vernon, a letter from the president of Princeton arrived expelling
the youngster from college.

On September 19, 1797, five years and a month after they had taken
him prisoner, the Austrians released Lafayette from his dungeon cell
and granted him safe passage out of the country. When the news
reached Mount Vernon, Washington could not restrain young Lafayette from leaving for France immediately—despite dangers of arrest
there. Washington gave his godson $300 (about $6,000 today) for
the voyage and took him and his tutor to Georgetown, where they

Sixty-six-year-old George Washington with his grandchildren at Mount Vernon. Standing behind him are his nephew Lawrence Lewis with Martha Washington. Lewis would later marry Martha's widowed daughter-in-law Eleanor ("Nelly") Parke Custis Stuart, seated right.

caught the stage to New York to embark for France. He gave the boy a letter for his father:

My dear Sir,

This letter will, I hope, be presented to you by your Son, who is highly deserving of such Parents as you and your amiable Lady.

He can relate, much better than I can describe, my participation in your sufferings—my solicitude for your relief—the measures I adopted (though ineffectually) to facilitate your liberation from an unjust & cruel imprisonment—and the joy I experienced at the news of its accomplishment. . . .

His conduct, since he first set his feet on American ground has been exemplary in every point of view—such as has gained him the esteem, affection & confidence of all who have had the pleasure of his acquaintance. His filial affection & duty, and his ardent desire to embrace his parents and Sisters . . . would not allow him to await the authentic account of this much desired event . . .

I could not withhold my assent to the gratification of his wishes, to fly to the arms of those whom he holds most dear.[41]

A week later, Washington received a letter from young Lafayette, attesting to his safe arrival at the Hamiltons in New York and his imminent departure for France:

> I have the hope of being after so long and cruel a separation at last united again to my parents and sister. I need not tell you, Sir, that if any thing can soften the painful remembrances of all their sufferings, it will be to hear from us, what a tender interest you took in them, what efforts you made to alleviate them and that the friendship with which you always honoured the father has induced you to receive the son under your roof with so much goodness! in your house I have been as happy as I could be separated from my family, and the time which I passed with you will never be forgot. . . .
>
> be so kind, Sir, as to accept the hommage of my fervent wishes for your happiness, and may you enjoy for a long time to come a life which has been so entirely consecrated to the good of mankind. I have the honour to be, Sir, with the utmost respect your most obedient humble servant
>
> G. W. Motier Lafayette[42]

14

"First in the Hearts of His Countrymen"

SEVENTEEN NINETY-EIGHT did not begin well for seventeen-year-old George Washington Parke Custis. Although he planned to abandon his studies after his dismissal from Princeton, his grandfather had other plans: he would continue studying at home! Like it or not, he would prepare for greatness.

"System in all things should be aimed at," began Washington's stern instructions to his grandson.

> From breakfast, until about an hour before Dinner (allowed for dressing, and preparing for it, that you may appear decent) I shall expect you will confine yourself to your studies; and diligently attend to them; endeavouring to make yourself master of whatever is recommended to, or required of you.
>
> While the afternoons are short, and but little interval between rising from dinner and assembling for Tea, you may employ that time in walking, or any other recreation.
>
> After Tea, if the Studies you are engaged in require it, you will no doubt perceive the propriety & advantage of returning to them, untill the hour of rest.
>
> Rise early, that by habit it may become familiar, agreeable—healthy—and profitable. It may for a while, be irksome to do this; but that will wear off; and the practise will produce a rich harvest forever thereafter; whether in public or private Walks of Life.

Make it an invariable rule to be in place . . . at the usual breakfasting, dining, and tea hours. It is not only disagreeable, but it is also very inconvenient, for servants to be running here, & there, and they know not where, to summon you to them, when their duties, and attendance, on the company who are seated, render it improper.

Saturday may be appropriated to riding; to your Gun, or other proper amusements.

Time disposed of in this manner, makes ample provision for exercise & every useful, or necessary recreation; at the same time that the hours allotted for study, *if really applied to it*, instead of running up & down stairs, & wasted in conversation with any one who will talk with you, will enable you to make considerable progress in whatsoever line is marked out for you: and that you may do it, is my sincere wish.[1]

As he laid down the law to his reluctant grandson, Washington received a letter from the steadfast George-Washington Lafayette that he had reached England safely. Shortly thereafter a letter came from Lafayette himself. He and his wife and two daughters had found safe haven in Denmark. "It is a Melancholy thought to Me," Lafayette wrote, "that While I Could Be So Happy at Mount Vernon, I am Still Almost as Separated from you as I have Been for five Years. . . . My dear General, the obligations I have to Your friendly and fatherly Care of My Son Georges." His letter was disjointed, affected by emotion, fragile health, and a lost facility for English. Emotions took over.

My Wife and daughters Beg their Most Affectionate Respects to Be Presented to You and to Mrs Washington to whom I Request to By Most tenderly and Respectfully Remembered—My Compliments Wait on My friend George Washington—How Happy I Shall Be to Hear My Son's particular, and Every day Repeated Accounts about you, Every Body, and Every thing that Surrounds You! it Shall to my Enchanted Mind Recall the liveliest Sentiments of My Heart, the Happiest Hours of My Life. Adieu, My Respected and Beloved General, You know the Veneration, Gratitude, and Love of Your filial friend

Lafayette[2]

George and Martha celebrated Lafayette's release at a gala birthday party for Washington in Alexandria, with granddaughter Nelly performing with her old music master for "twenty-five or thirty couples . . . we danced until two o'clock."[3]

Two weeks after issuing his instructions to his grandson, Washington realized the absurdity of imprisoning the boy in his own home. After a discussion with the boy's stepfather, Dr. David Stuart, Washington agreed to enroll him at a less demanding college in Annapolis, Maryland, but he simply could not suppress his unrealistic expectations and wrote to the principal: "Mr. Custis possesses competent talents to fit him for any studies, but they are counteracted by an indolence of mind which renders it difficult to draw them into action. . . . As his family, fortune and talents (if the latter can be improved) give him just pretensions to become a useful member of Society, in the Councils of his Country, his friends (and none more than myself) are extremely desirous that his education should be liberal, polished, and adapted to this end."[4]

After Custis enrolled, grandfather and grandson resumed their pointless correspondence of weekly admonitions, apologies, promises, angry recriminations, pleas for forgiveness, and more admonitions:

Custis: I have constantly in mind your virtuous precepts which I hope to benefit by.[5]

Washington: . . . it gives me . . . much pleasure to find that you are . . . disposed to prosecute your studies with zeal & alacrity. Let these continue to be your *primary* objects & pursuits; all other matters . . . are of secondary consideration.[6]

Custis: . . . could a repetition of those sentiments which I have allways avowed express my gratitude and obligations to you: freely should they be exercised, but it is sufficient that they are indelibly grounded on my mind and can never be erased. . . . What then could have been a greater misfortune to me than your displeasure, what a greater happiness than your confidence?"[7]

Washington: Your letter . . . gave us the pleasure . . . at hearing that you . . . [are] going on well in your studies. Prosecute these with deligence & ardour, and you will sometime hence, be more sensible than now, of the rich harvest you will gather from them . . .

with every good wish . . . & particularly the blessings of your Grand-mama, I remain your sincere friend and Affectionate

Go: Washington"[8]

Custis: I attend College regularly and am determined that noth-ing shall alienate my attention. Adieu Dearest Sir may Heaven proportion her reward to your merit, and the sincere and ardent prayer of

Geo. W. P. Custis[9]

With that, the boy's letters stopped, and, as Martha fretted, Wash-ington heard rumors of romantic escapades that made him lose his temper: "It is now four weeks since any person of this family has heard *from* you, although you were requested to write to some one in it, once a fortnight, knowing . . . how apt your Grandmama is to sus-pect that you are sick, or some accident has happened. . . . Recollect the saying of the wise man, 'that there is a time for all things' and sure I am it is not a time for you to think of forming a serious attach-ment. . . . But as I am willing to believe the report is groundless, and that you have not forgotten *so soon* the exhortation at parting, to foresake all things & cleve to your Books, until a regular & proper system of education is completed. . . . I wish to remain, so far as your own conduct will let me be, Your sincere friend, and Affectionate Advisor Go: Washington"[10]

The thought of Martha's "pretty little babe" eloping upset the entire Washington family. The Washingtons sent the boy's mother, Martha's daughter-in-law, Eleanor Calvert Custis Stuart, to Annapo-lis in the family coach with Washington's letter. After calming his mother, the boy replied to his grandfather:

The report, as mamma tells me, of my being *engaged* to the young lady in question is strictly erroneous. That I gave her reason to believe in my attachment to her, I candidly allow. . . . That I stated to her my prospects, duty, and dependence . . . I solemnly affirm. That I solicited her affection, and hoped, with the approbation of my family, to bring about a union at some future day, I likewise allow. The conditions were not accepted, and my youth being alleged . . . as an obstacle to the consummation of my wishes at the present time . . . I withdrew. . . . Thus the matter ended.

Let me once more, sir, on the shrine of gratitude, plight my faith to you; let me unclasp the sacred books of morality and lay my duty, nay, my all, at your feet. Your beneficence could not enhance your virtues; on my heart they are engraven as the benefactor, nay, the more than father of,

G. W. P. Custis[11]

Washington was all but apoplectic when he read the boy's letter; rather than reply in anger and regret his words, he postponed answering—indeed, never replied. Unnerved by the absence of any communication from his grandfather, the boy wrote again in mid-July, hoping "that my confession of both the circumstances of the case, and my error, has obliterated from your mind all unfavourable impressions. . . . I expect the College will adjourn in a fortnight."[12] Receiving no response, Custis sent a third letter, asking whether, when the college "breaks up" for vacation, "I leave it entirely or not."[13] That drew a response!

"The question . . . really astonishes me!" Washington exploded, "for it would seem as if *nothing* I could say to you made more than a *momentary* impression." Flushed with anger, Washington repeated all his previous admonitions, then threw his pen down in despair. He had said everything and could find no more words to lift his grandson to greatness.

In fact, the boy had already quit school.

It was fortunate that before he returned to Mount Vernon, his grandfather became engrossed in matters of state: "If the Constitution and your Convenience would admit of my Changing places with you," President John Adams had written, "or of my taking my old station as your Lieutenant civil, I should have no doubts of the Ultimate Prosperity and Glory of the Country."[14]

Adams told Washington he was raising an army because relations with France had deteriorated into undeclared war on the high seas. The French had sunk or captured upward of eight hundred American vessels and all but paralyzed American trade. Although Adams had sent a commission to Paris to discuss peace, French foreign minister Talleyrand had refused to negotiate unless the American envoys paid him a substantial bribe. Outraged by the French response, Adams asked Congress to strengthen national defenses.

"In forming an Army," he wrote to Washington, "I am at an immense Loss whether to call out all the old Generals, or to appoint a young [set]. If the French come here We must learn to march with a quick step, and to Attack, for in that Way only they are said to be vulnerable. I must tap you. Sometimes for Advice. We must have your Name, if you, in any case will permit Us to Use it. There will be more efficacy in it, than in many an Army."[15]

On July 2, Congress named Washington commanding general of the armed forces, and five days later abrogated the alliances with France from the Revolutionary War. A few days later, the secretary of war sent Washington his formal commission from the president.

President Adams sent a personal note extending "all the Apologies I can make" for asking Washington to return to public life. "My reasons for this measure, will be too well known to need any explanation to the Public. Every Friend and every Enemy of America, will comprehend them. . . . As I said in a former letter, if it had been in my power to nominate you to be President of the United States, I should have done it with less hesitation and more pleasure."[16]

Young Washington Custis exulted that his grandfather's return to public life had shifted the old man's focus away from the boy's academic failures. "I need not congratulate you," he wrote to his grandfather, "on an appointment which was allways designed by the Creator for one so fully capable of fulfilling it. Let an admiring world again behold a Cincinnatus springing up from rural retirement to the conquest of nations and the future historian in erasing so great a name insert that of the *Father of his Country*."[17]

Custis's euphoric words did little to dispel his grandfather's furor when the boy returned to Mount Vernon and announced his decision to end his formal education. The commander in chief's thunder and lightning hurt the boy deeply and sent him into a funk that left him hiding in the farthest recesses of the Mansion attic. Pressed by military matters, Washington threw up his hands in despair and consulted Washy's stepfather: "If you, or Mrs. Stuart could, by indirect means, discover the State of Washington Custis's mind, it would be to be wished. He appears to me to be moped & Stupid. says nothing—and is always in some hole or corner excluded from Company."[18]

In the end, Washington surrendered, sending a letter of capitulation to the principal of Washy's college: "Mr. Custis, I expected would have left . . . for Saint John's College; but, although he professed his readiness to do whatever was required of him, his dereliction to return, was too apparent, to afford any hope that good would result from it in the prosecution of his studies—and therefore . . . I [think] it best, upon the whole, to keep him here."[19]

Washington had some consolation for his failure with his grandson when his nephew Bushrod Washington came to Mount Vernon for dinner in early October and announced that President Adams had appointed him to the United States Supreme Court—a post he would hold until his death thirty-one years later.

Washington all but despaired of salvaging his grandson and turned his full attention to organizing an army to defend the United States. It would take almost every waking moment for the rest of the year. He estimated he would need twelve infantry regiments and a corps of artillery men and engineers to defend the nation against a French invasion. He named Alexander Hamilton second in command and promoted him to major general. Despairing of squeezing into his old uniform, Washington designed a new one—"a blue coat, with yellow buttons and gold epaulettes (each having three silver stars) linings cape and cuffs buff, in Winter, buff vest and breeches, in summer, a white vest and breeches of nankeen [brownish-yellow coarse cotton]." He ordered a white plume as "a further distinction" for the commander in chief's hat, as well as those of his staff.[20] Then he asked the dentist for a new set of teeth—and designed them as well.

"The upper teeth and bars do not fall back enough," he complained of his old set of teeth, "but stand more upright . . . by which means the bar . . . shoots beyond the gums and not only forces the lip out just under the nose, but by not having its proper place to rest upon frets, and makes that part very sore." The Father of His Country was not happy, and it showed in his portraits.[21]

On November 5, Washington broke the solemn promise he had made to himself and to Martha and left Mount Vernon for the capital, accompanied by Lear—now assigned the rank of colonel—and an entourage of aides and servants. Troops of light horse met their carriage at the Philadelphia city line, where General Washington and Colonel Lear mounted their horses and rode into the nation's capital to the tolling of church bells and cheers of thousands. Washington remained in the capital six weeks, during which time he effectively organized an army—on paper. He appointed his sister's son Lawrence Lewis commander of a Virginia cavalry troop, and, still hoping to inspire his incorrigible grandson to greatness, he appointed George Washington Parke Custis the rank of "cornet" in Lewis's company—the lowest commissioned rank in the army, but nonetheless the usual appointment for a young "gentleman" entering the military for the first time. His role would be to carry the company pennant—a conspicuous role that invariably drew more plaudits on parade than bullets in battle. Because the boy was a minor, Washington asked that his commission be withheld pending permission of his mother and grandmother.

Satisfied that the military would motivate his grandson to success, Washington left for Mount Vernon—then realized he would have to face Martha's wrath for putting her "pretty babe" at risk. Even worse, he envisioned the boy's outrage—and the public scandal—that would ensue if the boy's commission were revoked by order of his grandmother—the commander in chief's wife. As his coach rolled into Chester, just outside Philadelphia, Washington shouted at the driver to stop. He scratched a note marked "private" to the secretary of war, then sent an aide to deliver it as quickly as possible.

> Having requested that the Nomination of Mr Custis might be with held . . . until I could consult his Grandmother (Mrs Washington) and mother Mrs Stuart; I further pray that no mention of his name for such an Office may be made until the result is known; because, if their consent, being an only son, indeed the only male of his family, cannot be had, it would be better that the arrangement of him should pass *entirely* unnoticed, to prevent the uneasy sensations which might arise from disappointment if the knowledge of it should get to him.[22]

To his immense relief, he arrived at Mount Vernon to find his grandson in raptures over his appointment—and the opportunity, at last, to fulfill at least one of his grandfather's impossibly high expectations. Although Martha Washington fretted, the boy was a master at undermining his grandmother's resistance—a plaintive smile, a pout, a simple "Please?" Embracing her hand in his two hands or pressing it to his cheek, though used sparingly, invariably crushed her resistance. Her husband did the rest, assuring Martha that the likelihood of war was nil and promising to reassign her grandson to a noncombat role far behind the lines in the event of danger.

Washington spent Christmas morning in his study writing a long-overdue letter to Lafayette—his first since young George-Washington Lafayette had left Mount Vernon more than a year earlier. He apologized for his "long silence," explaining that he had returned to public life but assuring him of "the sincere, & heart felt pleasure I derived from finding . . . that you had not only regained your liberty, but was in the enjoyment of better health than could have been expected from your long & rigorous confinement; and that Madame la Fayette and the young ladies were able to survive it all." Washington penned page after page describing the events that had led to the current crisis with France but insisted that American policy was "to observe a strict neutrality." He ended his letter with familiar words: "I shall now only add what you knew well before, that with the most sincere friendship, & affectionate regard—I am always Yours." They were the last words Washington would ever write to his "adoptive son."[23]

Washington also sent a short letter to Lafayette's son, announcing the engagement of Washington's nephew Captain Lawrence Lewis to Martha's granddaughter Nelly Custis. Both grandparents exulted over another marital union of the two families.

"When the clouds which at present overcast the Political horizon are dispelled," he concluded to his French godson, "it would give all your friends great pleasure to see you in your old walks—and to none more than to your Sincere & Affectionate friend . . . Go: Washington."[24]

As the last year of the eighteenth century began, Washington grew annoyed with the failure of the War Department to begin recruiting troops for his army, but the impending wedding of his nephew to his adopted granddaughter took precedence, and on January 23 he went to Alexandria to do what he had never actually done, assume legal guardianship of the girl he and Martha had raised

Eleanor ("Nelly") Parke Custis,
Martha Washington's granddaughter,
at eighteen, before her marriage in the
Mansion at Mount Vernon to George
Washington's nephew Lawrence Lewis.
Portrait by James Sharples, 1796.

since early childhood. Still a minor at twenty, Nelly could not get a marriage license without her guardian's signature. So, for a few days at least, his and Martha's adored Nelly was truly his, legally, and he fussed like a mother rather than a father to have his new uniform ready for the wedding.

"There being some doubt in my mind respecting the Sort of Cuff & Pocket flap," he wrote to his Philadelphia tailor, "Whether the first shall simply turn up, or have a slash through it, with a flap the colour of the cloth (blue, with three buttons and holes) also embroidered; and whether the second shall have a cross pocket in the usual form, or slashed (that is inclining downwards). . . .

> Let your blue cloth be of the best and softest French or Spanish; and the finest you can procure, of a deep colour. And the Buff of the very best sort, fine, and not inclining to yellow or Orange. . . . The buttons are to be plain, flat, and of the best double gilt. . . .
>
> The waistcoat should be straight breasted, that is without lapels. and the Cuffs of the Coat neither large, nor tight; observing a just medium between the two.
>
> I again repeat my wish that they may be with me by the 22nd of Feby.[25]

The couple chose to wed on his birthnight—to pay homage to the aging patriarch—and, as Martha looked on in tears, he proudly gave their little granddaughter away at a candlelight ceremony in the Mansion at Mount Vernon. (The uniform he ordered arrived too late for the wedding.)

Shortly after his birthday, electrifying news reached Philadelphia and Mount Vernon that the American ship *Constellation* had captured the French Navy frigate *Insurgente*. The humiliating French naval defeat all but ended French outrages against American shipping. The French government sued for peace, and the American public's enthusiasm for war vanished. By the end of May, Washington once again referred to "the Seat of my retirement; where I rather hope . . . to spend the remnant of my life in tranquility; if one may judge from the appearance of both external, and internal causes. which present themselves to our present view."[26]

As spring blossoms embraced Mount Vernon, Washington found it impossible to maintain his icy demeanor toward his beloved grandson. Washy lacked genius, certainly, but was too winsome to maltreat. He dearly sought his grandfather's approval, but simply was not capable of climbing intellectual heights—or any other heights, for that matter.

"My Ward, Mr. Custis, having entered into the Service of his Country," Washington wrote to his merchant, "I wish to equip him with every thing suitable thereto; in a handsome, but not an expensive style.

> Let me pray you therefore to provide . . .
>
> A pair of Pistols & Horseman's Sword—Silver mounted
> A Saddle—best kind—& proper Halter. A handsome bridle he already has
> Holsters, & caps, to suit Pistols
> A proper Horseman's Cap—or Helmet
> A horseman's Cloak—suitable to the Unifm
>
> If any other necessary article, is omitted, it may be added to the above list. Let the cost accompany the Invoice, and the amount shall be paid so soon as it is made known.[27]

The renewal of Washington's affections so excited the boy that he spoke of nothing but galloping off to war and pestered his grandfather with "daily, fruitless enquiries . . . to know when . . . his Military equipments . . . may be expected."[28]

* * *

Early in June, Washington's old friend Patrick Henry died, and, with his own mortality in mind, he took stock of his assets and prepared a will. It opened simply:

"In the name of God amen. I George Washington of Mount Vernon, a citizen of the United States and lately President of the same . . ."

After issuing instructions to pay all his debts, the first provision of his will was simple and all-encompassing: "To my dearly beloved wife, Martha Washington I give and bequeath the use profit and benefit of my whole Estate, real and personal, for the term of her natural life."

The second provision was revealing:

> Upon the decease of my wife it is my will and desire, that all the slaves which I hold in *my own right* shall receive their freedom—To emancipate them during her [Martha's] life, would tho earnestly wished by me, be attended with such insuperable difficulties, on account of their intermixture by marriages with the Dower negroes* . . . it not being in my power . . . to manumit them—And whereas among those who will receive freedom according to this devise there may be some who from old age, or bodily infirmities & and others who on account of their infancy, that will be unable to support themselves, it is my will and desire that all who come under the first and second description shall be comfortably clothed and fed by my heirs while they live and that such of the latter description . . . be taught to read and write and to be brought up to some useful occupation . . . and I do hereby expressly forbid the sale or transportation . . . of any Slave I may die possessed of, under any pretence, whatsoever—and do moreover most positively, and most solemnly enjoin it upon my Executors . . . to see that this clause respecting Slaves be religiously fulfilled.[29]

Washington had 276 slaves, of whom 123 were his and 153 were Martha's dower slaves. Forty of his slaves and 58 of Martha's were children too young to work.

Washington provided "immediate freedom . . . to my mulatto man, William (calling himself William Lee)," his personal servant,

---

* Martha's slaves, inherited from her family and her previous husband and therefore not George's to dispose of.

to whom he bequeathed a lifetime annuity of $30 "independent of the victuals and *cloaths* he has been accustomed to receive." Washington also gave Lee the option of remaining at Mount Vernon at no cost "as a testimony of my sense of his attachment to me and for his faithful services during the Revolutionary War."

Washington made substantial bequests to the free school for poor and orphaned children at the Alexandria Academy, and to Liberty Hall Academy—the future Washington and Lee University. He bequeathed many personal items to close friends and loyal aides— "a pair of finely wrought steel pistols taken from the enemy in the Revolutionary war" went to Lafayette, for example. He gave Tobias Lear and his family lifetime, rent-free use of a home on two thousand acres of land adjacent to the Mansion Farm.

To each of his nephews he left a sword "accompanied with an injunction not to unsheath them for the purpose of shedding blood except it be for self-defence, or in defence of their Country and its rights." He left two thousand acres each along the Potomac to Fanny's boys George Fayette and Charles Washington, and he left his property at Berkeley Springs to his nephews George Steptoe and Lawrence Charles Augustine Washington, the two boys he had put through the College of Philadelphia.

"And whereas," his will continued, "it has always been my intention, since my expectation of having issue has ceased, to consider the grand children of my wife . . . whom we have raised from their earliest infancy . . . in the same light as I do my own relations . . . I give and bequeath to George Washington Parke Custis the Grand son of my wife and my ward and to his heirs, the tract I hold . . . in the *vicinity* of Alexandria containing one thousd two hundred acres more or less;—and my entire square . . . in the city of Washington."

To his granddaughter Nelly and her husband, his nephew Lawrence Lewis, he bequeathed the two-thousand-acre Dogue Farm, with its mill and distillery.

He bequeathed the crown jewel of his estate, the magnificent Mansion Farm at Mount Vernon, to the heir who had most lived up to his high expectations—his brother Jack's son Supreme Court justice Bushrod Washington. He also left Bushrod all his papers relating "to my civil and military administration of the affairs of this Country."[30]

In the fall, he and Martha received their usual invitation to the November ball in Alexandria, but he replied uncharacteristically that "alas! our dancing days are no more."[31]

As the last month of the old century began, the Washingtons looked forward to celebrating the arrival of the new one with the young Custis, Lewis, and Washington clans. Nelly Custis had given birth to her first child, at Mount Vernon on November 27, and Martha's granddaughter and namesake Martha Parke Custis Peter ("Patty")—gave birth to a "Manchild," as Washington put it, on December 3. The day was "clear & pleasant" according to his diary, and, as usual, he "rid" fifteen miles across the fields of his various plantations. After returning to the Mansion, he congratulated Patty's husband, then asked, "Have you succeeded, or are you likely to succeed, in procuring the Hemp seed I required?" The farm was always foremost in his thoughts.[32]

On December 9, Gouverneur Morris wrote Washington asking that he run for the presidency in 1800. Morris had served both in the Continental Congress and at the Constitutional Convention, and Washington had appointed him ambassador to France in 1792. Now resettled on his huge estate in Morrisania, New York, north of New York City, he had conferred with leading Federalists who had deemed President Adams "unfit for the Office he now holds. You will easily conceive," he told Washington, "that his Predecessor was wished for. . . .

> Recollect Sir, that each Occasion which has brought you back on the public Stage has been to you the Means of new and greater Glory. If General Washington had not become Member of the Convention he would have been considered only as the Defender and not as the Legislator of his Country. And if the President of the Convention had not become President of the United States he would not have added the Character of Statesman to those of a Patriot and Hero. . . .
>
> But you may perhaps say that you stand indirectly pledged to private Life. Surely Sir you neither gave nor meant to give such Pledge to the Extent of possible Contingencies. . . . Nay, you stand pledged by your former Conduct that when Circumstances arise which may require it you will act again. Those Circumstances seem

to be now imminent, and it is meet that you consider them. . . . Ponder them I pray.[33]

The letter reached Mount Vernon on December 16. Washington was dead.

On December 10, Washington had sent his farm manager an elaborately detailed plan for crops and operations on his River Farm for the year 1800 through 1803, which he insisted "be most *strictly*, and *pointedly* attended to and executed. . . . A System closely pursued . . . would move like *clock work* . . . and a reasonable and tolerably accurate estimate may be made of the produce. But when no plan is fixed, when directions flow from day to day, the business becomes a mere chaos."[34]

On December 12—a cloudy morning—he set out on his usual ride. "About 1 oclock it began to snow," he noted in his diary, "soon after to Hail and then turned to cold rain. Mer. 28 at night."[35]

Tobias Lear recalled the day in his journal:

> When he came in . . . I observed to him that I was afraid he had got wet, he said no, his great coat had kept him dry; but his neck appeared to be wet, and the snow was hanging on his hair. He came to dinner with out changing his dress.
>
> A heavy fall of snow took place on Friday, which prevented the General from riding out as usual. He had taken cold . . . and complained of having a sore throat—he had a hoarseness, which increased in the evening; but he made light of it, as he would never take anything to carry off a cold; always observing, "let it go as it came."

Washington then asked for a glass of his favorite Madeira and reminded Lear to write to his merchant in Philadelphia for more. Lear continues:

> In the evening, the papers having come from the post Office, he sat in the room, with Mrs Washington and myself, reading them 'till about nine o'clock. . . . On his retiring to bed, he appeared in perfect health, excepting the cold before mentioned, which he considered trifling, and had been remarkably chearful all the evening.

About two or three o'clk Saturday Morning he awoke Mrs Washington & told her he was very unwell, and had an ague [recurrent attack of chills, fever, and sweating]. She observed that he could scarcely speak, and breathed with difficulty—and would have got up to call a servant; but he would not permit her lest she should take cold.[36]

At daybreak, a housemaid entered Washington's room to make a fire, and Martha sent her for Lear, who rushed to Washington's bedside. "I found him breathing with difficulty—hardly able to utter a word intelligibly. I went out instantly—and wrote a line to Dr Craik, which I sent off by my servant, ordering him to go with all the swiftness his horse could carry him, and immediately returned to the General's Chamber. . . . A mixture of Molasses, Vinegar & butter was prepared, to try its effect in the throat; but he could not swallow a drop, whenever he attempted it he appeard to be distressed, convulsed, and almost suffocated."[37]

Martha was terrified and urged Lear to send for a second doctor, who lived closer—just across the river in Maryland.

"General Washington is very ill with Quincy [a throat infection]," Lear wrote. "Dr. Craik is sent for from Alexa. but has not yet come down. Mrs. Washington's anxiety is great, and she requests . . . you will come over without delay, as it is impossible for the General to continue long without relief. . . . He grows worse: can swallow nothing, and can scarcely breath."[38]

With doctors still miles away, Washington sent for his clerk, Albin Rawlins, who had experience bleeding sick slaves. The man hesitated to approach Washington's bedside. "Don't be afraid," Washington whispered. Rawlins cut into his patron's arm, only to hear a hoarse whisper: "The orifice is not large enough!"[39]

The blood nonetheless ran "pretty freely," according to Lear. "Mrs Washington, not knowing whether bleeding was proper or not . . . beg'd that much might not be taken from him lest it be injurious and desired me to stop it; but when I was about to untie the string, the general put up his hand to prevent it, and as soon as he could speak, he said, 'more.' Mrs Washington being still uneasy lest too much blood should be taken, it was stop'd after about half a pint was taken from him."

When the Maryland doctor arrived, he applied standard remedies—bathing, then "blistering" Washington's throat, then bleeding
him again. Forced inhalation of vinegar-laced steam sent Washington "into great distress and almost produced suffocation."

Dr. Craik, who had known Washington for forty-five years—
since the Fort Necessity campaign of 1754—arrived at ten. He ex-
amined his old friend, ordered a runner to fetch yet another doctor,
then bled Washington again—the third time that morning. Still
concerned about the justification for bleeding, Martha Washington
sent for a fourth doctor. By midafternoon the two other doctors
arrived and, after consulting with Dr. Craik, diagnosed Washington's illness as inflammatory "quinsy," a broadly used term of that
era for a variety of throat inflammations, including tonsillitis.*
With no other accepted remedies at their disposal,† they tried to
bleed Washington a fourth time, but by then they had drained
about eighty-two ounces of blood, or more than five pints, and left
him dehydrated and approaching hemorrhagic shock. As Lear noted,
"the blood ran slowly—appeared very thick." After feeling Washington's pulse, the doctors gave Washington a purgative of calo-
mel (mercurous chloride) and tartar emetic, both now known to be
poisonous substances that, in fact, gave Washington excruciatingly
painful cramps and diarrhea. In effect, his doctors, though meaning
well and applying all the most accepted medical techniques, were
actually killing him.

"His patience, fortitude & resignation never foresook him for a
moment," Lear reported. "In all his distress he uttered not a sigh nor
a complaint, always endeavouring to take what was offered him, or
to do what was desired.

"About half past 4 o'clk," Lear's journal continues, "he desired me
to ask Mrs Washington to come to his bed side—when he requested

---

* Modern physicians agree that Washington was suffering from an acute inflammation
of the upper respiratory tract, probably the epiglottis, the leaflike cartilage that opens
and closes the entry to the trachea, or windpipe.
† Although one doctor proposed a tracheotomy, then a controversial new procedure in
England that had never been tried in America, Craik and the other doctors rejected the
idea as too dangerous.

her to . . . take from his desk two Wills which she would find there, and bring them to him, which she did.

Upon looking at them he gave her [one] . . . to burn it, which she did, and then took the other & put it away. After this was done, I returned again to his bed side and took his hand. He said to me, *"I find I am going, my breath cannot continue long, I believed, from the first attack it would be fatal, do you arrange & record all my later Military letters & papers—arrange my accounts & settle my books, as you know more about them than anyone else."* The Physicians again came in (between 5 & 6 o'clk) and . . . asked him if he could sit up in the bed. He held out his hand to me & was raised up, when he said to the Physicians. *"I feel myself going, you had better not take any more trouble about me; but let me go off quietly; I cannot last long."* They found what had been done was without effect—he laid down again and they retired excepting Dr Craik. He then said to him, *"Doctor, I die hard, but I am not afraid to go, I believed from my first attack that I shd not survive it, my breath cannot last long."* The Doctor pressed his hand but could not utter a word. He retired from the bed side— and sat by the fire absorbed in grief. . . .

About ten o'clock he made several attempts to speak to me before he could effect it—at length, he said, *"I am just going, Have me decently buried, and do not let my body be put into the Vault in less than two days after I am dead."* I bowed assent. He looked at me again, and said, *"Do you understand me"*—I replied Yes, Sir, *"Tis well,"* said he. . . . Mrs Washington was sitting near the foot of the bed . . . the servants were standing in the Room near the door. . . . About ten minutes before he expired his breathing became much easier—he lay quietly—he withdrew his hand from mine & felt his own pulse—I spoke to Dr Craik who sat by the fire—he came to the bed side. The Generals hand fell from his wrist—I took it in mine and laid it upon my breast—Dr Craik put his hands over his eyes and he expired without a struggle or a Sigh! While we were fixed in silent grief—Mrs Washington asked, with a firm & collected Voice, *"Is he gone."* I could not speak, but held up my hand as a signal that he was. *"Tis well"* said she in a firm voice. *"Tis All now over. I have no more trials to pass through. I shall soon follow him!["]* . . . I kissed the cold hand, which I had 'till then held, laid it down, went to the fire and was for some time lost in profound grief. . . . About 12 o'clk the Corps[e] was brought down and laid

Martha Washington, sixty-nine, in 1801, two years after her husband's death. Portrait by Robert Field.

out in the large room. [Washington probably died from a combination of three causes: shock from loss of blood; asphyxiation, brought on by the inflammation of the epiglottis at the entry to his windpipe; and introduction of poisons into his weakened system.][40]

Four days later, on December 18, a procession of friends, relatives, military officers, Freemasons from Alexandria, and other admirers escorted Washington's coffin from the Mansion to the vault on the grounds of his beloved Mount Vernon. Lear cut a lock of his hair as a keepsake for Martha.

Congress set December 26 as a day of mourning in the capital, which held a funeral procession with an empty coffin, led by a riderless horse with boots reversed in its stirrups. With no other way to participate, cities, towns, and villages across the nation followed suit, staging mock funerals to display their grief. President Adams ordered the army to wear black sleeve bands for six months, then issued a formal message: "For his fellow-citizens, if their prayers could have been answered, he would have been immortal."[41] The Senate declared, "Ancient and modern names are diminished before him. . . . Let his countrymen consecrate the memory of the heroic General Washington, the patriotic statesman and the virtuous sage. Let them teach

Old burial vault. The original resting place of George and Martha Washington. Fearing its collapse, Washington designed a new vault, where his and Martha's remains were transferred in 1831.

their children never to forget that the fruit of his labors and his example are their inheritance."[42] For the formal religious service, Congress elected Washington's heroic comrade in the Revolutionary War Henry "Light-Horse Harry" Lee to give the eulogy that would echo in the hearts of American patriots for generations:

> First in war, first in peace and first in the hearts of his country-men, he was second to none in the humble and endearing scenes of private life. Pious, just, humble, temperate and sincere—uni-form, dignified and commanding. . . . Such was the man for whom our nation mourns.[43]

In the days and weeks that followed, congressmen, governors, mayors, and other notables across the nation delivered three hun-dred more eulogies, each more extravagant than the last. The plain-spoken Abigail Adams grew annoyed at the sometimes disingenuous euphoria. "Simple truth is his best, his greatest eulogy," she snapped. She pledged to wear nothing but black until spring and half mourning thereafter.[44] Martha Washington was touched; she had always admired Abigail and felt she could confide in her.

My dear Madam   Mount Vernon, January the 1st 1800

Accept the thanks of a heart opprest with sorrow but greatfull for your friendly sympathising letter.

To that almighty power who alone can heal the wounds he inflicts I look for consolation and fortitude.

May you long enjoy the happiness you now possess and never know affliction like mine

> with prayers for your happiness
> I remain your sincear
> Friend
> Martha Washington[45]

Martha Washington died about two and a half years later, on May 22, 1802.

Epilogue

AFTER HER HUSBAND'S DEATH, Martha Washington moved into a small room of her own on the third floor of the Mansion at Mount Vernon and never again slept in the bed or room she had shared with her husband for forty years. She burned all the letters she could find that she and her husband had ever written to each other— to prevent their ever being exploited or misinterpreted.

On December 27, 1799, President John Adams forwarded a copy of a congressional resolution to Martha Washington and asked "your assent to the interment of the remains of . . . your late Consort, General George Washington . . . under the marble monument to be erected in the capitol, at the City of Washington to commemorate the great events of his military and political life."[1]

Although deeply opposed to removing her husband's body from the land he so adored, she agreed. "Taught by the great example which I have so long had before me never to oppose my private wishes to the public will—I must consent to the request made by congress . . . and in doing this . . . I cannot say what a sacrifice of individual feeling I make to a sense of public duty."[2]

Before the sarcophagus for Washington's body was completed, however, Martha Washington died, and her body was placed beside his in the vault at Mount Vernon. Subsequent generations of Washingtons who inherited Mount Vernon prevented the removal of his body, and the sarcophagus beneath the Capitol dome remains empty.

New burial vault. Designed by Washington himself, it houses two marble sarcophagi behind the iron gate, one marked "Washington," the other "Martha, Consort of Washington." The stone tablet above the brick entrances bears the inscription "Within this Enclosure Rest the remains of Gen.l George Washington." The marble shafts commemorate Bushrod Washington, who inherited Mount Vernon, and his nephew John Augustine Washington, to whom he bequeathed the estate.

With the old vault at Mount Vernon in danger of collapse, Washington's heirs moved the Washingtons to a new vault in 1831—a structure that Washington himself had designed.

Lafayette and his son George-Washington Lafayette returned to Mount Vernon during a triumphal visit in 1824–1825 to celebrate the fiftieth anniversary of American independence. Washington and Custis descendants gathered with them for a tearful visit to George and Martha's tombs, after which George Washington Parke Custis— "Washy"—presented Lafayette with a ring containing a lock of Washington's hair. It is now on display at Lafayette's boyhood home, the Château de Chavaniac, in Auvergne, France.

*   *   *

George Washington Parke Custis never fulfilled Washington's ambitions for him. A wealthy indolent for most of his life, he tried his hand as a playwright, then as an artist, with no success. His *Recollections and Private Memoirs of Washington, by his Adopted Son* ran as a series of newspaper articles before being published as a book in 1860. Although the work is valuable for some of its insights, time had obscured and colored many of the author's memories, leaving the historical accuracy of some of his recollections in doubt. Custis's daughter Mary Anna married Robert E. Lee, who settled her in the elegant mansion that the federal government confiscated as a Civil War reparation and converted into the monumental centerpiece of Arlington National Cemetery.

George Washington bequeathed the Mansion and surrounding farm at Mount Vernon to his nephew United States Supreme Court justice Bushrod Washington, the son of Washington's beloved brother "Jack." Like his uncle George, Bushrod died without heirs and bequeathed it to his nephew John Augustine Washington, Jack's grandson. He, in turn, left the Mansion to his son, John Augustine Washington Jr., for whom it became too costly to maintain. Not only did he lack the skills in agronomy of his great-great-uncle, the swarms of visitors who had plagued Washington in the 1790s threatened to bankrupt him, and he appealed to Congress to buy it as a national monument. Congress refused, but a "Southern Matron" in South Carolina with a deep sense of patriotism issued a call "To the Ladies of the South" to "save American honor" by rescuing Mount Vernon from decay and ultimate destruction. Ann Pamela Cunningham formed the Ladies Association of Mount Vernon and, with help from former Massachusetts governor Edward Everett, raised $200,000 (equivalent to more than $4 million today) to purchase the Mansion and two hundred acres surrounding it from John Augustine Washington Jr. on April 6, 1858, and begin the restoration process that continues today.

Perhaps the most beautiful home in America, Mount Vernon remains in the hands of the Ladies Association, whose regent and vice regents across the nation volunteer the year around to maintain and restore the Mansion and grounds and search out and reacquire original furnishings.

With *no support* from either the state or national government, the Ladies Association also sponsors a wide-ranging and far-reaching educational program to restore to primacy in American schools the study of American history and the lives of Washington and the Founding Fathers.

Although George Washington had no issue, well over five thousand descendants of his extended family survive in virtually every state, occupation, and walk of life. Most of George Washington's immediate survivors remained farmers—as did more than 90 percent of the population of that time. Subsequent generations of Washingtons scattered across the nation, moving westward with other Americans along the ever-expanding frontier and entering every conceivable profession and occupation. By the end of the nineteenth century, their ranks represented a cross section of the American population, ranging from clergymen to coal miners. The twentieth century saw them produce Episcopal bishops, doctors, lawyers, authors, merchants, farmers, soldiers, war heroes, and average law-abiding citizens who differ from their neighbors only by their illustrious surname. Washington's nephew Bushrod was the sole Washington descendant to reach the highest ranks of government. All the rest were simply "Americans"—which, above all else, is what the private Washington actually was.

Notes

Introduction

1. George Washington (herein-after GW) to John Augustine Washington, July 18, 1755, in *The Papers of George Washington, Colonial Series, 1748–August 1755*, 10 vols., ed. W. W. Abbott and Dorothy Twohig (Charlottesville: University Press of Virginia, 1983–1995), 1:343.

2. GW to François-Jean de Beauvoir, Chevalier de Chastellux, April 25, 1788, in *The Papers of George Washington, Confederate Series, January 1784–July 1788*, 6 vols., ed. W. W. Abbott and Dorothy Twohig (Charlottesville: University Press of Virginia, 1992–1997), 6:227–230.

3. GW to Martha Washington, June 23, 1775, in *"Worthy Partner": The Papers of Martha Washington*, compiled by Joseph E. Fields (Westport, Connecticut: Greenwood Press, 1994), 161.

4. Mason L. Weems, *The Life of Washington* (Cambridge, Mass.: Harvard University Press, Belknap Press, 1962, reprint of ninth edition, in 1809, then titled *The Life of George Washington with Curious Anecdotes, Equally Honourable to Himself and Exemplary to His Young Countrymen*), 15–16. The book was originally published in 1800; Weems did not add the famous "cherry tree" fable until the fifth edition, in 1806. By 1825, when Weems died, twenty-nine "editions" had been published—many of them with so few changes that they merit the appellation of printings rather than editions. A century, thereafter, the total number of printings had reached eighty. The 1962 Harvard University Press edition was in its ninth printing in 1999.

Chapter 1. A Quest for Power and Glory

1. GW to John Augustine Washington, January 16, 1783, in *The Writings of George Washington, from the Original Manuscript Sources, 1745–1799*, 39 vols., ed. John C. Fitzpatrick (Washington, D.C.: U.S. Government Printing Office, 1931–1944), 26:43.

2. *Virginia Gazette*, August 25, 1774, cited in Freeman, *George Washington*, 1:92, 200.

3. GW to George William Fairfax, February 27, 1785, in *Writings*, Fitzpatrick, 28:83.

4. John J. McCusker, *How Much Is That in Real Money? A Historical Commodity Price Index for Use as a Deflator of Money Values in the Economy of the United States* (Worcester, Mass.: American Antiquarian Society, 2001), 34. Washington earned Virginia colonial pounds, each of which would be worth about $76 in today's currency.

5. Donald Jackson and Dorothy Twohig, eds., *The Diaries of George Washington*, 6 vols. (Charlottesville: University Press of Virginia, 1976–1979), 1:6.

6. GW to unknown recipient, n.d., in *Writings*, Fitzpatrick, 1:17.

7. Jackson and Twohig, *Diaries*, 1:9–11.

8. Release from Lawrence Washington, June 17, 1752, in *The Papers of George Washington, Colonial Series, 1748–August 1755*, 10 vols., ed. W. W. Abbott and Dorothy Twohig (Charlottesville: University Press of Virginia, 1983–1995), 1:51 (hereinafter *PGW, Col.*).

9. Jackson and Twohig, *Diaries*, 1:155.

10. GW to Horatio Sharpe, April 24, 1754, in *PGW, Col.* 1:85–86.

11. Jackson and Twohig, *Diaries*, 1:155.

12. Ibid.

13. Ibid., 1:156.

14. Ibid., 1:162.

15. Dinwiddie to GW, March 15, 1754, in *PGW, Col.* 1:75.

16. Jackson and Twohig, *Diaries*, 1:195.

17. GW to John Augustine Washington, May 31, 1754, in *PGW, Col.* 1:118.

18. Sarah Carlyle to GW, June 17, 1754, ibid., 1:145.

19. Daniel Campbell to GW, June 28, 1754, ibid., 1:151–152.

20. Dinwiddie to GW, June 1, 1754, ibid., 1:119–120.

21. GW to Dinwiddie, June 3, 1754, ibid., 1:122–125.

22. Fitzpatrick, *Writings*, 29:40.

23. GW to Robert Orme, March 15, 1755, in *PGW, Col.* 1:242–245.

24. Captain Robert Orme, aide-de-camp, to GW, March 2, 1755, ibid., 1:241.

25. Douglas Southall Freeman et al., *George Washington*, 7 vols. (New York: Charles Scribner's Sons, 1957), 2:21.

26. GW to William Byrd, April 20, 1755, in *PGW, Col.* 1:249–251.

27. GW to Carter Burwell, April 20, 1755, ibid., 1:252–253.

28. GW to John Robinson, April 20, 1755, ibid., 1:254–257.

29. GW to John Augustine Washington, May 28, 1755, ibid., 1:289–293.

30. Fitzpatrick, "Biographical Memoranda," October 1783, in *Writings*, 29:36–50, esp. 41–42.

31. Freeman, et al., *George Washington*, 2:64.

32. Ibid., 2:86.

33. Fitzpatrick, "Biographical Memoranda," *Writings*, 29:44.

34. GW to John Augustine Washington, July 18, 1755, in *PGW, Col.* 1:343.

35. William Fairfax to GW, July 26, 1755, ibid., 345–346.

36. S. Fairfax, Ann Spearing, Eliz[th] Dent to GW, July 26, 1755, ibid., 346.

37. Warner Lewis to GW, August 9, 1755, ibid., 358–359.

38. Philip Ludwell to GW, August 8, 1755, ibid., 358–359.

39. "Commission," August 14, 1755, ibid., 2:3–4.

40. GW "Address," January 8, 1756, ibid., 2:256–258.

41. Jared Sparks, *The Life of George Washington* (Boston: Tappan & Dennet, 1843), 72.

42. *Boston Gazette*, March 1, 1756, cited in Freeman et al., *George Washington*, 2:164.

43. *Virginia Gazette*, Williamsburg, no. IX, August 12, 1756.

44. GW to Robert Dinwiddie, October 10, 1756, ibid., 3:430–435.

45. Augustine Washington to GW, October 16, 1756, ibid., 3:435–437.

46. GW to John Stanwix, July 15, 1757, ibid., 3:306–308.

47. GW to Robert Dinwiddie, August 3, 1757, ibid., 3:359–361.

Chapter 2. An Agreeable Consort for Life

1. GW to Sarah Cary Fairfax, February 13, 1758, in *PGW, Col.* 5:93–94.

2. James Thomas Flexner, *Washington: The Indispensable Man* (Boston: Little, Brown, 1974), 134, citing Mercy Warren.

3. McCusker, *Real Money*, 34.

4. GW to Richard Washington, April 5, 1758, in *PGW Col.* 5:111–113.

5. April 7, 1760, ibid., 1:263.

6. GW to John Stanwix, April 10, 1758, ibid., 5:117–120.

7. GW to James Wood [c. July 28, 1758], ibid., 349.

8. George William Fairfax to GW, August 5, 1758, ibid., 371–373.

9. GW to Sarah Cary Fairfax, September 12, 1758, ibid., 6:10–13.

10. GW to Sarah Cary Fairfax, September 25, 1758, ibid., 41–43.

11. GW "Remarks, ibid., 122n.

12. Address from the Officers of the Virginia Regiment, December 31, 1758, ibid., 178–181.

13. To the Officers of the Virginia Regiment, n.d., ibid., 186–187.

14. Flexner, *Washington*, 42.

15. Resolution of the House of Burgesses, February 26, 1959, *PGW, Col.* 6:192–193.

16. Freeman et al., "Letter from George Mercer," *George Washington*, 3:6.

17. GW to John Alton, April 5, 1759, in *PGW, Col.* 6:200.

18. GW to Robert Cary & Co., May 1, 1759, ibid., 7:315–318.

19. Ibid.

20. GW to Richard Washington, May 7, 1759, ibid., 319–320.

21. Jackson and Twohig, *Diaries*, January 25, 1760, 1:228.

22. February 14–28, 1760, ibid., 238–248.

23. April 14, 1760, ibid., 266–267.

24. McCusker, *Real Money*, 34.

25. Judith S. Britt, *Nothing More Agreeable: Music in George Washington's Family* (Mount Vernon, Va.: The Mount Vernon Ladies Association, 1984), 14.

26. Jackson and Twohig, *Diaries*, March 25, 1760, 1:256.

27. GW to Robert Cary & Co., August 10, 1760, *PGW, Col.* 6:448–451.

28. Freeman et al., *George Washington*, 3:80.

29. Flexner, *Washington*, 42.

30. Freeman et al., *George Washington*, 3:79–80.

31. *PGW, Col.* 6:461–465.

32. Jackson and Twohig, *Diaries*, 1:283.

33. Guardian Accounts, *PGW, Col.* 7:86–93.

34. GW to Robert Cary & Co., November 3, 1762, ibid., 96–97.

35. Jackson and Twohig, *Diaries*, 1:299.

36. GW to Robert Cary & Co., November 15, 1762, in *PGW, Col.* 7:164–168.

37. GW to Robert Cary & Co., April 26, 1763, ibid., 202–205.

Chapter 3. "Fox Hunting . . . but Catchd Nothing"

1. GW to Robert Cary & Co., May 1, 1764, in *PGW, Col.* 7:305–306.

2. Ibid.

3. GW to Robert Cary & Co., September 20, 1765, ibid., 398–402.

4. Ibid.

5. Governor Francis Fauquier to the Lords of Trade, *Journ. House of Burgesses, 1761–65* (December 24, 1764):

303, cited in Freeman et al., *George Washington*, 3:123.

6. Martha Washington to GW, March 30, 1767, in Joseph E. Fields, *"Worthy Partner": The Papers of Martha Washington* (Westport, Conn.: Greenwood Press, 1994), 149.

7. Lund Washington to GW, August 17, 1767, ibid., 17–19; August 22, 1767, ibid., 19–20; September 5, 1767, ibid., 25–26.

8. GW to William Crawford, September 17, 1767, ibid., 26–32.

9. Jackson and Twohig, *Diaries*, 2:36–37.

10. GW to Scott, Pringle, Cheap, & Co., February 23, 1768, in *PGW, Col.* 8:68–69. They were wine merchants who drew from Washington's account with Cary & Co., which combined the wines with its own shipment to Washington.

11. GW to Jonathan Boucher, May 30, 1768, in *PGW, Col.* 8:89–91.

12. Jonathan Boucher to GW, June 16, 1768, ibid., 96–97.

13. Jackson and Twohig, *Diaries*, 2:61–67.

14. GW to Robert Cary & Co., June 6, 1768, in *PGW, Col.* 8:92–94.

15. Jonathan Boucher to GW, August 2, 1768, ibid., 122–125.

16. Jackson and Twohig, *Diaries*, 2:139.

Chapter 4. A Death in the Family

1. GW to George Mason, April 5, 1769, in *PGW, Col.* 8:177–181.

2. *Journal, House of Burgesses, 1766–1769*, 189, cited in Freeman et al., *George Washington*, 3:217.

3. Ibid., 218, in Freeman et al., *George Washington*, 3:221.

4. Harlow Giles Unger, *John Hancock: Merchant King and American Patriot* (New York: John Wiley & Sons, 2000), 114, citing *"Letters of a Farmer in Pennsylvania to the Inhabitants of the British Colonies,"* in *Pennsylvania Chronicle and Universal Advertiser*, December 2 and 12, 1767, and February 15, 1768.

5. Jackson and Twohig, *Diaries*, 2:156–157.

6. GW to Robert Cary & Co., July 25, 1769, in *PGW, Col.* 8:229–233.

7. "Advertisement," *Virginia Gazette*, Williamsburg, December 21 and 28, 1769, ibid., 280.

8. GW to Charles Washington, January 31, 1770, ibid., 300–304.

9. Invoice to Robert Cary & Co., July 18, 1771, ibid., 508–511.

10. Jackson and Twohig, *Diaries*, 2:235.

11. Freeman et al., *George Washington*, 3:185.

12. Ibid., 257–258.

13. Jackson and Twohig, *Diaries*, 2:309.

14. Ibid., 316.

15. Boucher to GW, December 17, 1770, in *PGW, Col.* 8:413–417.

16. GW to Boucher, January 21, 1771, ibid., 425–426.

17. Jackson and Twohig, *Diaries*, 3:73.

18. Ibid., 85.

19. GW to Jonathan Boucher, May 5, 1772, in *PGW, Col.* 8:40–41.

20. GW to Jonathan Boucher, May 21, 1772, ibid., 49–50.

21. GW to Daniel Jenifer Adams, July 20, 1772, ibid., 69–70.

22. GW to Benedict Calvert, April 3, 1773, ibid., 209–211.

23. Benedict Calvert to GW, April 8, 1773, ibid., 215–216.

24. Jackson and Twohig, *Diaries*, 3:183.

25. Ibid., 188.

26. GW to Burwell Bassett, June 20, 1773, in *PGW, Col.* 9:243–244.

27. John Parke Custis to GW, July 5, 1773, ibid., 264–267.

28. GW to Myles Cooper, December 15, 1773, ibid., 406–407.

29. William Crawford to GW, December 29, 1773, ibid., 418–421.

Chapter 5. The Glorious Cause

1. Unger, *John Hancock*, 174.

2. Jackson and Twohig, *Diaries*, 3:221n., citing George Washington Parke Custis, *Recollections and Private Memoirs of Washington* (New York: Derby & Jackson, 1860), 519.

3. Benson J. Lossing, *Mary and Martha, the Mother and the Wife of George Washington* (New York: Harper & Brothers, 1886), 126. The letter may have been an invention of Lossing, a romantic writer who claims it "was preserved by the family of her grandson, at Arlington House, so late as 1860, when I made the following copy from the original." Subsequent historians claim that if it existed, it was a forgery. "It is almost certainly forged," wrote Freeman et al. in *George Washington* 3:344n., for example. "None of Martha's surviving letters suggests the style or diction of this document." Philander D. Chase, longtime editor in chief of *The Papers of George Washington*, says he, too, finds "the authenticity of the letter to be very doubtful." I have no basis to disagree with such authorities, but suggest only that Martha almost certainly sent a note to Nelly to explain her absence and Lossing's letter—invented or forged—must certainly *reflect* Martha's sentiments at the time. For that reason alone, I have included it here.

4. Valentine Crawford to GW, May 6, 1774, in *PGW, Col.* 10:50–52.

5. Valentine Crawford to GW, May 7, 1774, ibid., 52–53.

6. Jackson and Twohig, *Diaries*, 3:250.

7. Ibid., xiii–xiv.

8. Bryan Fairfax to GW, July 3, 1774, in *PGW, Col.* 10:106–109. GW to Bryan Fairfax, July 4, 1774, *Col.* 10:109–111.

9. Valentine Crawford to GW, June 8, 1774, in *PGW, Col.* 10:88–91; William Crawford to GW, June 8, 1774, in *Col.* 10:93–94.

10. GW to George William Fairfax, June 10–15, 1774, in *PGW, Col.* 10:94–101.

11. William Wirt Henry, *Patrick Henry: Life, Correspondence and Speeches*, 3 vols. (New York: Charles Scribner's Sons, 1891), 1:213.

12. Bryan Fairfax to GW, July 17, 1774, in *PGW, Col.* 10:114–119; GW to Bryan Fairfax, July 20, 1774, *Col.* 10:128–131.

13. Jackson and Twohig, *Diaries*, 3:278n., from *Pennsylvania Packet*, September 19, 1774.

14. Freeman et al., *George Washington*, 3:377n., citing E. C. Burnett, ed., Silas Deane to Mrs. Deane, September 10, 1774, *Letters of Members of the Continental Congress*, 8 vols. (1921–1928), 1:28.

15. L. H. Butterfield, ed., *The Adams Papers: Diary & Autobiography of John Adams*, 4 vols. (New York: Atheneum, 1964), 2:117.

16. John Ferling, *John Adams: A Life* (New York: Henry Holt, 1992), 53.

17. GW to Robert McKenzie, October 9, 1744, *PGW, Col.* 10:171–172.

18. Jackson and Twohig, *Diaries*, 3:285.

19. John Adams to Mrs. Adams, September 25, 1774, in Freeman et al., *George Washington*, 3:385, citing Burnett, *Letters*, 1:47.

20. Jackson and Twohig, *Diaries*, 3:285n., citing J. Thomas Scharf and Thompson Westcott, *History of Philadelphia, 1709–1884*, 3 vols. (Philadelphia: L. H. Everts & Co., 1884), 1:235.

21. Jackson and Twohig, *Diaries*, 3:319.

22. GW to John Augustine Washington, March 25, 1775, in *PGW, Col.* 10:308–309.

23. Lord Dunmore to GW, April 18, 1775, ibid., 337–338.

24. James Cleveland to GW, May 12, 1775, ibid., 359–363.

25. GW to George William Fairfax, May 31, 1775, ibid., 367–368.

26. Freeman et al., *George Washington*, 3:426, citing Burnett, *Letters*, 1:102.

27. Freeman et al., *George Washington*, 2:67, citing Worthington C. Ford et al., eds., *Journals of the Continental Congress*, 34 vols. (Washington, D.C.: U.S. Government Printing Office).

28. Butterfield, *Adams*, 3:324–325.

29. Address to the Continental Congress, June 16, 1775, in W. W. Abbott, Dorothy Twohig, and Philander D. Chase, eds., *The Papers of George Washington, Revolutionary War Series, June 1775–April 1778* [in progress] 14 vols. (Charlottesville: University of Virginia Press, 1984–2004), 1:1–3 (hereinafter *PGW, Rev.*).

30. Ferling, *John Adams*, 127, citing Robert J. Taylor et al., eds., *Papers of John Adams*, 10 vols. (Cambridge, Mass.: Harvard University Press, Belknap Press, 1977–1983), 3:26.

31. Commission from the Continental Congress, June 19, 1775, *PGW, Rev.* 1:6–7.

32. GW to Martha Washington, June 18, 1775, ibid., 3–5.

33. Ibid.

34. GW to Burwell Bassett, June 19, 1775, ibid., 12–14.

35. GW to John Parke Custis, June 19, 1775, ibid., 15–16.

36. GW to John Augustine Washington, June 20, 1775, ibid., 19–20.

37. GW to Martha Washington, June 23, 1775, ibid., 27–28.

Chapter 6. "The Fate of Unborn Millions"

1. Freeman et al., *George Washington*, 3:515n.

2. Lund Washington to GW, October 5, 1775, in *PGW, Rev.* 2:115–117.

3. Martha Washington to Elizabeth Ramsay, December 30, 1775, in Fields, *"Worthy Partner,"* 164.

4. Ibid.

5. Mercy Warren to Abigail Adams, April 17, 1776, in *PGW, Rev.* 3:75n.

6. Fields, *"Worthy Partner,"* 164.

7. GW to Lund Washington, November 26, 1775, in *PGW, Rev.* 2:431–433.

8. Lund Washington to GW, January 17, 1776, ibid., 126–132.

9. Lund Washington to GW, March 7, 1776, ibid., 431–433.

10. John Parke Custis to GW, June 10, 1776, ibid., 4:484–486.

11. Martha Washington to Anna Maria Dandridge Bassett, August 28, 1776, in Fields, *"Worthy Partner,"* 172.

12. John Parke Custis to GW, June 10, 1776, in *PGW, Rev.* 4:484–486.

13. John Parke Custis to Martha Washington, June 9, 1776, ibid., 485n.–486n.

14. General Orders, July 2, 1776, in *PGW, Rev.* 5:179–182.

15. John Parke Custis to Martha Washington, August 21, 1776, in Fields, *"Worthy Partner,"* 170–171.

16. GW to Lund Washington, August 19, 1776, in *PGW, Rev.* 6:82–87.

17. September 30, 1776, ibid., 440–443.

18. GW to John Augustine Washington, November 6–19, 1776, ibid., 7:102–105.

19. GW to Lund Washington, December 10–17, 1776, ibid., 289–292.

20. Freeman et al., *George Washington*, 4:413.

21. GW to Samuel Washington, April 5, 1777, in *PGW, Rev.* 9:71–73.

22. GW to John Augustine Washington, April 12, 1777, ibid., 144–145.

23. Ron Chernow, *Alexander Hamilton* (New York: Penguin, 2004), 91.

24. Ibid., 87.

25. Harlow Giles Unger, *Lafayette* (Hoboken, N.J.: John Wiley & Sons, 2002), 41, citing George-Washington Lafayette [Gilbert Motier, marquis de La Fayette], *Mémoires, Correspondence, et Manuscrits du Général Lafayette, publiés par sa famille*, 6 vols. (Paris: H. Fournier, aîné, 1837).

26. Unger, *Lafayette*, 46.

27. Friedrich Kapp, *The Life of John Kalb, Major-General in the Revolutionary Army* (New York: Henry Holt, 1884), 137.

28. Martha Washington to Burwell Bassett, December 22, 1777, in Fields, "Worthy Partner," 175–177.

29. Lund Washington to GW, December 24, 1777, in *PGW, Rev.* 12:698–700.

30. Lossing, *Mary and Martha*, 168–171.

31. Lafayette to GW, December 30, 1777, in William A. Duer, ed., *Memoirs, Correspondence of General Lafayette, Published by his Family* (New York: Saunders and Otley Ann Street, 1837), 139–140.

32. Ibid.

33. GW to Major General Lafayette, December 31, 1777, in *PGW, Rev.* 13:83–84.

34. Lund Washington to GW, April 8, 1778, ibid., 14:429–431. The words cited are Lund's, but he is actually quoting GW's instructions from a previous GW letter.

35. Freeman et al., *George Washington*, 5:1.

36. Kapp, *John Kalb*, 158–159.

Chapter 7. An Affectionate Friend

1. Benson Bobrick, *Angel in the Whirlwind: The Triumph of the American Revolution* (New York: Simon & Schuster, 1997), 345.

2. George Washington Parke Custis, *Recollections*, 220.

3. Lafayette, Mémoires, 1:26.

4. Chernow, *Alexander Hamilton*, 114–115.

5. GW to John Augustine Washington, July 4, 1778, in Fitzpatrick, *Writings*, 12:156–158.

6. Freeman et al., *George Washington*, 5:93, citing Ford et al., eds., *Journals*, 13:110.

7. Freeman et al., *George Washington*, 5:39–40.

8. Unger, *Lafayette*, 92.

9. John Parke Custis to GW, September 11, 1777, in *PGW, Rev.* 11:201–204.

10. GW to John Parke Custis, October 10, 1778, in Fitzpatrick, *Writings*, 13:56–59.

11. GW to Marquis de Lafayette, July 4, 1779, ibid., 15:369–370.

12. GW to Marquis de Lafayette, September 30, 1779, ibid., 16:368–376.

13. Ibid.

14. GW to John Parke Custis, August 24, 1779, ibid., 16:164–168.

15. Jackson and Twohig, *Diaries*, 3:340–341.

16. GW to Philip Schuyler, January 30, 1780, in Fitzpatrick, *Writings*, 17:464–468.

17. Duer, *Memoirs*, 318.

18. GW to Marquis de Lafayette, May 8, 1780, in Fitzpatrick, *Writings*, 18:341.

19. Lafayette, *Mémoires*, 1:92–93.

20. GW to Lund Washington, May 31, 1781, in Fitzpatrick, *Writings*, 22:145.

21. GW to Lund Washington, April 30, 1781, ibid., 14–15.

22. GW to Colonel William Crawford, June 9, 1781, ibid., 194–196.

23. Ibid.

24. GW to Dr. John Baker, ibid., 129.

25. Freeman et al., *George Washington*, 5:327, citing *Jonathan Trumbull's Minutes*.

26. Freeman et al., *George Washington*, 5:427.

27. GW to the President of Congress, October 19, 1781, in Fitzpatrick, *Writings*, 23:241.

28. Jackson and Twohig, *Diaries*, 3:437n–438n.

Chapter 8. The Long Journey Home

1. GW to Secretary for Foreign Affairs [Robert Livingston], June 5, 1782, in Fitzpatrick, *Writings*, 24:315.

2. GW to Marquis de Lafayette, October 20, 1782, ibid., 25:278–281.

3. GW to Lund Washington, December 25, 1782, ibid., 470–473.

4. GW to David Rittenhouse, February 16, 1783, ibid., 26:136–137.

5. GW to Bartholomew Dandridge, June 25, 1782, ibid., 24:386–387.

6. GW to John Augustine Washington, January 16, 1783, ibid., 26:41–45.

7. GW to Bushrod Washington, November 17, 1788, ibid., 30:126–128.

8. Freeman et al., *George Washington*, 5:281.

9. GW to John Augustine Washington, January 16, 1783, in Fitzpatrick, *Writings*, 26:41–45.

10. GW to Bushrod Washington, January 15, 1783, ibid., 38–40.

11. GW to Marquis de Lafayette, March 23, 1783, ibid., 251–255.

12. Lafayette to GW, April 5, 1783, in Unger, *Lafayette*, 172–173.

13. Ibid.

14. GW to Marquis de Lafayette, April 5, 1783, in Fitzpatrick, *Writings*, 26:297–301.

15. GW to Charles Crookshanks & Company, May 15, 1783, ibid., 431.

16. GW to Lieutenant Colonel William Stephens Smith, May 15, 1783, ibid., 433–435.

17. GW to Boinod & Gaillard, February 18, 1784, in W. W. Abbott and Dorothy Twohig, eds., *The Papers of George Washington, Confederation Series,*

January 1784–September 1788, 6 vols. (Charlottesville: University Press of Virginia, 1992–1997), 1:126–127 (hereinafter *PGW, Confed.*).

18. GW to Barbé Marbois, July 9, 1783, in Fitzpatrick, *Writings*, 27:54–56.

19. Freeman et al., *George Washington*, 5:453, citing Rhode Island congressman David Howell in Edmund C. Burnett, ed., *Letters of Members of the Continental Congress*, 8 vols. (Washington, D.C., 1921–1926).

20. GW Circular to the States, June 8, 1783, in Fitzpatrick, *Writings*, 26:483–496.

21. GW to Daniel Parker, September 12, 1783, ibid., 27:150–151.

22. GW to Bushrod Washington, September 22, 1783, ibid., 160–161.

23. GW to Marquis de Lafayette, October 30, 1783, ibid., 215–218.

24. GW to George William Fairfax, July 10, 1783, ibid., 57–60.

25. GW to Marquis de Lafayette, December 4, 1783, ibid., 258–259.

26. John Marshall, *Life of Washington*, 5 vols. (Philadelphia: C. P. Wayne, 1804–1807), 2:57.

27. James Tilton to Gunning Bedford, December 25, 1783, in Fitzpatrick, *Writings*, 27:285n.

28. GW Address to Congress on Resigning His Commission, December 23, 1783, ibid., 284–285.

29. James Tilton to Gunning Bedford, December 25, 1783, ibid., 285n.

Chapter 9. A Broken Promise

1. GW to Lafayette, February 1, 1784, in *PGW, Confed.* 1:87–90.

2. Martha Washington to Hannah Stockton Boudinot, January 15, 1784, in Fields, "*Worthy Partner*," 193.

3. GW to John McDowell, March 5, 1798, in Fitzpatrick, *Writings*, 36:180–181.

4. GW to Benjamin Harrison, October 10, 1784, in *PGW, Confed.* 2:80–99.

5. GW to Lafayette, April 4, 1784, in *PGW, Confed.* 1:256–257.

6. Anastasie Lafayette, June 18, 1784, ibid., 456.

7. Lafayette to Adrienne, August 20, 1784, in Stanley J. Idzerda and Robert Rhodes Crout, eds., *Lafayette in the Age of the American Revolution: Selected Letters and Papers, 1776–1790*, 5 vols. (Ithaca, N.Y.: Cornell University Press, 1983), 5:403–404.

8. GW to Lafayette, July 25, 1785, in *PGW, Confed.* 3:151–155.

9. GW to Adrienne, Marquise de Lafayette, November 25, 1784, ibid., 2:150–151.

10. GW to Anastasie de Lafayette, November 25, 1784, ibid., 150.

11. GW to Lafayette, December 8, 1784, ibid., 175–176.

12. Jean Le Mayeur to GW, January 20, 1784, ibid., 1:64–65.

13. Jackson and Twohig, *Diaries*, 4:193–194n., citing *Virginia Magazine* 10 (1902–1903):325.

14. James Madison to Thomas Jefferson, January 9, 1784, in Freeman et al., *George Washington*, 4:27, citing *The Papers of James Madison*, 16 vols. (Charlottesville: University Press of Virginia, 1984–1989), 5:59.

15. GW to Mary Ball Washington, February 15, 1787, in *PGW, Confed.* 5:33–37.

16. Freeman et al., *George Washington*, 6:35, citing Wright and Tinling, eds., *Quebec to Carolina in 1785–1786, Being the Travel Diary and Observations of Robert Hunter, Jr., a Young Merchant of London*, 194.

17. Ibid., 6:36–37, citing Winslow C. Watson, ed., *Men and Times of the Revolution; or Memoirs of Elkanah Watson, Including Journals of Travels in Europe and America from 1777 to 1842* (New York, 1856), 243–244.

18. June 30, 1785, in Jackson and Twohig, *Diaries*, 6:157.

19. Freeman et al., *George Washington*, 6:37, citing Watson, *Men and Times*, 243–244.

20. GW to Francis Hopkinson, May 16, 1785, in *PGW, Confed.* 2:261–262.

21. Jackson and Twohig, *Diaries*, 6:135.

22. Freeman et al., *George Washington*, 6:44.

23. Benjamin Lincoln to GW, January 4, 1786, in *PGW, Confed.* 3:492–493.

24. George William Fairfax to GW, January 23, 1786, ibid., 517–521.

25. GW to John Beale Bordley, August 17, 1788, ibid., 6:450–454.

26. GW to William Pearce, October 6, 1793, in Fitzpatrick, *Writings*, 33:110–112.

27. GW to William Pearce, June 5, 1796, ibid., 35:79–82.

28. GW to Lafayette, May 10, 1786, in *PGW, Confed.* 4:41–45.

29. GW to Bushrod Washington, April 13, 1786, ibid., 18.

30. GW to Arthur Young, December 4, 1788, in W. W. Abbott, Dorothy Twohig, Philander D. Chase, eds., *The Papers of George Washington, Presidential Series, September 1788–May 1793*, 12 vols. [in progress] (Charlottesville: University Press of Virginia—University of Virginia Press, 1987–2005), 1:159–163 (hereinafter *PGW, Pres.*).

31. *Pennsylvania Packet*, March 7, 1786, in *PGW Confed.* 3:571–572.

32. GW to Charles Washington, February 14, 1787, ibid., 5:28–29.

33. John Jay to GW, March 16, 1786, ibid., 3:601–602.

34. GW to John Jay, May 18, 1786, ibid., 4:55–56.

35. GW to John Jay, August 15, 1786, ibid., 212–213.

36. GW to Jeremiah Wadsworth (Greene executor), October 22, 1786, ibid., 298–299.

37. Jackson and Twohig, *Diaries*, 5:93.

Chapter 10. *"God Bless Our Washington!"*

1. Henry Knox to GW, April 9, 1787, in *PGW, Confed.* 5:133–135.

2. Henry Knox to GW, March 19, 1787, ibid., 95–98.

3. GW to George Augustine Washington, May 17, 1787, ibid., 189.

4. GW to Alexander Hamilton, July 10, 1787, ibid., 257.

5. GW to George Augustine Washington, May 27, 1787, ibid., 196–199.

6. Jackson and Twohig, *Diaries*, 5:166–167.

7. Martha Washington to Fanny Bassett Washington, February 15, 1788, in Fields, *"Worthy Partner,"* 205–207.

8. William McWhir to GW, March 8, 1788, in *PGW, Confed.* 6:148.

9. Samuel Hanson to GW, March 16, 1788, ibid., 157–160.

10. GW to George Steptoe Washington, May 5, 1788, ibid., 262–263.

11. GW to Richard Conway, March 6, 1789, ibid., *Pres.* 1:368–369.

12. GW to Samuel Hanson, August 6, 1788, ibid., *Confed.* 6:429–430.

13. GW to George Steptoe Washington, August 6, 1788, ibid., 430–431.

14. John Jay to GW, April 20, 1788, ibid., 217.

15. Benjamin Rush to GW, April 26, 1788, ibid., 230–231.

16. GW to Dr. James Anderson, December 24, 1795, in Fitzpatrick, *Writings*, 34:405–410.

17. Gouverneur Morris to GW, November 12, 1788, in *PGW, Pres.* 1:103–105.

18. Alexander Hamilton to GW, September [30], 1788, ibid., 23–25.

19. Samuel Hanson, February 19, 1789, ibid., 321–322.

20. GW to George Steptoe Washington, March 23, 1789, ibid., 438–441.

21. GW to George Augustine Washington, March 31, 1789, ibid., 472–476.

22. John Langdon to GW, April 6, 1789, ibid., 2:29.

23. GW Address to Charles Thomson, April 14, 1789, ibid., 56–57. The address quoted is one of many similar drafts written with Tobias Lear. Historians are unsure which was the one he read to Thomson. Although they differ little in intent, all the different wordings are published in *PGW, Pres.* 2:56n. and 2:57n.

24. Martha Washington to John Dandridge, April 20, 1789, in Fields, *"Worthy Partner,"* 213–214.

25. Jackson and Twohig, *Diaries*, 5:445.

26. GW to Edward Rutledge, May 5, 1789, in *PGW, Pres.*2:217–218.

27. Ibid., 154–155, Tobias Lear's diary entry for April 30, 1789, cited in editor's introductory notes, "First Inaugural Address," and presumably drawn from Stephen Decatur Jr., *Private Affairs of George Washington, from the Records and Accounts of Tobias Lear, Esquire, His Secretary* (Boston, 1933).

28. Ibid.

29. Ibid.

30. Introductory notes to "First Inaugural Address," ibid., 155–157, citing Fisher Ames to George Richard Minot, May 3, 1789, in Ames, *Works of Fisher Ames*, 1:34–36; "one Philadelphia gentleman," in *Historical Magazine*, 3:184 (1859); and William Maclay, *Journal*, 9.

31. "First Inaugural Address," April 30, 1789, ibid., 152–177.

32. Martha Washington to Fanny Bassett Washington, June 8, 1789, in Fields, "Worthy Partner," 215–216.

33. Ibid.

34. Freeman et al., George Washington, 6:211.

35. Daily Advertiser, June 15, 1789, as cited in Freeman, ibid., 6:213.

36. Freeman et al., George Washington, 6:213, citing Abigail Adams to her sister Mary Cranch, June 28, 1789, in Stewart Mitchell, ed., New Letters of Abigail Adams, 1788–1801.

37. Freeman et al., George Washington, 6:213–214.

38. Martha Washington to Fanny Bassett Washington, summer 1789, in Fields, "Worthy Partner," 217.

39. Britt, Nothing More Agreeable, 30.

40. James Craik to GW, August 24, 1789, in PGW, Pres. 3:529–531.

41. GW to Betty Washington Lewis, September 13, 1789, ibid.; 4:32–36.

42. GW to Wakelin Welch & Son, August 16, 1789, ibid., 3:478–479.

43. October 5, 1789, in Jackson and Twohig, Diaries, 5:452–453.

44. GW to Lafayette, October 14, 1789, in PGW, Pres. 4:191–192.

45. Ibid.

46. Jackson and Twohig, Diaries, 5:479–480.

47. Ibid., 470–471.

48. GW to William Washington, January 8, 1791, in PGW, Pres. 7:211–213.

49. Independent Chronicle, November 27, 1789, p. 3.

50. Martha Washington to Fanny Bassett Washington, October 23, 1789, in Fields, "Worthy Partner," 219–220.

51. Martha Washington to Mercy Otis Warren, December 26, 1789, ibid., 223–224.

Chapter 11. "Tranquillity Reigns"

1. Jackson and Twohig, Diaries, 6:1.

2. Ibid., 6:5, 6, 9, 13.

3. John Adams to Abigail Adams, December 19, 1793, in John Bartlett, Familiar Quotations, 16th ed. (Boston: Little, Brown, 1992), 338:12.

4. Lafayette to GW, March 17, 1790, in PGW, Pres. 5:241–243.

5. GW to Lafayette, August 11, 1790, ibid., 6:233–235.

6. Harriot Washington to GW, April 2, 1790, ibid., 5:310–311.

7. Thomas Jefferson to his daughter Martha Jefferson Randolph, May 16, 1790, cited in Jackson and Twohig, Diaries, 77n., in Julian P. Boyd et al., eds., The Papers of Thomas Jefferson, 34 vols. [in progress] (Princeton, N.J.: Princeton University Press, 1950–   ), 16:429.

8. S. Ogden to Henry Knox, May 22, 1790, in Freeman et al., George Washington, 6:260n.

9. Boyd et al., Papers, 16:429.

10. Martha Washington to Mercy Otis Warren, June 12, 1790, in Fields, "Worthy Partner," 225–227.

11. Ibid.

12. Moses Seixas, warden of the Congregation of Yeshuat Israel of Newport, to GW, August 17, 1790, in PGW, Pres. 6:286n.

13. GW to the Hebrew congregation in Newport, Rhode Island, August 18, 1790, ibid., 284–286.

14. GW to George Steptoe Washington, December 5, 1790, ibid., 7:31–34.

15. GW to David Humphreys, July 20, 1791, ibid., 8:358–361.

16. GW to Lafayette, June 10, 1792, ibid., 10:4446–448.

17. GW to Tobias Lear, April 12, 1791, ibid., 8:84–86.

18. Tobias Lear to GW, April 24, 1791, ibid., 129–134.

Chapter 12. The Voice of Your Country

1. Thomas Jefferson to GW, May 23, 1792, in *PGW, Pres.* 10:408–414.

2. Harriot Washington to GW, May 28, 1792, ibid., 425–426.

3. Martha Washington to Fanny Bassett Washington, July 1, 1792, in Fields, *"Worthy Partner,"* 238–239.

4. Ibid.

5. Freeman et al., *George Washington*, 6:362, citing Henry Knox *Papers*, Massachusetts Historical Society.

6. Alexander Hamilton to GW, July 30–August 3, 1792, in *PGW, Pres.* 10:594–596.

7. GW to Thomas Jefferson, August 23, 1792, ibid., 11:28–32.

8. GW to Alexander Hamilton, August 26, 1792, ibid., 38–40.

9. Tobias Lear to GW, October 7, 1792, ibid., 198–201.

10. Alan and Donna Jean Fusonie, *George Washington, Pioneer Farmer* (Mount Vernon, Va.: Mount Vernon Ladies Association, 1998), 22.

11. GW to William Pearce, February 16, 1794, in Fitzpatrick, *Writings*, 33:268–271.

12. Directive to John Christian Ebbers, November 7, 1792, in *PGW, Pres.* 11:351–356.

13. GW to Anthony Whitting, November 25, 1792, ibid., 439–443.

14. Marquise de Lafayette to GW, October 8, 1792, ibid., 204–207.

15. Enclosure to the Marquise de Lafayette, January 31, 1793, ibid., 12:75–76.

16. Freeman et al., *George Washington*, 6:384n, citing William S. Baker, *Washington after the Revolution, 1784–1799* (Philadelphia: J. B. Lippincott, 1898), 250–251.

17. Anthony Whitting to GW, January 16, 1793, in *PGW, Pres.* 12:5–14.

18. Ibid.

19. GW to George Augustine Washington, January 27, 1793, ibid., 53–54.

20. Martha Washington to Fanny Bassett Washington, February 18, 1793, in Fields, *"Worthy Partner,"* 244.

21. GW to Frances Bassett Washington, February 24, 1793, in *PGW, Pres.* 12:210–211.

22. Freeman et al., *George Washington*, 7:6, citing *National Gazette*, February 27, 1793.

23. Second Inaugural Address, March 4, 1792, in *PGW, Pres.* 12:264–265.

24. GW to Frances Bassett Washington, March 17, 1793, ibid., 338–340.

25. Frances Bassett Washington to GW, March 28, 1793, ibid., 387–390.

26. Britt, *Nothing More Agreeable*, 44.

27. To the Provisional Executive Council of France, May 24, 1793, in *PGW, Pres.* 12:624–626n.

28. Meade Minnigerode, *Jefferson—Friend of France 1793: The Career of Edmond Charles Genet* (New York: G. P. Putnam's Sons, 1928), 184.

29. GW to the secretary of state, July 11, 1793, in Fitzpatrick, *Writings*, 33:4.

30. John Adams to Thomas Jefferson, June 13, 1813, in Lester J. Cappon, ed., *The Adams-Jefferson Letters: The Complete Correspondence between Thomas Jefferson and Abigail and John Adams* (Chapel Hill: University of North Carolina Press, 1959), 346.

31. Martha Washington to Fanny Bassett Washington, August 4, 1793, in Fields, *"Worthy Partner,"* 250.

32. GW to Tobias Lear, September 25, 1793, in Fitzpatrick, *Writings*, 33:104–106.

33. Martha Washington to Fanny Bassett Washington, January 14, 1794, in Fields, *"Worthy Partner,"* 254–255.

34. GW to Reverend James Muir, February 24, 1794, in Fitzpatrick, *Writings*, 33:281–282.

35. *Kentucky Gazette* (Lexington), April 5, 1794.

36. Martha Washington to Fanny Bassett Washington, September 29, 1794, in Fields, *"Worthy Partner,"* 276–277.

37. Freeman et al., *George Washington*, 7:210, citing William Spohn Baker, *Washington after the Revolution, 1784–1789* (Philadelphia, 1898), 289–290, which refers to "Diary of Robert Wellford," *William and Mary Quarterly*, First Series, 2 (1902):1–19.

38. Martha Washington to Fanny Bassett Washington, November 11, 1794, in Fields, *"Worthy Partner,"* 279–280.

39. Freeman et al., *George Washington*, 7:231, citing Fisher Ames to Christopher Gore, January 10, 1795, in Seth Ames, ed., *Works of Fisher Ames*, 2 vols. (Boston, 1854), 1:161.

40. GW to Edmund Pendleton, January 22, 1795, in Fitzpatrick, *Writings*, 34:98–101.

Chapter 13. Vine and Fig Tree Revisited

1. Alexander DeConde, *Entangling Alliance* (Durham, N.C.: Duke University Press, 1958), 427n., citing "Americanus" in the *Independent Gazeteer*; cited and reprinted in the *Virginia Herald and Fredericksburg Advertiser*, July 24, 1795.

2. GW to George Cabot, September 7, 1795, in Fitzpatrick, *Writings*, 34:299–301.

3. GW to Alexander Hamilton, November 18, 1795, ibid., 364.

4. Alexander Hamilton to GW, November 19, 1795, ibid., 364n.

5. GW to George-Washington Motier Lafayette, November 22, 1795, ibid., 367–368.

6. GW to Alexander Hamilton, November 23, 1795, ibid., 374–376.

7. GW to Alexander Hamilton, December 22, 1795, ibid., 404.

8. Alexander Hamilton to GW, December 24, 1795, ibid., 404n.

9. GW to George-Washington Motier Lafayette, February 28, 1796, ibid., 478.

10. GW to George-Washington Motier Lafayette, March 31, 1796, ibid., 35:8.

11. GW to William Pearce, June 5, 1796, ibid., 79–82.

12. GW to the secretary of war [James McHenry], May 29, 1797, ibid., 455–456.

13. Ibid.

14. Ibid.

15. Benjamin H. Latrobe's diary, July 16, 1796, ibid., 141n–142n.

16. GW to the secretary of war, July 18, 1796, ibid., 146–148.

17. Britt, *Nothing More Agreeable*, 52.

18. Farewell Address, September 19, 1796, in Fitzpatrick, *Writings*, 35:214–238.

19. GW to Washington Parke Custis, November 15, 1796, ibid., 281–283.

20. Eighth Annual Address to Congress, December 7, 1796, ibid., 310–320.

21. *Philadelphia Aurora*, December 21 and 23, 1796, in Donald H. Stewart, *The Opposition Press of the Federalist Period* (Albany: State University of New York Press, 1969), 533.

22. Freeman et al., *George Washington*, 7:432, citing Judge Airedale to Mrs. Airedale, February 24, 1797.

23. GW to George Washington Parke Custis, February 27, 1797, in Fitzpatrick, *Writings*, 35:402–404.

24. GW to John McDowell, March 5, 1798, ibid., 36:180–181.

25. GW to the vice president, February 20, 1797, ibid., 35:394.

26. GW to Henry Knox, March 2, 1797, ibid., 408–410.

27. Freeman et al., *George Washington*, 7:436, citing the recollections of Philadelphia's bishop William White in William Spohn Baker, *Washington after the Revolution, 1784–1799* (Philadelphia: J. B. Lippincott, 1898), 343.

28. Freeman et al., *George Washington*, 7:457, citing John Adams to Abigail Adams, March 5, 1797, in Charles Francis Adams, ed., *Letters of John Adams Addressed to His Wife*, 2 vols. (Boston: 1841), 2:244.

29. Stewart, *The Opposition Press*, 533–534, citing *Philadelphia Aurora*, March 5, 1797.

30. Elizabeth Willing Powel to GW, March 11 [13], 1797, in *The Papers of George Washington, Retirement Series, March 1797–December 1799*, 4 vols., ed. Dorothy Twohig (Charlottesville: University Press of Virginia, 1998–1999), 1:28–30 (hereinafter *PGW, Ret.*).

31. GW to Elizabeth Willing Powel, March 26, 1797, ibid., 51–53.

32. Ibid.

33. George Washington Parke Custis to GW, March 25, 1797, ibid., 48–50.

34. GW to George Washington Parke Custis, April 3, 1797, ibid., 69–70.

35. Martha Washington to Lucy Flucker Knox, n.d., in Fields, *"Worthy Partner,"* 304–305.

36. GW to Samuel Stanhope Smith, May 24, 1797, in *PGW, Ret.* 1:153–154.

37. George Washington Parke Custis to GW, May 29, 1797, ibid., 158–159.

38. GW to George Washington Parke Custis, June 4, 1797, ibid., 168–169.

39. GW to Lawrence Lewis, August 4, 1797, ibid., 288–289.

40. GW to George Washington Parke Custis, August 29, 1797, ibid., 325–326.

41. GW to Lafayette, October 8, 1797, ibid., 390–391.

42. George-Washington Motier Lafayette to GW, October 22, 1797, ibid., 421.

Chapter 14. "First in the Hearts of His Countrymen"

1. GW to George Washington Parke Custis, January 7, 1798, in *PGW, Ret.* 2:4–6.

2. Lafayette to GW, December 17, 1797, ibid., 1:534–536.

3. Eleanor Parke Custis to Elizabeth Bordley, March 20, 1798, in Jackson and Twohig, *Diaries*, 6:282n.

4. GW to John McDowell, March 5, 1798, in *PGW, Ret.* 2:118–119.

5. George Washington Parke Custis to GW, March 12, 1798, ibid., 138–139.

6. GW to George Washington Parke Custis, March 19, 1798, ibid., 149.

7. George Washington Parke Custis to GW, April 2, 1798, ibid., 219–220.

8. GW to George Washington Parke Custis, April 15, 1798, ibid., 239–240.

9. George Washington Parke Custis to GW, May 5, 1798, ibid., 252–253.

10. GW to George Washington Custis, June 13, 1798, ibid., 324–325.

11. George Washington Parke Custis, June 17, 1798, ibid., 335–336.

12. George Washington Parke Custis, June 17, 1798, ibid., 400–401.

13. George Washington Parke Custis, July 21, 1798, ibid., 437.

14. John Adams to GW, June 22, 1798, ibid., 351–352.

15. Ibid.

16. John Adams to GW, July 7, 1798, ibid., 389.

17. George Washington Parke Custis to GW, July 12, 1798, ibid., 400–401.

18. GW to David Stuart, August 13, 1798, ibid., 525–526.

19. GW to John McDowell, September 16, 1798, ibid., 579n.

20. GW to James McHenry, December 13, 1798, ibid., 3:250n.–265n.

21. GW to John Greenwood, December 7, 1798, ibid., 245–246.

22. GW to James McHenry, December 14, 1798, ibid., 267–268.

23. GW to Lafayette, December 25, 1798, ibid., 280–285.

24. GW to George-Washington Motier Lafayette, December 25, 1798, ibid., 279–280.

25. GW to James McAlbin, January 27, 1799, ibid., 340–342.

26. GW to Gouverneur Morris, May 26, 1799, in Fitzpatrick, Writings, 37:214–215.

27. GW to Clement Biddle, June 7, 1799, ibid., 231–232.

28. GW to James McHenry, July 14, 1799, in PGW, Ret. 4:186–187.

29. Last Will and Testament, July 9, 1799, in Fitzpatrick, Writings, 37:275–303.

30. Ibid. Washington had already disposed of most of his other thousands of acres—Dismal Swamp, the bounty lands at the Big Bend of the Ohio, and the lands at Great Meadows on the Youghiogheny River.

31. GW to Alexandria General Assemblies managers, November 12, 1799, in PGW, Ret. 4:402–403.

32. GW to Thomas Peter, December 3, 1799, ibid., 440.

33. Gouverneur Morris to GW, December 9, 1799, ibid., 452–453.

34. GW to James Anderson, December 10, 1799, ibid., 455–477.

35. Jackson and Twohig, Diaries, 6:377–378.

36. Tobias Lear's narrative account of the death of George Washington, December 15, 1799, in PGW, Ret. 4:542–546.

37. Ibid.

38. Fitzpatrick, Writings, 37:474.

39. Tobias Lear's narrative account of the death of George Washington, December 15, 1799, in PGW, Ret. 4:542–546.

40. Ibid.

41. Freeman, et al., George Washington, citing A. B. Hart, ed., "Tributes to Washington," 25–26.

42. Ibid., citing Hart, 21.

43. Ibid., 7:651, citing Annals of 7th Congress, 1:1310.

44. Ibid., 7:653, citing Stewart Mitchell, ed., New Letters of Abigail Adams, 1789–1801 (Boston: Houghton Mifflin, 1947), 229.

45. Martha Washington to Abigail Smith Adams, January 1, 1800, in Fields, "Worthy Partner," 333.

Epilogue

1. John Adams to Martha Washington, December 27, 1799, in Fields, "Worthy Partner," 327.

2. Martha Washington to John Adams, December 31, 1799, ibid., 332–333.

Selected Bibliography
of Principal Sources

Abbott, W. W., and Dorothy Twohig, eds. *The Papers of George Washington, Colonial Series, 1748–August 1755,* 10 vols. Charlottesville: University Press of Virginia, 1983–1995.

————. *The Papers of George Washington, Confederation Series, January 1784–September 1788.* 6 vols. Charlottesville: University Press of Virginia, 1992–1997.

Abbott, W. W., Dorothy Twohig, Philander D. Chase, and Theodore J. Crackel, eds. *The Papers of George Washington, Presidential Series, September 1788–May 1793.* 12 vols. [in progress] Charlottesville: University Press of Virginia—University of Virginia Press, 1987–2005.

————. *The Papers of George Washington, Revolutionary War Series, June 1775– April 1778.* 14 vols. [in progress] Charlottesville: University of Virginia Press, 1984–2004.

Adams, Charles Francis, ed. *Letters of John Adams Addressed to His Wife.* 2 vols. Boston: 1841.

Bobrick, Benson. *Angel in the Whirlwind: The Triumph of the American Revolution.* New York: Simon & Schuster, 1997.

Boyd, Julian P., et al., eds. *The Papers of Thomas Jefferson.* 34 vols. [in progress] Princeton, N.J.: Princeton University Press, 1950– .

Britt, Judith S. *Nothing More Agreeable: Music in George Washington's Family.* Mount Vernon, Va.: Mount Vernon Ladies' Association, 1984.

Butterfield, L. H., ed. *The Adams Papers: Diary & Autobiography of John Adams.* 4 vols. New York: Atheneum, 1964.

Cappon, Lester J., ed. *The Adams-Jefferson Letters: The Complete Correspondence between Thomas Jefferson and Abigail and John Adams.* Chapel Hill: University of North Carolina Press, 1959.

Chernow, Ron. *Alexander Hamilton.* New York: Penguin, 2004.

Custis, George Washington Parke. *Recollections and Private Memoirs of Washington.* New York: Derby & Jackson, 1860.

DeConde, Alexander. *Entangling Alliance*. Durham, N.C.: Duke University Press, 1958.

Duer, William A., ed. *Memoirs, Correspondence of General Lafayette, Published by His Family*. New York: Saunders and Otley Ann Street, 1837.

Ferling, John. *John Adams: A Life*. New York: Henry Holt, 1992.

Fields, Joseph E. *"Worthy Partner": The Papers of Martha Washington*. Westport, Conn.: Greenwood Press, 1994.

Fitzpatrick, John C., ed., *The Writings of George Washington, from the Original Manuscript Sources, 1745–1799*. 39 vols. Washington, D.C.: U.S. Government Printing Office, 1931–1944.

Flexner, James Thomas. *Washington: The Indispensable Man*. Boston: Little, Brown, 1974.

Freeman, Douglas Southall. *George Washington*. Completed by John Alexander Carroll and Mary Wells Ashworth. 7 vols. New York: Charles Scribner's Sons, 1957.

Fusonie, Alan and Donna Jean. *George Washington, Pioneer Farmer*. Mount Vernon, Va.: The Mount Vernon Ladies Association, 1998.

Henry, William Wirt. *Patrick Henry: Life, Correspondence, and Speeches*. 3 vols. New York: Charles Scribner's Sons, 1891.

Idzerda, Stanley J., and Robert Rhodes Crout, eds. *Lafayette in the Age of the American Revolution: Selected Letters and Papers, 1776–1790*. 5 vols. Ithaca, N.Y.: Cornell University Press, 1983.

Jackson, Donald, and Dorothy Twohig, eds. *The Diaries of George Washington*. 6 vols. Charlottesville: University Press of Virginia, 1976–1979.

Kapp, Friedrich. *The Life of John Kalb, Major-General in the Revolutionary Army*. New York: Henry Holt and Company, 1884.

Lafayette, George-Washington. [Gilbert Motier, marquis de La Fayette]. *Mémoires, Correspondence, et Manuscrits du Général Lafayette, publiés par sa famille*. 6 vols. Paris: H. Fournier, aîné, 1837.

Lossing, Benson J. *Mary and Martha, the Mother and the Wife of George Washington*. New York: Harper & Brothers, 1886.

McCusker, John J. *How Much Is That in Real Money? A Historical Commodity Price Index for Use as a Deflator of Money Values in the Economy of the United States*, 2nd ed. Worcester, Mass.: American Antiquarian Society, 2001.

——————. *Money and Exchange in Europe and America, 1600–1775: A Handbook*. Chapel Hill: University of North Carolina Press, 1978.

Minnigerode, Meade. *Jefferson—Friend of France 1793: The Career of Edmond Charles Genet*. New York: G. P. Putnam's Sons, 1928.

Sparks, Jared. *The Life of George Washington*. Boston: Tappan & Dennet, 1843.

Stewart, Donald H. *The Opposition Press of the Federalist Period*. Albany: State University of New York Press, 1969.

Twohig, Dorothy, ed. *The Papers of George Washington, Retirement Series, March 1797–December 1799*. 4 vols. Charlottesville: University Press of Virginia, 1998–1999.

Unger, Harlow Giles. *John Hancock: Merchant King and American Patriot*. New York: John Wiley & Sons, 2000.

——————. *Lafayette*. Hoboken, N.J.: John Wiley & Sons, 2002.

Weems, Mason L. *The Life of Washington*. 1800. Reprint, Cambridge, Mass.: Harvard University Press, Belknap Press, 1962.

Credits

Index